Making Love Last Forever

GARY SMALLEY

LifeWay Press®
Nashville, Tennessee

ISBN 0-8054-9791-9
Dewey Decimal Classification: 306.872
Subject Heading: LOVE\MARRIAGE

This book is a resource in the Home/Family category of the Christian Growth Study Plan.
Course CG-0207

Unless otherwise noted, Scripture quotations are from the Holy Bible,
New International Version, copyright © 1973, 1978, 1984 by International Bible Society

Scripture quotations marked RSV are from the Revised Standard Version of the Bible,
copyrighted 1946, 1952, © 1971, 1973.

To order additional copies of this resource: WRITE LifeWay Church Resources Customer Service,
One LifeWay Plaza, Nashville, TN 37234-0113; FAX order to (615) 251-5933;
PHONE 1-800-458-2772; order ONLINE at *www.lifeway.com*;
or visit the LifeWay Christian Store serving you.

Printed in the United States of America

Leadership and Adult Publishing
LifeWay Church Resources
One LifeWay Plaza
Nashville, Tennessee 37234-0175

Contents

Introduction

You are about to begin a voyage to Forever-Love. If you keep your eyes open throughout the voyage to three specific things, I believe you will get far more from your study.

First, stretch your mind to entertain the idea that you are responsible for your quality of life, no matter what your circumstances have been, are, or may become.

Second, be open to the idea that falling in love with life is the best way to equip yourself to stay in love with your spouse—forever. I've divided the course into two parts, offering two sets of principles. The first part is based on the critical truth: *You will never know the deep satisfaction of a life-long love with your spouse if you are not first in love with your life.* I'll give you five ways to enrich your life. Then in part 2 I'll present eight practical helps for understanding and, yes, loving your mate. These principles hold and can affect positive change in a relationship whether or not your spouse is willing to make personal changes in his or her lifestyle or attitude. Having said that, of course the ideal is for the two of you to work together at improving your relationship.

Third, work through the entire study and mark sections that you will need to come back to later. After you complete the course, go back to these sections and carefully work through them. Look for deeper insight as you "go for" a love that lasts forever.

You'll see that everything I teach or write about has a basic theme. I'm always trying to expose the age-old struggle between the life-giving principle of *honor* and the destructive emotion of *anger* that too often creeps in when we don't get what we expected. I see honor and anger as opposites, at two ends of a pole. And each of us make daily choices. As we choose anger over honor, we unknowingly or knowingly welcome the stress-producing, life-draining, divorce-creating thoughts that lead us down a path of personal and relational destruction. But choose honor and you choose life.

You're on the verge of a learning experience that could very well change your personal life and your marriage. Apply yourself to this material and God will apply the material to you.

How to Use Your Workbook

To gain the most from this study, let me suggest several things that I believe will help you along the way.

In Personal Study

 You and your spouse will each need a workbook. For your daily work you will each need a pencil and a Bible. We have printed most Scripture passages for you, but some are lengthy and will require the use of your Bible. Complete all written work on a daily basis.

 Conclude each week with Couple Time. This will help you begin to put into action what you've learned. Couple Time is located on the last page of each week's material.

 Set aside a time and place each day to complete your work; each daily assignment will usually take from 25 to 30 minutes. Getting in a routine early will set the tone for your involvement throughout the course. Take your time each day; Don't try to jump ahead, or complete several days' assignments in one sitting. Also, don't skip any assignments; each day builds on the previous day's discovery and leads to the next, so skipping over a day or two will rob you of crucial information and understanding. You will come to appreciate this time alone each day.

 Also set a time when you and your spouse can debrief the weekly material. This should occur before the weekly group session. As you protect this time together each week, you will grow to appreciate these special moments.

 Memorizing Scripture is a discipline you will be called upon to use in your study. This may be new to you. Consider the following ideas to help you further develop Scripture memorization. You and your spouse might covenant together and help each other memorize Scripture.

1. Read the verse and think about the meaning.
2. Write the verse on note cards, one phrase per card.
3. Glance at the first phrase and say it aloud. Glance at the next phrase and say both phrases aloud. Continue this process until you have said the whole passage.
4. Try to say the verse from memory later in the day. If you can't remember the entire verse, glance at the cards to refresh your memory.
5. Repeat the verse several times each day for a week until you feel the verse is firmly implanted in your mind.

In Preparation for Group Sessions

You and your spouse will gain the most from this study if you join other couples in a weekly group session. You may have received this workbook in an introduction to such a group experience. If not, consider inviting other couples in your church or community to join you. Use the *Making Love Last Forever Leader Kit* and *Leader Guide* to provide direction for your time together.

The group sessions will help clarify and amplify your understanding of the principles I present in the study. Be as faithful as possible to the group sessions, and you will reap even greater rewards from your personal study.

M*aking* Love Last Forever

could change your personal life

and your marriage.

WEEK 1

Love's Best-Kept Secret

Will our love last forever? It's the hope of every starry-eyed bride and groom who clasp hands and say "I do."

If your marriage is anything like mine, a few years after the wedding, you or your spouse—or both—were wondering why you had ever chosen this person to live with. "Till death do us part?" Impossible! "To love and to cherish?" You have got to be kidding!

I take much of the blame for the first disastrous years of my marriage. I was a wounded young man who had learned wounding tactics from a wounded, angry father. I knew how to lash out, clam up, lecture, and get my own way. My wife, Norma, learned to cope.

But for Norma and me something happened on the way to "forever." We discovered the principles I present in this study. We set a new course that has renewed our love and deepened our relationship. We are in love with life and with each other.

Is it really possible to marry and then see that starry-eyed love actually get better? The answer is, *Yes!*

In week 1 of part 1, you will—

- discover a love that endures no matter how tough the circumstances;
- understand that the choice for making love last rests with you since you can't change others but you can change yourself;
- determine to take responsibility for future choices;
- acknowledge that your future choices do not have to be chained to past mistakes and failures and,
- make a commitment to take responsibility for the quality of your life and marriage.

Day 1 Forever-Love Is Possible	Day 2 You Can Choose to Get on Course	Day 3 You Can Take Responsibility for Future Choices	Day 4 You Can Accept the Reality of the Past and Live Beyond It	Day 5 You Can Be 100 Percent Responsible for Your Choices

A key verse to memorize this week:

"I can do everything through him [Christ] who gives me strength" (Philippians 4:13).

Day 1

Forever-Love Is Possible

Whenever I see love win out in a marriage that looked hopeless, my confidence is increased, and I've found ways to help almost anyone stay in love despite impossible odds. Take this seemingly "ship-wrecked" relationship. Who would have thought John and Sharon would reconcile and eventually enjoy a good marriage?

It was 11:00 p.m. when the phone rang. My wife, Norma, and I were already in bed. At the other end of the line was John, a popular, local business executive. He was locked in a major argument with his wife, Sharon, and the dispute was so fierce he was saying things like, "I'm sick of trying. I want to get on an airplane and fly to another state. I just don't have any energy left to stay with this woman."

Before he took such a drastic step, however, he was making one last attempt to reach out for help. "Is there anything you can do for us?" he asked. "Can we come over tonight and talk with you?"

Norma and I had a quick discussion and invited them to come over.

John and Sharon came to our home, and the argument continued in front of us. The issue they were facing was serious: he was addicted and out of control sexually, and to add insult to injury, he had given her a sexually-transmitted disease. She was nauseated by his behavior and disgusted with him.

Despite the gravity of the situation, a couple of things happened that night that are comical in hindsight—especially if you like seeing Murphy's Law lived out. For instance, at one point in their arguing, she kicked our coffee table, driving it toward me and causing it to cut my leg. At another point, Sharon was nearly breaking my fingers in an effort to get out of my grasp so she could run outside and attack John. (Norma had taken him into the front yard in the hope of cooling things down a bit.)

By 12:30 or 1:00, I had been beat up, yelled at, and deprived of sleep, so I felt I had earned the right to say something to this couple. (They hadn't allowed us to give them any advice up to this point.) I began, "Well as I've listened to both of you, I think there's something you can start working on even tonight."

What robs our love for life the most is not what happens to us, but how we choose to respond and grow from it.

But John looked at his watch and said, "I am so tired. I am so discouraged. I don't have any more energy. I've got to leave." And with that they both left.

I fell asleep that night thinking, *This will never work out.*

I share this extreme case because unfortunately study after study indicates that more than 50 percent of the marriages in this country end in divorce. It doesn't have to be that way. With time and work, John and Sharon acted on most of the principles found in these pages and their relationship turned around.

 How is your marriage relationship right now? Circle all the words below that describe your marriage at this moment.

Loving	In crisis	In conflict
Hurtful	Needing help	Intimate
Growing	Painful	Changing
Great	Impossible	Immature
Mature	Distant	Christ-centered

Any good marriage can grow and any poor marriage can make it. The choice rests in the hands of both spouses. We can develop an attitude and then take positive steps toward growing a marriage that's rooted in the love of Jesus Christ. The couple I just described went through months of counseling and hard work. Now, several years later, they are in love.

The Bible describes the most intimate and profound love we can experience as *agape. Agape* is biblical love, the kind of love God has for us and we in turn express to others. First John 4:19 says, "We love because he first loved us." God's forgiving unconditional, and unselfish love in Christ makes it possible for us to love others.

How deep is your marital love right now? I would like you to evaluate your love relationship using 1 Corinthians 13. At the end of the study, we will do this again and see how you have grown.

Take a survey on your love relationship. Put your name on each line at the place that represents where your love for your spouse is right now. Put your spouse's name where you experience that quality of love from your spouse.

1 CORINTHIANS 13 LOVE

Patient — Impatient

Kind — Unkind

Not jealous — Jealous

Not boastful — Boastful

Humble — Proud

Agape is biblical love, the kind of love God has for us and we in turn express to others.

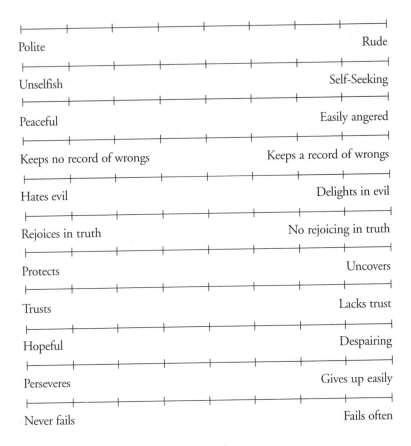

Polite	Rude
Unselfish	Self-Seeking
Peaceful	Easily angered
Keeps no record of wrongs	Keeps a record of wrongs
Hates evil	Delights in evil
Rejoices in truth	No rejoicing in truth
Protects	Uncovers
Trusts	Lacks trust
Hopeful	Despairing
Perseveres	Gives up easily
Never fails	Fails often

In 1 Corinthians 13, the apostle Paul calls us to a deeper love relationship.

After looking over the list, you may feel down about your marriage relationship. Remember, if the couple I described can make it, any marriage can make it! Scripture declares, " 'Everything is possible for him who believes' " (Mark 9:23).

You may face immanent disaster without knowing it. Do you know that the *Titanic* was warned six separate times to slow down, change course, and take a southern route before it finally hit an iceberg and sank? However, the captain erroneously believed that the ship could not sink. If only he had changed directions.

Your marriage may be very healthy right now and need only small course corrections to be better. That's wonderful. Thank the Lord. But, your marriage may need a major course change in order to avoid disaster. Commit yourself right now to discovering what's needed and together with your spouse change. Remember, your love can deepen and grow through the power and motivation of God's Spirit.

Love's best-kept secret is not to change or exchange your spouse. It's to change your own course. The remainder of this week we will explore factors that will help you believe love can grow and change is possible through Jesus Christ.

 Write a prayer thanking God for your spouse and for the ability to grow and change in your relationship.

_____

_____

Day 2
You Can Choose to Get on Course

For some couples, today's title may be difficult to believe. Once we get off course in our relationships, we develop attitudes and behaviors that often reinforce the negative aspects and move us further from the positive aspects of our marriages. We *can* discover the deep satisfaction that comes from being in love. It's that simple. It's your choice.

"My choice?" you ask. "But you don't know what I've been through. You don't know the person I married. You don't know our problems."

 Begin this day by admitting where you are in your marriage. Put and *x* on the line that expresses you feeling about your marriage:

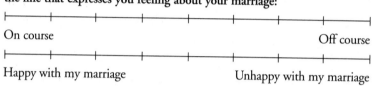

On course   Off course

Happy with my marriage   Unhappy with my marriage

If you find yourself putting an *x* toward the negative side of each line, then you may be wondering if anything in your marriage can change. I want you to know that love for life is possible no matter what your circumstances.

 Think of the problems that arise in your marriage. What do you believe causes them? Check the two or three most frequent causes of problems or conflict in your marriage.

- ❏ Unfortunate circumstances
- ❏ Differences of opinion
- ❏ Differences in backgrounds
- ❏ Sexual problems
- ❏ Bad choices
- ❏ Money
- ❏ Health problems
- ❏ Poor communication
- ❏ Personality differences
- ❏ Other:_____

A person who continually blames others or his or her circumstances becomes what Stephen Covey calls "the reactive person."[1] These people allow circumstances or others to rob them of their quality of life. We can become "proactive" persons who take responsibility for our own lives.

If our marriages are to improve, change must begin with ourselves, not others or circumstances. A sudden windfall of money or a drastic change in circumstances can change people; but people are only truly changed when they make a choice to be changed by God's truth and become empowered by His Spirit.

Believe it! In short, here is the formula:

We can't change other people.

We can change ourselves.

As we change, people around us adjust their responses and make decisions according to our new behavior.

As Christians we are being changed; we have been given the power to change. Read the following passages, and write down how change happens.

BIBLE PASSAGE	HOW WE ARE CHANGING
Therefore, if anyone is in Christ, he is a new creation; the old has gone, the new has come! (2 Corinthians 5:17).	_____ _____ _____ _____
And we, who with unveiled faces all reflect the Lord's glory, are being transformed into his likeness with ever-increasing glory, which comes from the Lord, who is the Spirit (2 Corinthians 3:18).	_____ _____ _____ _____ _____
Therefore, I urge you, brothers, in view of God's mercy, to offer your bodies as living sacrifices, holy and pleasing to God—this is your spiritual act of worship. Do not conform any longer to the pattern of this world, but be transformed by the renewing of the mind. Then you will be able to test and approve what God's will is— his good, pleasing, and perfect will (Romans 12:1-2).	_____ _____ _____ _____ _____ _____ _____ _____

What I am today is the result of the choices I've made in the past.

Let me give you an example of how someone who finally chose to take responsibility for his own emotional well-being began to change. When Richard first came to see me, he was not a happy man. Picking up the phone to call a counselor was a first step in acknowledging his dissatisfaction with life and was a warning that something was wrong. He was frustrated, disappointed, and fearful things were never going to change. Yet a wee bit of hope prompted some changes in his life.

Richard was in his 50s, a husband and dad, a classy dresser, and the president of his own large company. After more than 30 years of marriage to Gail, he'd grown tired of her nagging, even hatefulness. But he had also grown tired of expecting Gail to change and meet his relational needs as she had in the early days of their marriage. Even though he hated the thought, he was contemplating divorce. But before he took that drastic step, he sought out and acted on my advice.

After the usual counselor-client preliminaries, I asked what had brought him to me. He answered, "I'm aware of my part in messing up with my wife and kids. I've spent so much time building this company. Even though it's late, I want to have a better relationship with them. I'm very successful financially, but I'm not very happy, and neither are my family members. I don't know how to go about changing things, especially after being the way I've been for so many years."

Then he added something highly significant. "I didn't have much of a relationship with my own dad," he said. "In fact, he was always too busy for me, just the way I've been with my family."

That was a key factor in Richard's past failure as a husband and father. His own dad never built a close relationship with him, and that pattern probably had gone back for several generations. Richard's model of a parent was weak, and Richard didn't get the opportunity to see a man loving his wife. His grandfather's example got passed from generation to generation. Richard didn't know any other approach.

If Richard had been hooked on the blame game (where you "win" by finding someone else to blame for everything wrong in your life), he could have stopped his growth at this point. With a little bit of new insight, he could have said, "OK it's mostly my father's fault!" Or he could have said, like so many workaholic people, "But I was providing for my family! I did it all for them, so they could have a better standard of living. If they can't understand my good motives, it's their problem. Hang this 'relationship' bit."

If Richard *had* chosen to blame his father for his own problems, he might have had some justification. Research shows that people raised under strong, controlling, and rejecting parents may, in turn, reject and control their own families.[2]

Richard was no longer looking for a scapegoat. He took responsibility for his response to the way he had been parented. At this point Richard learned two powerful truths.

- What I am today is the result of the choices I've made in the past.
- I am 100 percent responsible for all the choices I've made.

 How do you feel about these truths? Check one box.

❑ I agree totally   ❑ I agree in part   ❑ I totally disagree

Why?

_____

_____

Richard began to distance himself from the age-old rationalization: *The devil made me do it.* Richard no longer was going to empower his father to ruin his relationships. He took responsibility for himself. He said things like, "No more, Dad; I'm not going to follow your example any longer. I'm going to discover what I need to do for myself and for my wife and children and finally find satisfaction in these vital areas of my life." All he needed was some guidance to start avoiding the icebergs and sail toward warmer seas.

I am 100 percent responsible for all the choices I've made.

Richard began working on his relationship with his son and wife. Slowly, significant changes were made in his life, family, and marriage all because he made a choice to take responsibility for his emotional well-being. He had the courage to move beyond the status quo.

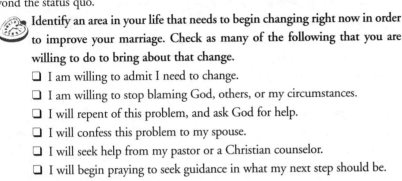 Identify an area in your life that needs to begin changing right now in order to improve your marriage. Check as many of the following that you are willing to do to bring about that change.

❑ I am willing to admit I need to change.

❑ I am willing to stop blaming God, others, or my circumstances.

❑ I will repent of this problem, and ask God for help.

❑ I will confess this problem to my spouse.

❑ I will seek help from my pastor or a Christian counselor.

❑ I will begin praying to seek guidance in what my next step should be.

Are you wondering if you have the courage, power, and ability to change? Do you at times feel like a failure for not following through with decisions to change that you have made in the past? You are already taking significant steps toward changing. You are involved in this study which will help you grow and mature in Christian marriage. You are beginning to face realistically the need for change.

If it's difficult for you to believe you can make the choice to change, memorize the following Scripture. If you believe you can change, repeat the following Scripture three or four times out loud to remind yourself of God's awesome power at work in you through Jesus Christ.

"I can do everything through him [Christ] who gives me strength" (Philippians 4:13).

---

1 Stephen R. Covey, *The Seven Habits of Highly Effective People* (New York: Simon & Schuster, 1989), 71.
2 Irene and Herbert Goldenberg, *Family Therapy: An Overview* (Pacific Grove, C.A.: Brooks, Cole, 1980, 1985).

Day 3
You Can Take Responsibility for Future Choices

In spite of past failures and painful decisions, we can take responsibility for our futures by deciding to make positive and healthy choices today for our families and marriages. Like Richard did in yesterday's material, we can take responsibility to make things right. What steps can we take today that will shape a better future for our marriages and families?

Forever-love begins with two steps:

1. Forever-love says "I'll take responsibility for my own choices—past, present, and future."
2. Forever-love accepts the reality of the past but lives beyond "the blame game."

Let's look at each of these steps and discover how to take them. When we take responsibility for our past choices, we must first realize that not everything we experience now is the consequence or result of our choices. Yes, certain choices made by others dramatically affect us today. In the Bible, the choices made by Adam and Eve affect the whole of humanity until the end of history. Choices made by our parents affect who we are today. Tomorrow, we will explore how to deal with past choices made by others that continually affect our lives. But today let's examine choices we have made that are significantly affecting our marriages right now.

 Briefly describe or list any major decisions you made in the past which are having negative consequences in your marriage right now.

_____

_____

Instead of trying to second guess yourself on what you might have done differently, approach the past negative choices you have made from a different perspective. There are biblical ways you can face these past realities. The most important first step you can take is to repent. *Repent* means to both admit what's wrong and to change direction. An easy way to remember the action of repentance is: Admit it. Quit it. Reframe it. You'll most likely never forget it, but you can place new meaning on old actions.

Look at each of the following Scriptures about facing past sin and failure. Underline each action or attitude that we are told to take in responding with repentance.

If we confess our sins, he is faithful and just and will forgive us our sins and purify us from all unrighteousness (1 John 1:9).

You were taught, with regard to your former way of life, to put off your old self, which is being corrupted by its deceitful desires; to be made new in the attitude of your minds; and to put on the new self, created to be like God in true righteousness and holiness (Ephesians 4:22-24).

Therefore, since we are surrounded by such a great cloud of witnesses, let us throw off everything that hinders and the sin that so easily entangles, and let us run with perseverance the race marked out for us. Let us fix our eyes on Jesus, the author and perfecter of our faith (Hebrews 12:1-2).

R epent *means to admit what's wrong and to change direction:*

Admit it.

Quit it.

Reframe it.

14

Godly sorrow brings repentance that leads to salvation and leaves no regret, but worldly sorrow brings death (2 Corinthians 7:10).

Brothers, I do not consider myself yet to have taken hold of it. But one thing I do: Forgetting what is behind and straining toward what is ahead, I press on toward the goal to win the prize for which God has called me heavenward in Christ Jesus (Philippians 3:13-14).

 There comes a point at which you must let go and let God set you free from past bondages, sin, and guilt. The death of Jesus Christ on the cross for your sins has set you free from sin (see Romans 8). What sin are you still clinging to that damages and hinders the love in your marriage? If there is a past bondage, briefly write it here.

_____

_____

It's time to give that to Jesus Christ. If you are unwilling to surrender that past sin, or if you have tried to do so and it still plagues your marriage, I encourage you to seek guidance from your pastor or a Christian counselor. The past can be cleansed by Jesus Christ, but that is your decision. You can continue to feel guilty and let guilt affect your marriage if you so desire, but why would you want that? Let it go.

 Why not do that right now? Below is a drawing of a cross representing Jesus Christ. If there are past sins or failures you have not released, write them on the cross. Or, if you have released and confessed those sins, write a prayer of thanksgiving to Jesus praising Him for what He has done in your life.

In closing, pray this prayer out loud:
Lord Jesus, thank you for the privilege of repenting of past sins. Thank you for forgiving me. Grant me the courage to take responsibility for my own choices—past, present, and future. Amen.

Day 4

You Can Accept the Reality of the Past and Live Beyond It

Let's return to our story about Richard. He had experienced many hurts from his dad. Still, Richard accepted the truth of his past. He looked realistically at what his father had done to him, and he decided to take the "good" and discard any of the "bad" as he saw it. He didn't want his past to control his present and future.

I know what it feels like to grow up with an angry father. I know my father's behavior affected me, along with my brothers and sisters. At times I used to wish things had been different. But they weren't. Now I have to take what was given to me and do the best I can with the available resources. This has truly been a releasing and joyful experience. I'm free to take the counsel of others—friends, family, books—and decide to do what I believe is best for me and my family. I don't have to waste time wishing things had been different. I'm free to choose my response to everything that happens or doesn't happen to me.

While we can't succeed by blaming the past for our current unhappiness, we do need to understand and interpret our inherited tendencies so we can consciously grow beyond them. If we don't, I've found, we usually remain "frozen" at a lower maturity level.

 God intends for us to grow as Christians, not stay at the same place all our lives. Two Scripture passages come immediately to mind. Read each passage and underline the phrases that refer to growth in the Christian life.

> Therefore, if anyone is in Christ, he is a new creation; the old has gone, the new has come (2 Corinthians 5:17).

> Then we will no longer be infants, tossed back and forth by the waves, and blown here and there by every wind of teach and by the cunning and craftiness of men in their deceitful scheming. Instead, speaking the truth in love, we will in all things grow up into him who is the Head, that is Christ (Ephesians 4:14-15).

That growth may not always be steady and consistent. At times we grow slowly. At other times, we may regress or surge ahead suddenly.

 List four or five events in your marriage that resulted in major decisions or conflicts for you as a couple. Those times may have been exciting and challenging or dangerous and stormy. Choose a variety of events. Then place an *x* on the line next to each event to identify the speed at which you both grew and matured after that event. You may have grown slowly and marked 10 miles an hour. You may have grown quickly and significantly and marked 60 miles an hour.

16

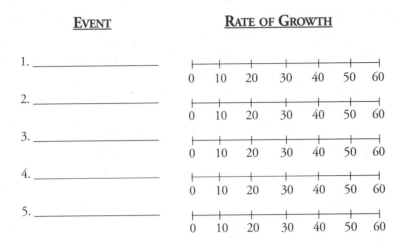

EVENT	RATE OF GROWTH
1. _____	0 10 20 30 40 50 60
2. _____	0 10 20 30 40 50 60
3. _____	0 10 20 30 40 50 60
4. _____	0 10 20 30 40 50 60
5. _____	0 10 20 30 40 50 60

Here's a personal illustration of what happened to me in a time of real growth. On one of our first family trips to Hawaii, Norma, the kids, and I were all excited about hitting the sand and being together. As we prepared to go down to the beach for the first time, however, I was delayed for some reason. Everyone else wanted to get going. But I explained, "I'm just not ready."

"OK," they said, "we'll go on ahead. Come find us when you're ready. We'll be right down here." They pointed up the beach.

"Sounds fine," I told them.

About half an hour later, I left the hotel room and went looking for my family. I walked up and down the beach as far as I could go in both directions, but I couldn't find them. As time went on, I started feeling irritated and hurt. *Wait a minute,* I thought. *We're here in Hawaii as a family to be together, but they've deserted me! I've been rejected!* Basically, I was pouting and showing my immaturity.

I didn't find them, so I went back to the hotel and waited impatiently. Eventually they came in, and I was sulking. "What's wrong with you?" they asked.

"You left me," I said glumly.

"We told you where we were going," they responded.

"Yeah, well, I went there, and you weren't there," I accused.

"We meant the other beach just a little farther down," they said.

"Well, that wasn't very clear!" I insisted, unwilling to be appeased.

After that, I wouldn't speak to anybody. Thank God for our son, Greg, who has always had the capacity to confront his father. "Dad," he said cautiously and respectfully, "I thought you wanted a 'new generation' with our family—to be a better father than your own dad was in a lot of ways."

"I do," I insisted, glaring at him.

"Dad," he said, "is this really the kind of example you want to pass on to me?"

"No," I had to admit grudgingly. "And I realize I've asked you guys to help me when I'm not responding well."

Now, here's the really interesting thing. My wife said, "You know, this is exactly how your father acted when he was upset. He would be angry, sulk, be silent, and close everyone out." And she had said to me in the past, "The worst thing you can

Growth may not always be steady and consistent. At times we grow slowly; other times we regress or surge ahead.

do to me is become silent, because then I feel we're not connected." That was my way of punishing the family when I wasn't happy with them, and that was also some of my dad coming out in me.

Greg was in high school when this conflict occurred, and as it escalated, he intervened. "OK," he said, "let's get this solved. Let me hear your side, Mom. Let me hear your side, Dad. Dad, don't you understand what you did here? OK, Mom, do you understand? Good. That fixes it." He actually helped us solve that minor skirmish. No wonder he's getting his doctorate in counseling!

By handling the situation so directly and drawing the comparison to my father, my family made me see the level of immaturity at which I was stuck. It's important for us to take such a look at our level of maturity from time to time. And when we find we are thinking only of ourselves, a lot of that can be traced right back to our past. One expert says the worst thing a husband can do if he wants his love in marriage to last is to close out the family with the "silent treatment."[1] That was me. But I don't have to let this type of behavior continue. I understand my past, but I'll be hanged before I will allow it to determine my future.

I learned an important biblical truth I want to share with you as a couple. We do tend to learn behavior, bad habits, and carry on the sins of our parents (see Exodus 20:4). As a result, we need to identify the negatives we've received from our parents, admit, quit, and reframe them. God's power in our lives breaks every past sin and curse on us through the power of Jesus Christ.

 List two negative habits, behaviors, or attitudes you exhibit that came directly from one or both of your parents.

_____

_____

List one action you will take to eliminate one of these attitudes/behaviors.

_____

You can choose not to live with those destructive things from the past. When you assume full responsibility for your present and future, you come to a place where you—like thousands of others—can make a deep commitment to your spouse and kids: "I don't want to be bound to the past anymore. I want a 'new generation,' a fresh start." Again, you don't have to do this alone. The resources at your disposal start—but certainly don't end—with this study.

 In closing, pray thanking God that in Jesus Christ He broke every past sin in your life, and you can live as a "new person" in Him.

[1] Howard Markman, Scott Stanley, and Susan Blumberg, *Fighting for Your Marriage* (San Francisco: Josey-Bass, 1994), 22.

You can choose not to live with those destructive things from the past.

Day 5
You Can Be 100 Percent Responsible for Your Choices

What about you? Have you come to the place where you're willing to take full responsibility for the quality of your own life? Can you—like John and Sharon and Richard and Gary Smalley—turn away from the blame game, no matter how difficult your past has been, and embrace the great, freeing truth that you will be as content as you choose to be?

Be willing to say with the apostle Paul, "I am not saying this because I am in need, for I have learned to be content whatever the circumstances. I know what it is to be in need, and I know what it is to have plenty. I have learned the secret of being content in any and every situation, whether living in plenty or in want. I can do everything through him who gives me strength" (Philippians 4:11-13).

I trust you will, and I know that if you do, the rest of this book is going to be like a trip to a buried treasure chest for you. You'll find insights all along the way that will help you make your life the best it can be.

 On the line below, mark with an x where you are right now in taking full responsibility for your life.

0%	50%	100%

If you're a victim of abuse, you're probably going to need help to deal with your situation and to rediscover love for life and your spouse. And if others react negatively to the changes you try to make, the going won't be easy. You still **choose your own response** to each situation, and you can decide to be persistent and hopeful. If you do, I can almost guarantee your future will be better than your past.

Beginning next week, we will explore the critical issue of draining unresolved anger from your life. It causes more pain, drowns more marriages, sinks more children than any other power I know. You'll not only see the damage it does, but you'll see how you can keep it far removed from you and your loved ones.

 This week we have studied, in one form or another, nine forever-love principles. I have summarized each principle below. After each one, indicate whether you agree or disagree with the principle. Then place an *x* on the line indicating the effectiveness of this principle in your marriage.

• **Forever-love does not work to change or exchange a spouse. Instead, it's up to us individually to change our response and mind-set.**

❑ Agree   ❑ Disagree

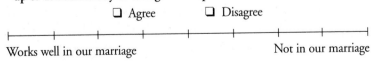

Works well in our marriage   Not in our marriage

Love for life is possible no matter what your circumstances.

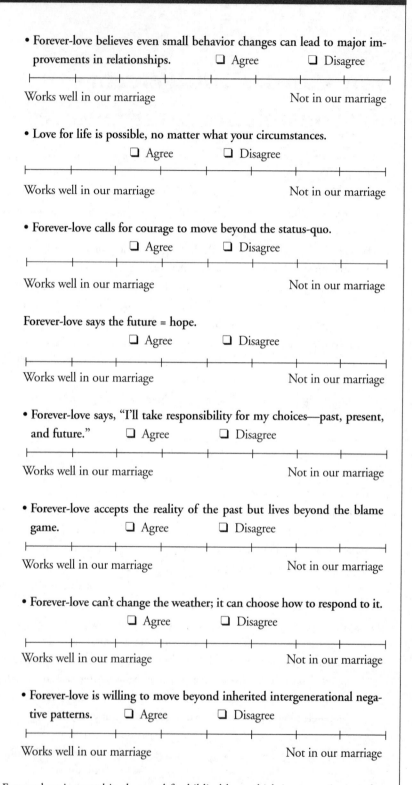

• Forever-love believes even small behavior changes can lead to major improvements in relationships. ❏ Agree   ❏ Disagree

├───────┼───────┼───────┼───────┼───────┼───────┼───────┤
Works well in our marriage   Not in our marriage

• Love for life is possible, no matter what your circumstances.
❏ Agree   ❏ Disagree

├───────┼───────┼───────┼───────┼───────┼───────┼───────┤
Works well in our marriage   Not in our marriage

• Forever-love calls for courage to move beyond the status-quo.
❏ Agree   ❏ Disagree

├───────┼───────┼───────┼───────┼───────┼───────┼───────┤
Works well in our marriage   Not in our marriage

Forever-love says the future = hope.
❏ Agree   ❏ Disagree

├───────┼───────┼───────┼───────┼───────┼───────┼───────┤
Works well in our marriage   Not in our marriage

• Forever-love says, "I'll take responsibility for my choices—past, present, and future." ❏ Agree   ❏ Disagree

├───────┼───────┼───────┼───────┼───────┼───────┼───────┤
Works well in our marriage   Not in our marriage

• Forever-love accepts the reality of the past but lives beyond the blame game. ❏ Agree   ❏ Disagree

├───────┼───────┼───────┼───────┼───────┼───────┼───────┤
Works well in our marriage   Not in our marriage

• Forever-love can't change the weather; it can choose how to respond to it.
❏ Agree   ❏ Disagree

├───────┼───────┼───────┼───────┼───────┼───────┼───────┤
Works well in our marriage   Not in our marriage

• Forever-love is willing to move beyond inherited intergenerational negative patterns. ❏ Agree   ❏ Disagree

├───────┼───────┼───────┼───────┼───────┼───────┼───────┤
Works well in our marriage   Not in our marriage

Forever-love can't change the weather; it can choose how to respond to it.

Forever-love is rooted in the word for biblical love which is *agape*. *Agape* is the unconditional love in our marriage that we freely give and do not have to earn. Later in this study, we will explore how to give love unconditionally. Let's review the qualities of *agape* that we surveyed on day 1.

Read 1 Corinthians 13:4-8 below. Circle the qualities that need to grow most in your marriage and underline the qualities that are currently strongest in your marriage.

> Love is patient, love is kind. It does not envy, it does not boast, it is not proud. It is not rude, it is not self-seeking, it is not easily angered, it keeps no record of wrongs. Love does not delight in evil but rejoices with the truth. It always perseveres. Love never fails. But where there are prophecies, they will cease; where there are tongues, they will be stilled; where there is knowledge, it will pass away (1 Corinthians 13:4-8).

In the remainder of part 1, we will explore five choices you need to make as a couple. Let me overview these upcoming choices.

Forever-Love Choices

1. From past experiences, everyone has some degree of buried anger. The average person has little or no idea how damaging forgotten or ignored anger can be—alienating loved ones, sabotaging relationships. And worse yet, most people don't even know how much destructive anger they're carrying around—like a ball and chain, it weighs one down. But we can **choose to break free of that destructive anger.** I'll show you how to detect your own level of anger. I'll also show seven ways to release anger's control over you and your relationships.

2. We have a second choice to make. We can choose a disastrous route, ignoring the value of any trials that come our way. Or we can **choose to see that every painful encounter contains a "pearl of love"** that we can use to add to a priceless collection. When we face adversity, we don't have to get bitter. We can use the adversity to make love grow bigger and better.

3. Next, we will discuss the perils of "putting all your eggs in one basket." If you **choose to diversify your life interests,** you increase your chances of remaining satisfied with life and staying in love.

4. Choosing to allow people and circumstances to "take away" your love for life can lead to a relational disaster. You'll discover two great truths that transformed my attitude, my wife's attitude, and increased the safety we feel with each other because we **choose to avoid past patterns of sabotaging love.**

5. Finally, each of us must **choose whether or not we will establish our personal spiritual journey.** Being disconnected from a living and loving God is like untying and pushing away a life jacket, thinking we're better off without it. It is the fuel we need to move into warmer water, away from damaging icebergs.

As you close this week, complete the Couple Time page with your spouse.

May God give you the courage and commitment to take responsibility for choices that will change you and your marriage.

Couple Time

For you to complete

The most important thing I learned about myself this week is:

_____

One quality of forever-love that needs to grow in my marriage is:

_____

One quality of forever-love that is the strongest in my marriage is:

_____

One bad attitude or behavior from my parents which affects my marriage that I will eliminate is:

_____

For you to share with your spouse

1. Sit together facing one another and take turns sharing how each of you completed the above section.

2. Pray 1 Corinthians 13:4-8 for each other as a prayer of hope and affirmation. As you pray, put your spouse's name in the place where *love* is in the text. Here is an abbreviated version to help you.

> (Name) is patient.
> (Name) is kind.
> (Name) does not envy.
> (Name) does not boast.
> (Name) is not proud.
> (Name) is not rude.
> (Name) is not self-seeking.
> (Name) is not easily angered.
> (Name) is keeps no record of wrongs.
> (Name) does not delight in evil but rejoices with the truth.
> (Name) always protects, always trusts, always hopes, always perseveres.
> (Name) never fails.

Conclude by giving each other a hug.

Handling Anger

Unresolved anger can do tremendous damage and even destroy relationships.

Let me tell you how anger worked its damage in the life of my friend, Larry, who for nine years was angry at *me*. He thought the anger would go away, but it didn't.

At one time we were great friends. Then I sensed there was a wall between us. We were still casual friends, and I attributed any "distance" between us to the fact that we no longer lived in the same city. We now live halfway across the country from each other. And anyway, I figured that if there were anything wrong between us, he would talk about it.

Well, not long ago, I was staying in a hotel in the town where Larry lives. While I was there, I got a call from him. "We've got to talk," he said.

"All right," I said, "about what?"

"I've been upset with you for about nine years now," he answered, amazing me. As he went on, I was even more appalled. "I've been really angry with you all that time, and I can't shake it," he said, his voice quivering. "I've tried to tell myself I would get over it in time, but it won't go away. I think about it a lot. Now it's affecting what I do in my job and my other relationships, too. I don't want to live like this anymore. I have to get this thing resolved. Can we meet?"

Words like that from a friend make you sick to your stomach. I asked myself, *What did I do? What does this involve?* Of course I agreed to meet with him.

We got together in a restaurant, and there the story came out, though it took about five hours. Larry cried, I cried, and at one point it got so emotional that his nose started bleeding. One messy scene! But he finally got out his deep anger.

The problem grew out of a decision we had made nine years before. Together we were going to confront a guy with whom we both had major disagreements. This was a very serious situation, and we were equally upset. We went to see the man, and when we got there, the guy said to me, "I'll discuss the problems you and I have with each other, but I'd rather not have both of you ganging up on me."

So I talked it over with Larry, who agreed to leave the conversation—and the scene. I remember, as we parted, telling Larry I was sorry and that we would talk later. But as things turned out, Larry thought I had sided with "the other guy" and deserted him as my friend. I had actually doubled Larry's anger. I left him with his anger toward the other person and now also hurt from me.

So Larry walked away thinking, *How could Gary have done this to me? We were going to talk to the man together, and he just discarded me, like I'm not of any value.* Yet I had never understood what I had done or how my friend felt about it until that day in the restaurant.

Most of us bury our anger so quickly we don't know what we're doing.

When I heard his feelings and how the incident had affected him for nine years, I grieved deeply. I had not intended to give more loyalty to our adversary than to my good friend.

Fortunately, our relationship was healed that day. We cried together, hugged each other, and sought each other's forgiveness. The anger was finally drained out of my friend, but not before he had suffered depression and other signs of unhappiness for nine years. And since that time, we've gone on to develop a deeper friendship.

Some might say that Larry was "overreacting" and in time would have gotten over it. That's what he thought would happen, but it didn't. There are thousands of people who wish they could shake off the effects of old offenses, but the truth is, many just can't. And because they aren't able to "get over it," the damage continues inside them, sometimes for years.

Before you dismiss this week's study as being not for you because you're not an "angry person," let me point out that most of us bury our anger so quickly we don't know what we're doing. Then it does its sneaky damage. It often leads to our lashing out at others. Or it gets turned inward, where it can become depression. Some may pretend it's "not there," but it is.

This week you will:

• learn how unresolved anger threatens marriages and relationships;
• discover the obvious and hidden effects of anger on ourselves, our relationships with others and with God;
• uncover seven steps to unload anger;
• begin to come clean with unforgiveness in your life;
• develop skills for releasing anger in yourself and others.

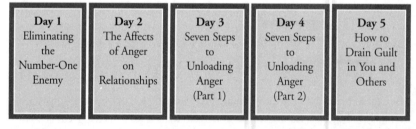

Day 1	**Day 2**	**Day 3**	**Day 4**	**Day 5**
Eliminating the Number-One Enemy	The Affects of Anger on Relationships	Seven Steps to Unloading Anger (Part 1)	Seven Steps to Unloading Anger (Part 2)	How to Drain Guilt in You and Others

As you study and pray this week, be open and honest with yourself and God. Be willing to confront unforgiveness and unresolved anger in your own life.

I invite you to memorize and meditate on this verse in the coming week.

> In your anger, do not sin: Do not let the sun go down while you are still angry, and do not give the devil a foothold (Ephesians 4:26-27).

Day 1
Eliminating the Number-One Enemy

There's a major destroyer of love on the loose; I've found it to be the leading cause of divorce and the single greatest thief of one's love for life. It may already be at work in your life and marriage.

Before I tell you what the major destroyer of love is, what do you believe it to be? From the following list, check what you think is the most destructive force in marriage today.

- ❏ Financial problems
- ❏ Sexual problems
- ❏ Poor communication
- ❏ Hatred

- ❏ Unresolved past guilt
- ❏ Unforgiveness
- ❏ Forgotten, unresolved anger
- ❏ Personality conflicts

The number one destroyer on my list is choosing to ignore *forgotten, unresolved anger,* not just the kind that gnaws at one's stomach night after night, but the type that quietly disappears. At least I used to think it disappeared. But when we bury anger inside us, **it's always buried** *alive!* And when we aren't even aware of its presence, it does its damage, destroying like rust on a car, like moths in a dark closet. But it doesn't have to remain buried; it doesn't have to wreak its havoc in our lives and relationships. There is hope—as we choose to root it out.

The Bible doesn't identify anger as a sin. Rather, the real sin is unresolved anger. Read the following passages and summarize what each says.

Everyone should be quick to listen, slow to speak and slow to become angry, for man's anger does not bring about the righteous life that God desires (James 1:19-20).

_____
_____
_____
_____
_____

See to it that no one misses the grace of God and that no bitter root grows up to cause trouble and defile many (Hebrews 12:15).

_____
_____
_____
_____

Forgive us out debts, as we also have forgiven our debtors. And lead us not into temptation, but deliver us from the evil one. For if you forgive men when they sin against you, your heavenly Father will also forgive you (Matthew 6:12-14).

_____
_____
_____
_____
_____
_____

How do you and your spouse usually handle your anger? *Check* the ways you handle anger and *circle* the ways your spouse handles anger.

- ❑ Flash quickly and release quickly.
- ❑ Smolder for a long time and remember for a long time.
- ❑ Express anger honestly trying not to project blame or degrade the other person.
- ❑ Put down and say hurtful things to the person with whom I'm angry.
- ❑ Keep anger to myself, not expressing it to others.
- ❑ Avoid confrontation by not talking directly to the person I'm angry with but talking to others about my anger.

Anger affects our relationships with family, others, God, and ourselves.

Anger affects our relationships with family, others, God, and ourselves. It springs from three separate emotions—**fear, frustration,** and **hurt.** In fact, when we strip anger down to its deepest level, we discover a thread running through all aspects of anger—*unfulfilled expectations.* **Frustration** is not receiving what we expected from others or circumstances. **Hurt** is when we don't hear the words or receive the actions we expected from others or circumstances.

And **fear** is either dreading that what we expect will not come as we wish, or expecting that something bad is going to happen. In his book *Banishing Fear from Your Life,* Charles Bass clearly explains, "The process by which fear provokes anger is relatively simple: we use anger to cope with fear." He goes on to tell a wonderful story of counseling a couple "who interacted with a fear/anger reaction." From the husband and wife he heard two completely different stories.

The husband's version? "Every time I come home, Mary is waiting for me with a chip on her shoulder. I hate to go home. As I drive home, I get more and more tense. When I get home and see her waiting for me with her hands on her hips, it just makes me mad, and I tie into her before she can get the jump on me."

The wife's story? "Joe is always mad at me over something. He always comes home in a bad temper. I really have to stand up to him to defend myself."[1] For both people a smoldering anger was fueled by a fear of the other's anger.

There's a wonderful line in the classic Christmas carol written by Phillips Brooks. "O Little Town of Bethlehem" refers to "the hopes and fears of all the years." If those hopes aren't realized and those fears are, anger can settle in—anger at ourselves, at specific others, at the more generic world, at God. We feel the need to blame our unhappiness on someone or something.

Anger can become our chosen response from something happening to us outside of our control. It's a normal response, even a good response when it's controlled. But we are the ones **who choose** to hold on to anger or let it go. We can choose to see its powerful potential for destruction and take the steps to reduce it within us. It's an iceberg sinking our love.

 When you get angry, which emotion is usually at the root of your anger? At the top of the next page is a list of different situations. Write the words fear, frustration, or hurt on each line at the point that best illustrates the intensity level you feel each of the three emotions.

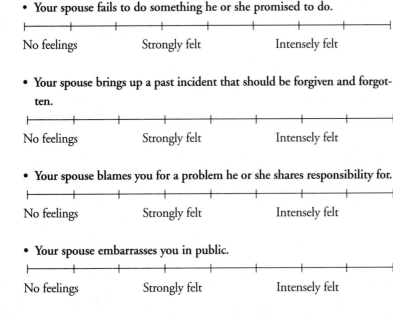

- **Your spouse fails to do something he or she promised to do.**

No feelings   Strongly felt   Intensely felt

- **Your spouse brings up a past incident that should be forgiven and forgotten.**

No feelings   Strongly felt   Intensely felt

- **Your spouse blames you for a problem he or she shares responsibility for.**

No feelings   Strongly felt   Intensely felt

- **Your spouse embarrasses you in public.**

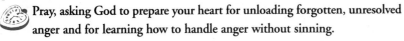

No feelings   Strongly felt   Intensely felt

This week you will explore the effects of anger on your relationship with your spouse and others. You'll also discover constructive ways to unload anger.

Pray, asking God to prepare your heart for unloading forgotten, unresolved anger and for learning how to handle anger without sinning.

---

[1]Charles Bass, *Banishing Fear from Your Life* (Garden City, N.Y.: Doubleday, 1986), 18-19.

Day 2
The Effects of Anger on Relationships

What effects do angry emotions have on your relationships? They cause distance from other people, God, ourself, and maturity as well as making us miserable.

Distance from Other People

One of the most common results or symptoms of deep anger is *relational distance*, an unwillingness and inability to let others get close. It seems to block our ability to give and receive love. You're sincerely trying to develop a satisfying and loving marriage, but the anger in either you or your mate can greatly inhibit your efforts. Consider this truly unfortunate story of a couple that had been married about 17 years. The husband knew things were not going well; he wanted to do something about it, and he asked me for help. Because he lived in a different state, we had to communicate by phone and letter.

This long-distance counseling continued off and on for about three years. Sometimes I wouldn't hear from him for months. And then one day he called to say, "I really appreciate all your help, but I'm leaving my wife."

I can't stand that kind of call! I dislike divorce, and I dislike "losing" a couple I've been trying to help. *Failure!* I thought. Again, that's not exactly what I said to him. I asked, "Why are you giving up?"

"Well," he answered, "when I woke up this morning, she was standing by the bed with a knife in her hand."

Whoa, I thought, *that could motivate a person to leave, couldn't it?*

But *why* did nothing the husband tried work? Why did their relationship get to the point of knife wielding and eventually divorce? The one time I talked with the wife, I discovered an extreme bitterness toward her mother because of a series of childhood incidents. For years, without even realizing the implications, she had carried this deep-seated anger toward her mom, and it poisoned her relationship with her husband. She had been so hurt by her mother, that she had decided unknowingly she was never going to let anyone get close enough to hurt her again. No matter what advice I gave her husband, and no matter how hard he tried to love her, his efforts were doomed. She simply wouldn't let him get near her heart. It's as if angry people can't allow others to get too close! The forgotten hurt holds them at arm's length, sabotaging relationships.

Could there be a forgotten hurt that's sabotaging a relationship you have with your spouse or another person? Take a moment right now and think about this.

 If anything I have described sounds familiar in your relationship, ask God to reveal to you any forgotten or past hurts that may be damaging your marriage. List three that come to mind. Ask God to help you remember.

_____

_____

 Pray seeking insight, revelation, and wisdom to deal with your past hurt.

Distance from God

A second consequence of unresolved anger can be spiritual blindness or feeling particularly distanced or alienated from God. A recent Gallup poll revealed that over 90 percent of Americans say they believe in God. That's great as a base, starting point. But in my counseling, I've observed some reverse correlation between anger and faith. It seems the greater a person's unresolved anger, the more difficulty that person has developing a meaningful spiritual life. The spiritual side of life offers us love, asks us to be loving and sensitive toward others, but anger appears to darken the heart, making it impossible to see the "call" or receive the love offered us from God. Anger can function like an automatic rheostat, turning down the spiritual light that could be shining within and from us. First John 2:9 says, "Anyone who claims to be in the light but hates his brother is still in the darkness."

Relational distance seems to block our ability to give and receive love.

Fill in the circle indicating the closeness of your relationship with God.

My relationship with God is: ○   ○   ○
                             Intimate   OK   Distant

If you find yourself distant from God, ask, "Am I angry with God over a situation from the past when I was hurt, frustrated, or fearful?"

Distance from Oneself

Another consequence of unresolved anger is a lowered sense of self-worth. In this case the anger and low self-worth are so intertwined and circular that it's hard to separate causes and effects. Let's say a child's—or an adult's—personal sense of being or boundary was drastically, maybe repeatedly, violated. Hurt, frustration from feeling helpless, and fear lead to anger. And that anger can set in and take this form: *I can't be worth much if others—and "life"—treat me like this.* The anger prompted by someone else's actions or attitudes can quickly become anger or blame or guilt directed at oneself. Such anger turned inward can become depression.

 The Bible describes this destructive cycle as the sins of the parents being passed on to future generations. Underline in the following text what it says about the parents' sins being passed on to future generations.

> You shall not make for yourself an idol … You shall not bow down to them or worship them; for I, the Lord your God, am a jealous God, punishing the children for the sin of the fathers to the third and fourth generation of those who hate me, but showing love to a thousand generations of those who love me and keep my commandments (Exodus 20:4-6).

 I have listed a few ways to break this destructive cycle. *Check* those you are trying. Circle those you may need to try.

- ❑ Confront past guilt—real or false
- ❑ Confess unresolved anger to a Christian friend, counselor, or pastor
- ❑ Pray about the anger
- ❑ Repent of the anger and bitterness
- ❑ Be reconciled to your parents
- ❑ Other: _____

If you continue to carry unresolved anger inside of you without acting to let go of it, you will experience ongoing pain. If you are not taking any of the above actions, your inner pain is increasing.

The greater the pain we carry inside, the greater the temptation to engage in addictive behaviors to get relief—temporary relief. The addictive behavior can include an unhealthy addiction to another person. According to a world renown psychiatrist, unchecked anger is a critical element in the most common psychiatric disorder: passive-dependent personality disorder. People with this personality disorder come to believe they cannot live a quality life without being cared for by another person.

It seems the greater a person's unresolved anger, the more difficulty that person has developing a meaningful spiritual life.

Passive-dependents set themselves up for emotional bankruptcy, because no one can ever fill them. No amount of praise or affirmation is ever enough. They are endlessly angry because people are continually disappointing them.[1]

The only one who can fully meet your needs is God. Are there people in your life that you count on to meet all your needs? Check any of the people listed below that you depend too much on to meet your emotional needs.

❑ Spouse   ❑ Friends   ❑ Children

❑ Mother   ❑ Boss or others at work   ❑ Other: _____

❑ Father   ❑ Support group at church

Anyone that you checked on the the list will also be a constant source of frustration for you. Why? They will never be able to live up to all of your expectations. In the next few days, you will learn ways to unload your anger and begin to release your need to depend on others more than God.

Angry, dependent people are locked into a pattern of living where they must have others, but when they get them, they smother them and usually kill the relationship. They find someone else, and the same thing happens. As they continue to fail, their anger—fueled by hurt (feeling abandoned) and frustration (feeling a failure) and fear (of being alone)—can alienate them from themselves and others, eating away at them just as if they actually turned on themselves and gnawed at their ankles until they reached the bone.[2] Is anger destructive, or what?

The cycle of anger and the sense of low self-value feeding off each other also can produce physical problems. So many people today go to the doctor and complain of backaches, neck aches, or headaches. But when the doctor looks into it, he can't find any physical cause of the pain. And some doctors are concluding that this epidemic of aches and pains may be the outworking of buried anger. The anger alienates us from our own bodies.

List any physical problems you have for which there seems to be no diagnosable cause. Could fear, frustration, or hurt from buried anger be the cause?

_____

_____

Distance from Maturity

This last "distance" caused by anger is connected to all those previously mentioned. Unresolved anger freezes our emotional maturity level near where it was when the hurtful offense occurred. Let's suppose your parents divorced when you were 12 years old. You were devastated, and the "anger container" inside you began to fill. In all likelihood, you also got stuck near that emotional level. You may have an adult body, but you've probably got the heart of a wounded 12-year-old.

The only one who can fully meet your needs is God.

Maybe you're not the angry person but you live with one. In that case, you may find yourself asking from time to time, *Why is he so childish? Why does she say those off-the-wall, immature things that hurt us?*

Anger Has Power to Keep You Miserable

Read that subhead again. Allow the truth to sink in: *Anger has the power to keep you miserable.* Jesus intends for you to be filled with joy. Is past anger robbing your joy?

Read John 16:33 and complete the sentence that follows.

> "I [Jesus] have told you these things, so that in me you may have peace. In this world you will have trouble, But take heart! I have overcome the world."

What Jesus has given me that nothing can rob is _____.

Unresolved anger and blame can imprison us, bind us, and make us miserable at heart and miserable to live with. Conversely, there is truth to the song that says, "Freedom is a state of mind." You can break free of unresolved anger. You may need further insight and support to break free, but that freedom is available. And it is a key to staying in love with life and for life.

At the end of this week's study is an *Anger Inventory* (page 42). Complete it now. If your score is high, then the next two days of study are critically important to you.

Ask God to begin to heal past anger in your life caused from fear, frustration, and hurt.

---

[1]M. Scott Peck, *Further Along the Road Less Traveled* (New York: Simon & Schuster, 1993), 39.
[2]Ibid., 63.

Day 3
Seven Steps to Unloading Anger (Part 1)

Today and tomorrow we will study seven steps toward unloading anger. Think of anger in terms of a dangerous substance that's compressed into a spray can. Some of these steps or tools will drain a little at a time, while others may let out half of it all at once. Some bring immediate results, while others give help over a longer period. Even though some may cause you to think, *I don't know if I can do that,* none of them are impossible. I've seen all of them work for me and thousands of others. Try them. After several weeks you'll find yourself saying, *You know, I don't have that same sick and empty feeling I had before.* Why? Because your under-pressure anger is going, going, nearly gone.

As a Christian, you are growing and changing, maturing in Jesus Christ. The following passage describes this change. Read Ephesians 4:22-27 and describe the change taking place in you through the power of Jesus Christ.

You were taught, with regard to your former way of life, to put off your old self, which is being corrupted by its deceitful desires; to be made new in the attitude of your minds; and to put on the new self, created to be like God in true righteousness and holiness.

Therefore each of you must put off falsehood and speak truthfully to his neighbors, for we are all members of one body. "In your anger do not sin." Do not let the sun go down while you are still angry, and do not give the devil a foothold.

_____

_____

Aren't most of your actions motivated by the desire for gain or the fear of loss?

Everyday it's our privilege to choose the overcoming power of Christ's forgiveness. You may contemplate the most obvious way to get the pressure out of the can: let it explode in one violent rip. But let me caution that you are the "can" that may well be hurt in the blast. Consider these more healthy steps.

1. Define the Offense

Think about it. Aren't most of your actions motivated by the desire for gain or the fear of loss (or a combination of the two)?

Those hopes and fears—expectations and losses—can trigger anger. We get angry because someone (maybe even our own mortal, inadequate self) is taking something away from us that we don't want to lose, or we're being denied something we want to gain. We blame something or someone for a loss—maybe even the loss of an unfulfilled dream or the loss of peace of mind. The first step is to analyze and define exactly what happened, what you've actually lost or were denied.

There was a man toward whom I was very angry for six years. When I looked at that situation and tried to name my loss, I realized I felt he had stolen some of my dignity. Maybe deeper than that, because we were coworkers and our conflict made me feel I couldn't stay in the same organization, I also felt he had taken my future. I had enjoyed that job—had thought I was finally where I wanted to be in life—and then, because the place "wasn't big enough for both of us," I felt deeply resentful.

Another personal story leads into my second point. When my brother, Ronnie, 4 years older than I, died at the age of 51, I was angry with him for months. He had been an angry person himself; he was generally distrustful of people and somewhat explosive at times. He didn't like doctors, so he refused to get checkups.

I would tell him, "Ronnie, heart trouble runs in our family. We've inherited this. You've got to get your cholesterol and your heart checked."

But he would respond, "I don't like doctors. They rip you off." And he would refuse to go.

Finally he had a heart attack and had to go. But even then, he wouldn't follow the doctor's instructions for how to take better care of himself. He figured, *I'm strong. I'll be all right.*

We were just getting to be closer friends when he died, and I got angry. Getting past that anger took time, and it meant I had to face the reality of my loss: I had lost a brother and a friend. Just admitting what I had lost and allowing myself to feel it (see step 2) helped a lot to get rid of my frustration and anger.

What about your own anger? Think of the things others have done that are still playing on that video tape in your mind. What did they deny you?

Is there anger from the past that you can specifically name? What is it? Briefly describe your anger.

_____

_____

*C*onfession *literally means "to agree" with God.*

When we store anger, it is plain and simple … it's sin! With admitting your anger, you need to confess that anger to the Lord. Confession is admitting and recognizing sin in your life. Confession literally means "to agree" with God. He knows the anger is there. Agree with God. Confess the anger.

First John 1:9 says that "if we confess out sins, he is faithful and just and will forgive us our sins and purify us from all unrighteousness." Write a prayer of confession. If you have a spouse and/or Christian friend to pray with, confess that anger to that person and ask them to pray with you.
Lord Jesus, I confess that …

_____

_____

2. Allow Yourself to Grieve

The second step in unloading anger is to allow yourself to grieve your loss. You've identified and written down what happened in the offense. Now accept that your pain—your sense of loss—is real; this person—your mate, boss, friend, parent, or maybe even yourself—did take something from you or deny you something. Don't minimize it! He or she didn't treat you with respect. Say the words: "You hurt me!"

Think of someone who has hurt you and you have not let go of the hurt or grieved the loss. Say out loud to yourself and God:
(The person who hurt you) *really hurt me. God help me to forgive them for* (the hurt).

You *are* angry, so look at it realistically. It's not only OK to grieve your loss, whatever it is, for a period of time, but grieving is also essential for your healing.

Elisabeth Kubler-Ross found that people go through stages of grief whenever they learn of their impending death: denial, anger, bargaining, depression, and acceptance. M. Scott Peck adds that we go through these same stages of grief every time we're about to grow in psychological or spiritual maturity.[1] If the conscious, grieving process feels painful, think of it in terms of final results: You're about to have an important "growth spurt" in your life. At the final stage of acceptance you will be able to say, *Yes, I can live with the loss; I can see beyond the loss.*

 What is the loss? Check any of the following things that describe your loss.

❑ Loss of pride   ❑ Loss of respect or dignity

❑ Loss of money or property   ❑ Loss of relationship

❑ Other:_____

Now speak and then surrender the loss to the Lord. Pray, *Lord I surrender to you both my hurt and my loss of* _____.

3. Try to Understand Your Offender

The third step in resolving anger—trying to understand your offender—may seem impossible and the benefits of it incomprehensible. It may take a while, but as soon as you can do it, I assure you, it can speed your release. Some of the healing power of this step is just in trying it. As you attempt to understand the person and why he or she might have committed the offense, you set a process in motion: You may well see how your offender could have acted out of his or her own hurt.

Read Romans 15:1-7 below. Underline the words or phrases that speak most directly to you.

> We who are strong ought to bear with the failings of the weak and not to please ourselves. Each of us should please his neighbor for his good, to build him up. For even Christ did not please himself but, as it is written: "The insults of those who insult you have fallen on me." For everything that was written in the past was written to teach us, so that through endurance and the encouragement of the Scriptures we might have hope. May the God who gives endurance and encouragement give you a spirit of unity among yourselves as you follow Christ Jesus, so that with one heart and mouth you may glorify the God and Father of our Lord Jesus Christ. Accept one another, then, just as Christ accepted you, in order to bring praise to God.

Accepting and trying to understand my offender has meant a lot to me personally. When I did, it was like draining half of my anger "can" at once. Let me explain. Remember the man I was angry with for six years? I was so tied up inside that I would wake up early in the morning thinking things like *I'm going to get revenge* and *I hope something bad happens to him today.* I was grinding away, playing the old tape in my head. Then one day, a person I was counseling came in with an article clipped from a magazine. The client said, "This article really describes me and tries to help people like me understand how they can get better. Would you read it? Maybe it will give you a better understanding of me, and you can use some of the ideas to help me."

"Sure," I said. I took the article home that night, though frankly I wasn't thrilled with the idea. But as I started to read it, I was amazed. I thought it described my own offender to a T! It was the first time I had any understanding of him and why he may have acted as he did. *So that's why he was such a jerk to me,* I thought. *That's why he did all those things. It makes all the sense in the world. No wonder!*

As I gained some understanding of the potential pain in his life, I actually felt twinges of compassion for him. I hadn't planned it or expected it at all. But realizing his hurtful actions toward me could be caused by his own hurtful experiences helped me see everything in a new light. He was an anger-filled, sabotaging man.

As soon as I understood for the first time just how wounded my offender might be, my attitude changed; a great pressure behind my anger was released.

Think of Jesus dying on the cross for you and me. Did He understand those who were crucifying Him? Yes, He must have in order to say, " 'Father, forgive them, for they do not know what they are doing' " (Luke 23:34). Will you demonstrate that kind of understanding, forgiveness, and love?

People hurt us because they were first wounded.

 **Fill in the blanks to identify the first three steps to unload your anger.**

1. _____ the offense.

2. Allow yourself to _____.

3. Try to _____ your offender.

 **Close in prayer, forgiving the person from the past who hurt you.**

------

[1]M. Scott Peck, *Further Along the Road Less Traveled,* 63.

Day 4
Seven Steps to Unloading Anger (Part 2)

We are continuing our steps from yesterday. Let's get started.

4. Release Your Offender
This step in dealing with anger involves giving up your desire for revenge, releasing your offender from your wish to get even. This step sometimes comes "naturally" once you have understood some of the causes of the offensive behavior toward you.

Read Romans 12:19 below and briefly summarize what it says about revenge.

Do not take revenge, my friends, but leave room for God's wrath, for it is written: "It is mine to avenge; I will repay," says the Lord.

_____

_____

_____

_____

Releasing your offender can drain several ounces of resentment at once and it usually involves learning how to forgive. Forgiving someone for a few offences toward you doesn't compare to your life time of offences toward God—and everyday He forgives you! (Matthew 18). The original definition of _forgiveness_ actually means that you untie or release someone. As long as you remain bitter and unforgiving, you're tied to that person with emotional knots. Being untied involves a conscious and deliberate release of the offender through an act of forgiveness.

Jesus teaches in the Sermon on the Mount that we receive forgiveness as we forgive others (see Matthew 6:12-15).

 Below is a cup representing the crucible of your life. Shade with a black pen or pencil the cup up to the level of unforgiveness in your life. In the unshaded part, write the words _God's Forgiveness_.

Look at the cup closely. You cannot receive any more of God's forgiveness until you empty yourself of unforgiveness. Are you ready to forgive? It's a good idea to say forgiving words out loud picturing the person you are forgiving, preferably with someone else present, because the impact is more powerful. In my forgiveness of the coworker who had so offended me, I said the words aloud but alone. I took several hours, and I relived those situations in which I had felt such deep hurt. In my mind's eye I was with him again in those painful incidents, but I was also observing "from a corner of the room." In this private scenario, as we came to a place where he had given offense, I would stop him and say, "I forgive you. I'm untying you from the emotional ropes that have held me to you. I release you."

 Is there a person you need to release, to forgive? If so, what do you need to say to that person without being hurtful or vengeful? Write what you would say to that person.

The original definition of forgiveness _actually means that you untie or release someone._ Jesus teaches that we receive forgiveness as we forgive others.

An important though difficult part of releasing someone is giving up the expectation that the person will eventually see the error of his or her ways and take the initiative to make things right with you. Be willing to forgive without expecting ever to see a reciprocal action in kind from the other person.

5. Look for Pearls in the Offense

You can overcome anger by searching for "hidden pearls" in the offense committed against you. Some good can come of any bad situation if you'll just look for it. Find the good, and you can be grateful for it. Gratitude and anger can't coexist. This is another step that can drain a lot of anger all at once. It's an alternate choice you can make in how you respond to hurt, fear, or frustration.

We will say more about pearl hunting next week. Keep reading.

 Think of one thing you have learned from a past hurt. Write it below.

_____

_____

6. Put Your Feelings in Writing

Another helpful step in working through anger is to put your feelings in writing in the form of a letter to the person who offended you. I'm not saying you have to mail the letter. But when you spell out your hurts, frustrations, and fears, it's almost as if your anger is released through the ink of the pen. You may not feel the effect immediately, but you can in time. What do you write?

- Clarify what you lost or were denied
- Describe what caused you pain and led to your anger
- Talk about your resultant feelings
- Express your desire to set aside and live beyond your anger
- Say that you wish to know the freedom that comes with forgiveness
- State how you would like your offender to respond

Normally, I don't encourage the people to send such letters to—or confront—their offenders; the offender usually reacts badly and increases the offense. It can make the problem worse for everyone involved.

As an old proverb says: Do not reprove a fool, or he will hate you and spread all sorts of lies about you (see Proverbs 9:7). Foolish people (often angry, emotionally blind people) can't see their faults and shortcomings. Being confronted with their hurtful actions and words can threaten them with so much pain that they may respond by lashing out—hating you for forcing them to look at what they cannot face; they may subsequently do whatever they can to discredit you.

As I said before, I generally advise against mailing a letter written to an offender. Just writing the letter can help unload some of your resentment, whether you mail it or not.

When you spell out your hurts, frustrations, and fears, it's as if your anger is released through the ink of the pen.

Below is a sheet of stationery. Write a letter like I have described.

Its never easy to reach out in a loving way to those who have hurt us.

7. Reach Out to Your Offender

This last step in resolving anger may well be the hardest. It doesn't come naturally, and it requires a huge act of the will, not to mention a high degree of maturity and love. But when you're able to do it, it can release a lot of anger.

What does this involve? Finding some way to help in the healing of the person who offended you. I suspect this sounds impossible, but I've seen its benefits to those who can get to this point.

You may never be able to do this. I'm not saying you *should* do it. But I'm saying that if you *can* come to the place where you can have some compassion for the person because of the pain he's also been through, it can provide a great healing for you. Guaranteed: He is wounded, sick, and in need of healing. I've tried to do this myself for people who have offended me. It has been very emotional, but I could feel my anger releasing. I know it won't be easy for anyone.

It's never easy to reach out in a loving way to those who have hurt us.

Complete this sentence, adding the name of someone who offended you.
One way I could reach out to _____ would be

_____

Pray, asking God for the power through His Spirit to take these seven steps and unload your past anger in a healthy, constructive, biblical way.

Fill in the blanks to list the seven steps or ways to unload anger.

1. _____ the offense.

2. Allow yourself to _____.

3. Try to _____ your offender.

4. _____ your offender.

5. Look for _____ in the offense.

6. Put your feelings in _____ .

7. _____ out to your offender.

Day 5
Using the Steps to Drain Your Own Guilt

You may be the offender. You may have "provoked" someone to choose anger because of your hurtful, frustrating actions or words. The pain of your own guilt may have turned into anger toward yourself. Consider this statement as a step that reaches out to heal both the offended and you, the offender: *Each of the steps mentioned to get rid of your anger can also be used in reverse to release anger in someone you have offended (and anger-produced guilt in you, the offender).*

Remember the story of my friend Larry, who was angry with me for nine years? Let's just imagine a different scenario from what actually happened. Suppose right from the beginning I had been aware I had wounded him. Suppose I had called him that very week, met him for coffee, and analyzed or named my offense, apologized, made some explanation for my actions, and sought his forgiveness? I could have helped loosen the lid on his anger and the guilt that would have been eating at me.

In 1 Samuel, we read the stories of how Saul hated David though David had not sought to hurt Saul. David actually reached out to Saul attempting to release him from his anger.

 Read the following passages from the account of Saul and David and briefly write what David did to reach out to Saul. (For the complete account, read 1 Samuel 18; 19:9-10; 24; and 26.)

Saul's Attitude
When Saul realized that the Lord was with David and that his daughter Michal loved David, Saul became still more afraid of him, and he remained his enemy the rest of his days (1 Samuel 18:28-29).

David Spares Saul's Life

"You are more righteous than I," he [Saul] said. "You have treated me well, but I have treated you badly. You have just now told me of the good you did to me; the Lord delivered me into your hands, but you did not kill me" (1 Samuel 24: 17-18).

David Spares Saul's Life—Again

David answered, "The Lord rewards every man for his righteousness and faithfulness. The Lord delivered you into my hands today, but I would not lay a hand on the Lord's anointed" (1 Samuel 26:23).

Is there unforgiveness in your life?

Remember the steps?

1. Define the offense
2. Allow yourself to grieve
3. Try to understand your offender
4. Release your offender
5. Look for pearls in the offense
6. Put your feelings in writing
7. Reach out to your offender

These are all steps that add up to forgiveness and will release you from the anger that can otherwise eat away at your insides.

 Is there unforgiveness in your life? Which of the above steps do you need? Underline the ones you have taken and circle those you need to take.

Let me share a story that illustrates these elements. I have a friend who played professional baseball. At one point in his life, he came to a startling realization: *I really didn't enjoy playing baseball as much as my father did. He forced me to play from the time I was a little guy. He was my coach and inspiration. In fact, I didn't even see him a lot except for baseball. And the bottom line is that I'm angry at him for the way he raised me.*

He came to that understanding in a movie theater. He was in his late 40s by that time (his father was in his early 80s), and he and his wife were watching the film *Field of Dreams*. As he sat there looking on, he just started crying, then sobbing. *What in the world is going on?* he wondered. And his wife was giving him a *What's wrong with you?* look. But he just sat there crying, even after the credits had run.

"Honey, the movie is over," his wife said as the lights came up.

"I don't know what's going on with me," he said, "but this movie brought out all kinds of feelings about my dad. Honey, I don't know if you'll understand this, but I'd like to go see him right away. I really feel I need to. What do you think?"

"That's fine," she said.

My friend called his mother that night and said, "Mom, I'm going to fly up and see Dad. Make sure he's home tomorrow night, because I'm coming up to do something with him."

So he got up there and told his dad what he wanted to do, and the father replied, "What! You flew all the way up here for us to go to a movie?"

"That's right, Dad, I want to watch this movie with you." That's all he told him.

They went to the theater together, and this time they both sobbed all the way through. At the end of the movie, they drove to an all-night restaurant, where they talked over how they felt. By early morning, this son had forgiven his father, and they were reconciled in a way that neither had ever before experienced.

I understand *Field of Dreams* has had a similar healing effect for many fathers and sons. In this case, although the whole process took place rather quickly, my friend used many of the steps described this week. He clarified and grieved his loss—as a young man he hadn't realized his own goals and dreams. He forgave his father and reached out to heal both him and their relationship.

I trust that these steps of forgiveness can help you or someone you love drain away all kinds of anger. To the extent that you can experience inner healing, you'll be better equipped to love the people around you.

For the sake of our society as well, we need to see families healed and brought back into harmony. We need to say "Enough is enough" and start learning how to forgive each other. When that spreads, just watch what happens in our world! I pray you'll be right at the heart of that movement.

Remember how Peter denied he knew Jesus (see Matthew 26:69-75)? Remember how Judas betrayed Jesus (see Matthew 26:47-56)? Contrast how Judas handled his guilt and how Jesus and Peter handled Peter's guilt. Read the passages and complete the sentences that follow.

> "I have sinned," he [Judas] said, "for I have betrayed innocent blood." … So Judas threw the money into the temple and left. Then he went away and hanged himself (Matthew 27: 4-5).

> The third time he [Jesus] said to him [Peter], "Simon son of John, do you love me?"
>
> Peter was hurt because Jesus asked him the third time, "Do you love me?" He said, "Lord, you know all things; you know that I love you."
>
> Jesus said, "Feed my sheep" (John 21:17).

Judas handled guilt by _____.
Jesus and Peter handled Peter's guilt by

_____.

If you are willing to forgive and be forgiven, then pray the following prayer out loud: *Lord Jesus, forgive me of my unforgiveness toward (those you have not previously forgiven). Now Jesus, forgive me and cleanse me through Your shed blood. Amen.*

To the extent that you can experience inner healing, you'll be better equipped to love the people around you.

Anger Inventory

While this is not a scientifically-constructed test, it can give you some idea of where you stand in regard to your anger or your potentially anger-producing background. To take the inventory, rate each statement below on a scale from 0 (very low) to 10 (very high) for how much it applies to you.

_____ 1. I have frequently recurring minor health problems.

_____ 2. I tend to have difficulty remaining close to people. Others have even said I am "cold."

_____ 3. I continually fail to see the pitfalls in business deals.

_____ 4. I have little interest in religious matters.

_____ 5. I have many doubts about the existence of God.

_____ 6. I tend to see religious people as "a bunch of hypocrites."

_____ 7. I tend to be judgmental or overly critical of people.

_____ 8. I have a general inability to see my own shortcomings.

_____ 9. My image is very important to me. What I wear and drive are big concerns.

_____ 10. I often struggle with feelings of low self-value.

_____ 11. I often fail to see that my words or actions hurt the feelings of others.

_____ 12. My parents divorced before I turned 18.

_____ 13. I think one or both of my parents drank too much alcohol.

_____ 14. My parents seemed addicted to drugs or other substances.

_____ 15. My parents abused me.

_____ 16. My parents seemed too distant or neglectful to me.

_____ 17. I felt that my parents were too controlling of me.

_____ 18. I often struggle with feelings of discouragement or depression.

_____ 19. I seem to be at odds with several people for long periods of time.

_____ 20. I tend to be overly controlling of my mate, children, or friends.

_____ 21. I have general feelings of anxiety; I can't put my finger on what it is that I'm uneasy about.

_____ 22. I have sometimes thought about suicide.

_____ 23. I have had a hard time forgiving others when they hurt or frustrate me.

_____ 24. I have a hard time confronting others when they hurt me, and I know I'm not that good at getting my anger out.

_____ 25. I find myself overly busy most of the time.

_____ 26. I find it easier to blame others than to take responsibility for my mistakes.

_____ 27. I often overreact to what others say or do to me.

_____ 28. I feel I'm motivated far too often by fear of failure.

_____ 29. I often wish people who have hurt me could be punished somehow.

_____ 30. I frequently think that I've been cheated out of important areas of life.

_____ 31. I get into fights with others that sometimes result in physical aggression, such as throwing things, slapping, or hitting.

_____ 32. I don't really trust anyone other than myself.

_____ **Total score (Add the 32 numbers of your ratings)**

You may wish to discuss your results with your mate, a friend, or a trained counselor. If your total score is more than 100, the up-coming studies are especially important for you. If your score is more than 200, you may want to see a counselor trained in helping people uncover and deal with anger.

Couple Time

For you to complete

The most important thing I learned this week about unresolved anger is:

_____

_____

The step of resolving and unloading past anger that I need to focus on the most is:

_____

_____

One way my relationship with the Lord has deepened this week is:

_____

_____

One person I need to reach out to is:

_____

For you to share with your spouse

1. Sit down together facing each other and take turns sharing how each of you completed the above section.

2. Read Ephesians 4:25-32 out loud to one another. Share which verse speaks the most directly to each of you and why.

3. Complete this sentence for each other.
One way that we need to handle our anger in the future in a more godly way is:

_____

4. Ask for forgiveness from each other for any past unresolved anger. Pray for one another asking God to forgive you as you forgive each other.

You Can Choose to Turn "Sand Storms" Into Pearls

I could be happy, I could be in love with life, if only … Most not-yet-happy people have one or more "great" ways to finish that sentence. *If only my spouse would drop dead. If only I had a spouse. If only I lived in a better neighborhood. If only I were to win the lottery.* They could love life if only they could somehow reduce the number of their troubles, leave behind the frustrating, anger-producing negatives—as a snake slithers out of and leaves behind its skin.

But just the opposite is true! Without some painful encounters, our quality of life is diminished. Scott Peck begins his classic book *The Road Less Traveled* with a now famous line: "Life is difficult." He continues: "This is a great truth, one of the greatest truths."[1]

On these two counts I agree, and I also say that contained in every difficulty are good and great things that we can learn to appreciate—that we can use for our benefit and enrichment.

All our trials, great and small, can bring more of the two best things in life: love for life and love for others. But only those who take full responsibility for their responses to trials find these loves in their lasting form.

No one can escape his or her share of life's problems. One might try to, like old Charlie, who thought he could find true happiness by escaping the pressures of life. With this hope, he entered a monastery where silence was the rule—the only exception being chapel prayers. Every 5 years, however, you could speak two words to the abbot. At the end of his first 5 years there, Charlie chose his words carefully: "Bad food," he said. After 5 more years, Charlie said, "Hard bed." Finally, after 15 years, Charlie declared, "I quit!"

Disappointed, the abbot responded, "I'm not surprised. Ever since you came, all you've done is complain."

Trials, hardships, hurts, and all the other painful experiences we encounter are like personal "sand storms." They might blind us, sting us, irritate us, and anger us. But as we respond to them, we have a choice I introduced in the previous chapter: *After a trial we can get better or bitter.*

We can find the road to a love that lasts forever as we get to the place where we regularly use our "sand storms" to our advantage. I call the process of transforming hurts into benefits *pearl counting*. I use that word picture because the pearl found within an oyster started with an irritating piece of sand. Those precious jewels are ours for the taking.

In fact, every trial contains *several* pearls. Once I caught on to this principle, I got excited about seeing how many I could find in each crisis. Some provide a whole "necklace" suitable for prominent display. The more pearls, the greater your riches.

But you might ask, "What good comes out of my business going under, or having been abused as a child, or my mate's serious illness, or … ?" Although those situations are initially devastating, they each eventually can produce a set of beautiful, valuable pearls. Not too quickly. It usually takes at least four years for an oyster to add layer after layer of secretions to make the larger, valuable pearls.

As you dig into your tribulations and discover the gems buried within, your self-worth will soar, and so will your ability to give and receive love. One of the greatest life-giving principles I've found is that all trials, big or small, can add to our "love chest" if we search for it.

This week you will …

- learn how to discover the pearls in every trial;
- develop the skills to avoid panic-thinking and extreme reactions to circumstances no matter how painful;
- understand how to give and find priceless pearls;
- begin to list strengths and write down your trials;
- search for benefits from each trial and find ways to turn pearls into loving action.

Contained in every difficulty are good and great things that we can learn to appreciate.

Day 1	Day 2	Day 3	Day 4	Day 5
Dig Up the Pearls in Every Trial	Avoid Extreme Thoughts	Allow Yourself to Grieve Your Pain	Count Precious Pearls (Part 1)	Count Precious Pearls (Part 2)

As you study and pray this week, I encourage you not to become discouraged when trials and difficulties arise. You can learn, grow, and discover pearls from every difficulty.

I invite you to memorize and meditate on this verse in the coming week.

> "In this you greatly rejoice, though now for a little while you may have had to suffer grief in all kinds of trials. These have come so that your faith—of greater worth than gold, which perishes even though refined by fire—may be proved genuine and may result in praise, glory and honor when Jesus Christ is revealed" (1 Peter 1:6-7).

[1]M. Scott Peck, *The Road Less Traveled* (New York: Simon & Schuster: 1978), 15.

Day 1
Dig Up the Pearls in Every Trial

At age 38 Terry Brown had finally found his dream bride, Janna. But one week before their wedding, Terry received a midnight call from his brother: Their mother had been diagnosed with acute cancer; doctors gave her only 24 hours to live. Terry flew to Florida the next day to be by her side, where he and his brothers stayed until she slipped into a coma. Meanwhile, Janna came to me in tears, wondering what she could do to support Terry and asking if they should postpone their ceremony.

As Terry's mother lingered on life support, other family members urged Terry to go forward with his wedding plans; no one knew for sure how long she would last.

As it turned out, the mother lived until her son's wedding, which took place as originally planned. That evening, following the ceremony, Terry heard that his mother, without regaining consciousness, had slipped away earlier in the day.

At this point, Terry and Janna's plans did change. The next morning, when they were supposed to be starting their honeymoon, they flew to Florida for what would be the first of three memorial services. Then, still on their "honeymoon," they flew to Chicago for the funeral.

We can all sympathize with Terry's loss and the unfortunate timing. But follow with me and see what they did in response to their tragedy.

Several months after the wedding, I listened as they explained their response to the terrible events. He confessed that even though he was losing the mother he had loved for 38 years—though he knew she wanted more than anything to be with him for his long-awaited wedding—he was gaining the closest friend he had ever known. He said it was a strange, conflicting set of emotions. On one hand, he was losing a most important loved one. On the other hand, he was feeling so encouraged by and such a tender tug toward Janna, who was demonstrating such unconditional love for him. She was far more concerned for him and his feelings than she was for her honeymoon. Through this terrible situation, he could see her friendship in action—unbelievably supportive, caring, and relaxed.

This traumatic beginning of their life together convinced them that they would be able to go through almost anything. The crisis was so bonding for them—he later admitted that the whole week was the most encouraging time of his life. His bride's love for him far exceeded anything he had imagined possible.

Because Terry had previously learned the secrets of pearl counting, he was somewhat aware of these positive possibilities while still in the midst of the funeral (honeymoon) week. He just started looking for—expecting—something good to come out of that mess. And it did! Terry found pearls: a deeper bond with Janna, the assurance that he has a friend committed to him even in hard times.

 From where do trials come? List one or two sources of trials in life.

God can bring out pearls no matter what the source of the trial may be.

Compare your items with mine. Add any sources of trials you thought of that I have missed. Then think about the past year of your life. Rate the sources of most of your trials by placing a 1, 2, or 3 in the blank by your top three.

_____ God
_____ Other people
_____ The world
_____ Satan
_____ Enemies
_____ Trying circumstances and situations
_____ Problems I have created
_____ Other: _____
_____ Other: _____

Obviously, God does not create every trial. But, He can work in every circumstance to strengthen and comfort us. God can bring out pearls no matter what the source of the trial may be. Our response to difficulties remains the key. When difficulties, trials, and problems arise, what is your normal response?

Check your usual feelings when faced with a difficulty or a trial.

❑ Anger   ❑ Frustration
❑ Depression   ❑ Joy
❑ Discouragement   ❑ Gratitude
❑ Hope   ❑ Anticipation
❑ Confusion   ❑ Other:_____

What pearls have you discovered in the trials you have faced?

God works for good in every situation—including suffering and trials—if we allow Him. Read the following Scripture from Romans 8:28. Then, in your own words, describe how God works for good in difficult situations.

We know that in all things God works for the good of those who love him, who have been called according to his purpose (Romans 8:28).

_____

_____

Think of a situation in the last year when you experienced trials. What pearls did you discover from that situation? Describe the trials and the pearls.

_____

_____

What attitude does God desire you to have when you face a trial? Below is a list of attitudes Paul mentions in Philippians 4:4-13. Check those attitudes that need the most cultivation in your life as you face trials and difficulties in your marriage and other relationships.

- ❏ Joy
- ❏ Have true and noble thoughts
- ❏ Seek excellence
- ❏ Be content
- ❏ Be thankful
- ❏ Focus on what's pure
- ❏ Praise God
- ❏ Do not be anxious

Ask the Lord in prayer to give you the attitudes you need to find pearls in every difficulty you face. Write your prayer below.

_____

_____

Day 2
Avoid Extreme Thoughts

When we hit hard times, we often overreact and panic. "This is the absolute worst thing that could happen!" "Nobody has ever gone through anything as devastating as this circumstance!" The truth is neither of those statements is true.

Try to refocus some of your energy away from all that's bad to searching for anything that could possibly be good in the trial. Try to think of what new opportunities this situation may bring.

Check the following questions you most need to ask yourself when facing a trial so that you will not be overcome with panic.

- ❏ What can I learn from this?
- ❏ What new opportunity does this present?
- ❏ How can I pray more effectively?
- ❏ In what way is this bringing me closer to God?
- ❏ What does this crisis reveal about my character?
- ❏ How can God use this trial to produce a pearl in my life?
- ❏ What future happiness lies ahead as a result of this trial?

Relax. Most trials are not as bad as they seem at the time. As Mark Twain once said, "I am an old man and have known a great many troubles, but most of them never happened."

One extreme but subtle thought we can try to avoid might be boiled down to: *I am the center of the universe.* A recent *Newsweek* cover featured a big, bold word: "Exhausted." The inside story, titled "Breaking Point," paints a picture of a frazzled

America—stressed as never before. Why? Because "we have cell phones in the car and beepers in our pockets, and we carry them to Disneyland, to the beach, to the bathroom."[2] We think the world will fall apart if we don't respond now. When everything becomes an emergency only we can fix, life quickly becomes out of control.

Facing an emergency, the human body revs up, ready for the challenge: increased heart-rate, constricted muscles and arteries, pumped adrenaline. That ready-to-fight stance may serve us well to ward off physical attack, but "it's horribly suited to the unremitting pressures of modern life."[3] Extreme thoughts hurt us physically and psychologically; we too often turn daily challenges into "dog attacks."

Even the threat of a real dog attack can prompt unnecessarily wild thoughts, such as, *This is it. I'm a dead man.* I know. I've been there. Years ago I was at a speaking engagement in Florida and scheduled to stay in a private home. My very first evening, well after dark, I was dropped off, my ride drove away—and then I discovered I was locked out of the house. No key. No one at home. I knew I was at the right house. I knew I was expected. What to do?

I walked over to the front window to see if it would open. No. It was locked. I thought I'd try a back door. As I fumbled my way to the back, I saw that the yard was surrounded by a substantial iron fence. I tried to open the gate. Yes. Success.

I entered, closed the gate, made my way up the back walk, and met my worst nightmare—a huge dog. Our eyes met; he immediately saw the fear in mine. Sensing his victory, he bolted toward me with what seemed to be incredible speed. I knew I was a dead man. The adrenaline kicked in. I was ready to fight him off with nothing but my bare hands and maybe my teeth—though I knew his teeth would win.

He sped over to me, put on his brakes, and slid down the walk until he was right on top of my shoes. Then he instinctively did what he was trained to do: He started licking my feet!

I leaned over, petted him, and said, "Nice doggie. Good doggie!" Meanwhile, my heart was beating so hard, it felt as if my whole body were that one pumping organ!

Anyone would have extreme thoughts with a huge dog racing toward him. I tell the story to illustrate a larger point: in real life, most of our trials are something like that "dog attack"; the perceived threat or even the perceived damage doesn't match the reality of the actual damage.

Even when the damage is real (even if I had been mauled by the dog), that trial still leads to the creation of one or more pearls—there for the finding.

⏱ **In Philippians 4:8, Paul gives us a list of thoughts we need to have at the time of testing, trials, and difficulties. These thoughts are the opposite of extreme thoughts. Mark an x on the line where your thoughts usually are when facing a crisis.**

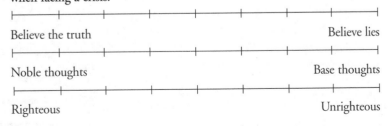

Believe the truth   Believe lies

Noble thoughts   Base thoughts

Righteous   Unrighteous

Think of what new opportunities this situation may bring.

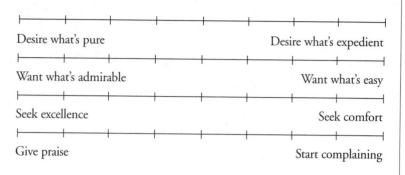

Desire what's pure							Desire what's expedient
Want what's admirable							Want what's easy
Seek excellence							Seek comfort
Give praise							Start complaining

Panic thinking sees trials as crises; God's perspective sees them as producing pearls.

When our thoughts and attitudes conform to the mind of Christ (1 Corinthians 2:16), then we can face any trial that life has to offer. At times, those trials come completely without warning like with my friend, Tom.

Several years ago, Tom went through the most agonizing trial of his life. With no recognized warning, one day his wife left him. She meant business; the separation quickly led to a divorce.

In Tom's own words, it was like a "sand hurricane." He had always wanted a happy marriage, and he had no clue as to why his wife had aborted their relationship. The accompanying tailspin is not uncommon in such situations. Tom was hopelessly depressed. He questioned why he should even go on living.

But Tom gradually regained a proper focus on life; that extreme thinking proved faulty. He realized that his life was not utterly destroyed, and he felt a growing desire to help others facing a trauma similar to his.

So Tom went back to school, eventually completing his Ph.D. He gained extensive counseling experience. In time he started a national organization, Fresh Start, which specializes in helping people through the trauma of an unwanted marital break-up. He told me, "As I look back, my divorce has turned out to be the greatest and most rewarding experience of my life."

During his crisis Tom thought nothing could ever match the pain he felt. But that pain was redeemed. Tom's life-career opened up as a result of his own pain. Tom has remarried, and the relationship he has with his new wife and children is better than he had imagined possible.

As I've grown older I've conditioned myself to avoid extreme "panic" thinking. If we can slowly reverse our thinking from "all that we're losing" in any trial to "all that we will eventually gain," we'll become much more positive and not so easily shaken by negative circumstances. Just think how much easier you'll be to live with once you grasp this principle. Your mate or friends might throw a party in celebration! You might throw your own love-for-life party.

Panic thinking sees trials as crises. God's perspective is that any irritation or trial in life can produce a pearl.

If you are facing a crisis or trial, are you willing to pray this prayer?

Lord Jesus, thank you for the opportunity to discover a pearl in this trial. Give me eyes to see and ears to hear what good you will do in my life in the midst of this trial. Amen.

---

[1]LynNell Hancock, "Breaking Point," *Newsweek*, 6 March 1995, 59.
[2]Geoffrey Cowley, "Dialing the Stress-Meter Down," *Newsweek*, 6 March 1995, 62.

Day 3

Allow Yourself to Grieve the Pain

Even though I urge people to keep an optimistic outlook when confronted by a negative experience, it's still important to allow yourself to figure out what took place, analyze how it makes you feel, and *feel* the pain associated with the event. By not using this last key, you can stuff the feelings so deep that you think you've solved the problem—when actually you're simply denying the problem.

Remember "counting pearls" is the fifth step in releasing unresolved anger. It is one step in a larger process that involves working through grief—accepting the reality of one's trial and one's loss. I've never found an exception. There are pearls in every trial, not before but during and especially following our grief. Another way to say this is: *don't waste your tears.*

 When you experience pain, what is your first reaction? Check your normal reaction to pain and loss.

- ❑ Tears
- ❑ Repression
- ❑ Complaining
- ❑ Anger
- ❑ Stoic outlook
- ❑ Become negative
- ❑ Depression
- ❑ Faith
- ❑ Grief
- ❑ Denial
- ❑ Optimism
- ❑ Hope
- ❑ Other: _____

Don't hold back the tears or the grief. Grief is a gift from God to release our pain when loss occurs. People grieved in healthy ways in the Bible.

 Read the following Scriptures that report two accounts related to Jesus— one during His ministry and one at His death and resurrection. Briefly describe the grief expressed.

On his arrival, Jesus found that Lazarus had already been in the tomb for four days.

When Jesus saw her [Mary] weeping, and the Jews who had come along with her also weeping, he was deeply moved in spirit and troubled. "Where have you laid him?" he asked.

"Come and see, Lord," they replied.

Jesus wept.

Then the Jews said, "See how he loved him!" (John 11:17,33-36).

They asked her [Mary], "Woman, why are you crying?" "They have taken my Lord away," she said, "and I don't know where they have put him" (John 20:13).

Grief is a gift from God to release our pain when loss occurs.

Expressing grief is appropriate. God comforts us when we grieve. He also expects us to use the pain we have experienced and the tears we have shed as pearls to comfort others in their pain.

 Read 2 Corinthians 1:3-5 below. Underline the portion of this Scripture that speaks most meaningfully to you.

> Praise be to the God and Father of our Lord Jesus Christ, who comforts us in all our troubles, so that we can comfort those in any trouble with the comfort we ourselves have received from God. For just as the sufferings of Christ flow over into our lives, so also through Christ our comfort overflows.

Now we get to the specifics of how to find those pearls in the "sand storms" of our lives. These steps are not something we use just for a short time after a trial; we continue using them until our thinking actually changes and we realize the positive results—until we find the pearls in every trial. You will have victory over your pain only when you feel and see the benefits to you. What do I mean by *benefits*? More connection with others, yourself, God. An underlying heart-happiness. New opportunities. Keep reading to identify more pearly gems.

Counting pearls is transforming *bitter* into *better*. When you're bitter, you're angry and feel low self-worth. When you're better, you feel grateful and enjoy an elevated sense of self-value and happiness.

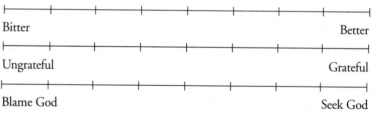 **Before we explore the specific steps in counting pearls, let me ask you a question. Are your trials producing character in you which enables you to serve the Lord and others better, or are you filling up with misery, self-pity, and bitterness? Mark an x to indicate where you are right now.**

Bitter   Better

Ungrateful   Grateful

Blame God   Seek God

Hebrews 12:15 warns us about bitterness: "See to it that no one misses the grace of God and that no bitter root grows up to cause trouble and defile many."

 Write a prayer of confession for any bitterness in your life. Or, write a prayer thanking God for transforming your pain into pearls.

_____

_____

Counting pearls is transforming bitter *into* better.

Day 4
Count Precious Pearls (Part 1)

To get a handle on the basics of the pearl-counting process, look at the chart on page 54, get a pencil, and get ready to fill in the chart. This entire chart is *positive.* It may not seem like it at first, as the chart will include a list of trials or crises. But when you've completed the chart, you'll see how your crises have brought you numerous benefits. The benefits aren't simply vague character traits; you'll find specific pearls that fit into every area of life. Let's discuss what each column is about.

1. My Life-long Strengths

 Complete this sentence:
I'm glad I'm alive because _____

_____

Self-appreciation is a healthy exercise in personal value.

Naming your strengths might be an easy assignment. But it's a hard challenge for some people. Self-appreciation is not an unhealthy, narcissistic indulgence but a healthy exercise in personal value. It's a realistic look at yourself.

 What do you like about yourself? This is not the time to be overly humble. List what you like about yourself in the box below.

Count Precious Pearls

My Life-long Strengths	My Most Painful Trials	My Support People	My Pearls from Each Trial	My Loving Action Because of Each Trial

What we're looking for is an accurate view of the positive things about you and what you truly appreciate about who you are. What types of activities do you do well?

List what you do well in the box below.

> *What do you truly appreciate about who you are?*

How are your people skills? Hobbies? What do you bring to relationships that others appreciate? If you can't think of several strengths about yourself, ask your mate or friends—and read on. It gets better!

Make a list of all the strengths you have not yet listed.

Transfer what you wrote in each box to column 1, My Life-long Strengths, on the chart on page 54.

2. My Most Painful Trials

Think back over your whole life history. List below the most painful trials you've experienced—your personal "sand storms." Include ones that have lowered your sense of self-value or caused you shame or guilt. It may be too hurtful to list some, but I encourage you to list any—and all—as you're able. If the listing process does become unbearable, focus on two or three, and deal with others at another time. Also begin thinking positively about your sand storms. List the pearls you have gleaned from them.

STORM	PEARL
_____	_____
_____	_____
_____	_____
_____	_____
_____	_____

I have searched for every pearl in each major "storm" of my entire life. Because of that, I can honestly say there is nothing that remains negative about me in my mind. Don't misunderstand me; I don't see myself as even close to perfect, and others may still see negative things about me, but I've done my best to turn everything around to a positive inside my own heart. I get to spend every day bathing in a pool of value about what has happened to me. It's like soaking in "pearl water."

The negatives in my life started early. Let me name one particular negative—a poor academic record and a resulting poor self-image—that I've come to see as a positive. My parents didn't place a high premium on academics. Neither one of them had gone far in school. Their lack of interest had an discouraging effect on my life. Besides that, we moved often. I changed schools every year, and sometimes twice a year. In first and second grade I was in California, where they were experimenting with some new educational philosophy that didn't last long. It was one of those "The child will learn when he's ready" approaches that didn't suit me well. Apparently I wasn't ready to learn, because by third grade I was far behind my peers.

Further complicating the issue was a move to Washington state. By the time I got to the end of third grade, my parents were told things like, "We'd really like to see Gary be a leader in school," and, "We want to see Gary mature around the others." The translation was clear: *I had flunked third grade.*

To this day, my kids tease me mercilessly over this issue. "Dad, how could you flunk third grade?" they'll ask. Then we all laugh together.

Truthfully, I was deeply embarrassed for many years about having failed a grade. It was a secret I tried to keep as private as possible. Once I completed this pearl-counting exercise, however, I was able to turn it all around. You'll see how this occurs as you read on.

 Before you leave this category, you may want to number your trials in the order of their severity. Give the worst pain you endured a number one, next, a number two, and so on. Transfer the list you made to column 2, My Most Painful Trials, on the chart on page 54. List them in the order of their severity. Close today's study in prayer, thanking God for seeing you through.

Day 5

Count Precious Pearls (Part 2)

3. My Support People

Think about the people who have helped you through some of your more serious trials. I would imagine your spouse would be on top of the list if it's a recent trial. Others would be folks like your parents, a professional counselor, a minister, a friend, or your extended family. In the midst of a trial, you may have prayed for God's wisdom and understanding.

Make a list of those people who helped you through your trials and storms.

_____

_____

 Transfer these names to column 3, My Support People, on the chart on page 54. Tremendous support may be right near you—and that support can help you as you move to column 4.

4. My Pearls from Each Trial

Here is the very *heart and life* of finding your own pearls. These pearls are more valuable than the earthy pearls one strings for a necklace; but they are so treasured that you can encase them on your heart's favorite trophy shelf.

 In column 4, My Pearls from Each Trial, on the chart on page 54, list the positive aspects of each painful encounter in your life. Besides your own answers, ask for the input of those who know and love you—the support team you identified in column 3. They can often add a perspective to your suffering that you may have overlooked.

Also look at column 1 and the personal strengths you identified. Have any of those strengths come as a result of particular trials? Where did you gather those strengths? Often they come from what you've learned by trial and error—in every sense of the phrase.

The next true story will give you a more specific example of how a trial can be turned into precious pearls.

Remember it is *always* possible to find treasure in physical trauma. George was a typical, hard-driving executive. He looked 10 years younger than his age—45. Great job, great family life. It was a classic case of "George is the last guy I thought would have a heart attack!"

But that's exactly what happened.

On a Tuesday afternoon, in the middle of an upper-management strategy session, George complained of chest pains, then collapsed on the boardroom table. As he was rushed to the hospital by the paramedics, George just kept repeating his wife's name: "Barb, Barb, Barb." And Barb was at the hospital waiting when George arrived.

He was wheeled directly into the operating room. After hours that seemed like days, the surgeon appeared at the waiting room door to assure Barb that George was going to be all right. "But he *must* take it slow," the doctor warned.

Barb took it upon herself to ensure that George experienced a full recovery. She helped him with his slow and steady climb back to a normal life. George can barely get through recounting this time in his life without choking up. "Barb was the most amazing helper I had ever seen," he says. "For all the years we were married, I had prided myself on a healthy physique—so much so that I secretly doubted if Barb would even be interested in me if I let myself go—or worse yet, got sick."

Remember it is always possible to find treasure in physical trauma.

George continues, "But it was through this horrible trial that I saw a side of Barb that had been hidden in the 21 years we had been married. I was treated to a glimpse of a woman who loves me unconditionally. Her love isn't dependent on my good looks, firm physique, or good health. She just loves me —no matter what. I wouldn't wish a heart attack on anybody, but I do have to say it has been the greatest aid in strengthening our marriage. I now see life so differently. I've slowed down; I smell the roses. I can honestly say I'm glad it happened to me." That's a glimpse of finding very precious pearls as a result of a life-threatening sickness.

For years I saw nothing positive about my poor academic record. Flunking third grade and being a poor reader and speller were completely negative for me. But I now see positives in my entire educational development.

One such benefit is this very book you're reading. Can you imagine how amazed all my elementary-school teachers would be if they knew I've written twelve books? And for reasons beyond my understanding, some of the books have actually won awards! How can this be?

Most of the reason goes back to my being a poor reader. In those years "learning disability" tests weren't given. But if they had been, I wouldn't be surprised if I had been placed in that category. Since I know the struggle of a poor reader, I realize a book must possess a certain excitement about it that will keep the reader's attention. My goal is to make a book as understandable as possible. I also appreciate the concept of "salt," that special "thirst creator" that makes me want to keep reading.

I work hard at achieving these things in my books. It's not uncommon for me to go through twenty or more rewrites of each chapter to reach that ideal blend of content, excitement, and "salt." I'm still not the greatest reader. So if a chapter doesn't interest me or force me on, I redo it until it does. I'm very grateful today that I had a weak childhood training–not that this is license for anyone to do poorly in school. But if life deals you a painful "piece of sand," turn it into a pearl and use it in a way that can benefit you and others.

5. My Loving Action Because of Each Trial

When major disasters strike, priorities have a way of realigning. Most people first search for their family members, not their belongings. Suffering has a way of bringing people together; the most important things on earth come into sharper focus. This increased interest in being with and helping others during a crisis is a demonstration of love.

The key to this final column in your chart is understanding how love works. It's as simple as this: *We use love or we lose it.* We take hold of a new appreciation for "connections," reorganized priorities, and new sensitivities that we've gained in hard times; and we share the new joy with others—or we lose the joy.

David and Linda were attending one of my seminars and realized how they needed to find any value they could in a devastating loss. Five years earlier, their precious daughter, Sara, had died just two hours after birth. David and Linda both lived the following years carrying anger, resentment, and frustration.

After allowing themselves time to feel the pain of their grief—their loss—they gained enough strength to start their own hunt for any good that could come from this tragedy. And what did they discover? David and Linda now realize how they appreciate the little things in life that they once had taken for granted. But Linda found a more specific way to use her search for pearls to help someone else.

She writes, "A friend of mine lost her brother and sister-in-law in a tragic auto accident. As a result, three young girls were left as orphans. But over the last three-and-a-half months, I've been able to talk to this friend. When she expresses hurt, frustration, and agony, I can say, 'I know what you're feeling,' and really mean it!"

Linda goes on to say, "I thank God I had Sara for the short time I did, because I learned so much from her death. I'm so much more alert to the suffering of others. I can be an understanding companion to my friend and her family, and I look forward to helping more, because of my experience. When I'm with those three girls, they know I not only love them, but I deeply understand their loss as well. I can tell they know I understand and care. Through searching for treasure, I feel my daughter's death has finally given me a purpose. I still miss her a great deal, but I can now help others like I never dreamed I would. And helping them has been so rewarding."

I know of nothing more helpful to those who suffer than to at least begin the slow process of breaking through the cocoon of anger and the feeling of being cheated in life. The crisis of breaking out is the opportunity of a lifetime!

 List in column 5, My Loving Action Because of Each Trial, on the chart on page 54 all the ways you can share your pearls with others.

Write 1 Peter 1:6-7, the memory verse for the week, on the lines below.

_____

_____

_____

_____

 Pray that God will not only transform your pain into pearls but that He will give you opportunities to share your pearls with others.

We use love or we lose it.

Couple Time

For you to complete

The most important thing I learned this week about facing difficulties and trials is:

_____

_____

One pearl I have discovered that I can share with others is:

_____

One attitude in facing trials that needs to grow in my life is:

_____

One way I will avoid extreme thoughts is:

_____

For you to share with your spouse

1. Sit down facing one another and take turns sharing how you completed the above section.

2. Read the following verses together out loud:

   "Not only so, but we also rejoice in our sufferings, because we know that suffering produces perseverance; perseverance, character; and character, hope. And hope does not disappoint us, because God has poured out his love into our hearts by the Holy Spirit, whom he has given us" (Romans 5:3-5).

Share together:
• What means most to me from this verse is _____.
• One person with whom we need to share some of our pearls is

_____

3. Hold hands. Pray the following prayer: "My beloved, all that I think of you, will be true, noble, right, pure, love, admirable, excellent and praiseworthy. In Jesus' name, Amen" (based on Philippians 4:8).

WEEK 4

How to Balance Expectations and Reality

The wider the gap between what we expect and the reality of what we experience, the greater the potential for discouragement and fatigue. The insights this week are based on this foundational statement. The gap between expectations and reality is like a drain through which we lose the *joie de vivre*—the joy or love of life.

I'm grateful to Dr. Dan Trathen of Denver for helping me work through the lessons in the following preventive plan. When you hit a crisis situation—when reality opens a trap door—don't let your energy drain away. Here's how you can minimize the trauma of any future crisis you face.

Crises are inevitable. Some are predictable, called life-cycle crises. Some are beneficial. All can be redeemable. But, there are specific ways by which you can protect yourself. As you run with me through the next story, you'll see a truth about life in general, and you may begin to see that there is something you can do to prevent energy loss.

Creeping Sun and Slithering Snakes

When I was about 12 years old, I got the scare of my life. It was the worst thing that ever happened to me. In fact, I'm amazed I'm alive today to tell this story.

My family was living in the state of Washington, out in the country. One fall day I was outside playing with my best friend. Having great fun, we weren't paying much attention to the clock. As the sun crept toward the horizon, we suddenly realized it was time to be heading home. So, like the two adventurous boys we were, we decided to take a shortcut through a wooded area.

We had no path to follow, but that didn't bother us. We were just running along, the wind whistling past our ears. And then, all of a sudden, we heard this deafening and horrifying rattling sound very close by. We stopped, froze, and listened. The sound was all around us, and it seemed to be coming from everywhere at once.

We looked at the ground. It was moving. We were in the middle of a field of rattlesnakes! Hundreds of them, all sizes. They were striking out blindly in all directions.

My friend and I knew we didn't have long to live.

Fortunately, we had the presence of mind to jump up on a snake-free log that had fallen but was well above ground. We yelled for help at the top of our lungs, but we were too deep into the woods for anyone to hear.

"What are we going to do?" my friend shouted.

"I don't know," I answered, "but we've got to do something soon because it's getting dark!" *Will the snakes crawl up onto our log?* I wondered.

Then one of us got the idea of breaking long branches off the log and using them as extended arms or "swords" to flip the writhing, rattling creatures out of our way as we cleared a path to make our escape. And that's what we did. One snake at a time—what seemed like one *inch* at a time—crying all the way, we made a path to the edge of that sea of snakes. The slightest slip or fall would have landed us on top of a half dozen of them, but we kept moving.

We only had about 30 feet to cover to get into the clear, but it seemed to take forever. When we finally left the last snake behind, we were trembling and exhausted. But we gathered our remaining strength and ran home as fast as we could to report our near-death experience.

I'd like to use this childhood crisis to symbolize all of life's crises and how we can reduce the energy loss and shorten the duration of the trauma they cause. So, in the coming week, you will explore:

- how to narrow the gap between expectations and reality in a relationship;
- how to understand, develop, and implement life priorities;
- how to balance expectations with experienced realities and outcomes;
- ways to bring our expectations in line with reality; and,
- how best to change expectations and take responsibility for the change.

Day 1 Disaster Protection	**Day 2** Identify Priorities	**Day 3** Compare Expectations Against Reality	**Day 4** Align Expectations with Reality	**Day 5** The Best Ways to Change

Memorize and hide in your heart this Scripture for setting priorities in life: " 'Seek first his kingdom and his righteousness, and all these things will be given to you as well' " (Matthew 6:33).

Day 1
Disaster Protection

When a crisis strikes, we can be like two boys running along near the safety of home and suddenly finding themselves in the middle of a field of deadly snakes—smack in the midst of a seriously unpleasant, potentially disastrous, situation.

As you can imagine, my friend and I weren't prepared to deal with rattlesnakes that day so many years ago. We were just wearing sneakers, jeans, and t-shirts—easy for a snake to bite through—and we had no weapons except our sticks. But suppose things had been a little different. Suppose instead of wearing low-cut sneakers, we had been prepared for the *reality* we faced; suppose we had been wearing hip-high boots made of multiple layers of strong, thick leather—so strong that a snake's fangs would break off before they could penetrate to the skin underneath.

If I had been wearing such a pair of boots and knew they would protect me, my whole attitude would have been different. Instead of being terrified, thinking I would die at any moment, I would have walked right into that mass of snakes with confidence! I would have simply kicked them out of my path as I made my way to the other side of the field. *Go ahead, take your best bite, make my day!* I would have challenged them boldly. And the preventive boots would have kept me safe.

What kind of "hip boots" can we wear to protect us in all of life's crises? What can shield us from the harmful effects of such situations?

 Our disaster protection begins with our relationship with God. We can spiritually arm ourselves to face any upcoming crisis in life. Paul describes our spiritual armor. Read the Scripture below and circle each aspect of God's armor that's available to us in protecting ourselves.

> Therefore put on the full armor of God, so that when the day of evil comes, you may be able to stand your ground, and after you have done everything, to stand. Stand firm then, with the belt of truth buckled around your waist, with the breastplate of righteousness in place, and with your feet fitted with the readiness that comes from the gospel of peace. In addition to all this, take up the shield of faith, with which you can extinguish all the flaming arrows of the evil one. Take the helmet of salvation and the sword of the Spirit, which is the Word of God (Ephesians 6:13-17).

Once we are armed spiritually, we must maintain our spiritual walk with a thick pair of hip boots. What do I mean?

We "put on a thick pair of hip boots" by maintaining balance in our life. To switch metaphors and use a common cliché: *If we've put all our eggs in one basket and that basket falls to the ground, our life expectations are dashed.* But if we carry several baskets, each holding a different life interest, and then drop one causing disappointment in one area of life, we are able to maintain strength, hope, and joy because we're still holding several baskets.

At the top of the next page are baskets representing three areas of our lives. Write on the eggs in each basket different expectations you have for that area of your life. For example, one expectation in your marriage may be to pray with one another or to affirm each other daily. A career expectation may be to complete a degree or get a certain promotion.

*D*isaster protection begins with our relationship with God.

We "put on a thick pair of hip boots" by maintaining balance in our lives.

Here's an illustration of what can happen when the "hip boots of balance" aren't worn. Two years ago Gene's life fell apart. His small business went bankrupt. The business was most of his identity. He'd given it so much time and attention that his wife and children were "distant" housemates, providing little support in his despair. Gene's friends—business-related "contacts"—also scattered like frightened birds when he filed his court papers. Nonwork friends? He had none. Where was God? It had been a long time since Gene had paid any attention to faith.

With no intimate friends, distance at home, no spiritual center, and the loss of his career, Gene felt overwhelmed. Nowhere. Hopeless. At age 42, Gene took his own life. A two-word note was found by his body. His message to the world: "I failed." Maybe Gene's basic failure was that he had neglected to develop any "life support" outside his business.

Let me contrast that with another story. Granted, this is not as drastic as a foreclosure, nevertheless it was a severe career crisis for a young man—my son Greg.

As each of our children formed a career path, we began to share a dream that someday we could all work together, maybe speaking on the same platform.

Not long ago Greg felt he was finally ready to make part of our dream come true. He was prepared to stand in front of a large audience and teach some of the principles I regularly present in seminars. As you can imagine, I was thrilled.

I invited Greg to join me and speak at an upcoming seminar. I said Greg was ready—but nervous and apprehensive. As the day approached he was losing sleep and feeling nauseated because of performance anxiety.

The big moment soon came for Greg to get up and address the audience. For me, proud papa, it was a magical experience—one I'll never forget. My years of fatherly dreaming were about to be rewarded. As I introduced him to the group, I had to stop for just a second to wipe my misty eyes.

Greg stood, approached the podium to warm applause, and turned to address the audience. He started off relaxed, saying what a delight it was to share the platform with his dad. Then, halfway through his presentation, Greg experienced a major crisis. He went blank. Right there, in front of two thousand people, with every eye in the room on him, he forgot what he was supposed to say next. Without going into all the details, simply put, he bombed the rest of the presentation. Afterwards he pulled me aside and whispered, "Dad, can you give me any helpful advice?"

I looked into his eyes and told him soberly, "Son, remember this: *It's always the darkest just before it goes totally black!*"

As we laughed, Greg shot back, "Thanks a lot for your encouragement, Dad!"

I tell that story because it illustrates so well the core message I want to get across during this week's study. For just as Greg found himself in a crisis that drained away much of his energy, so any of us can experience a crisis at any time. If the crisis occurs in one of the most important areas of our lives, such as our job, marriage, children, friends, or our spiritual side, we can suffer massive loss of emotional and mental energy. But Greg was already doing something that allowed him to recover quickly from his crisis and regain his strength and the ability to move forward.

 Share a recent time when you experienced a crisis in your life.

_____

_____

Balance your expectations with reality.

Fortunately, there's a way to overcome a crisis and regain equilibrium quickly. It worked for Greg, and it can work for you. Let me explain. Greg experienced a crisis in the career area of his life. For the moment, the failure drained him, frustrated him, caused him pain, and dragged him down. But in four other major areas of his life, he was doing well. As a husband, his marriage was solid and fulfilling. As a father, he had a great relationship with his child. Spiritually, he felt he was on good terms with God. As a friend, he had several buddies who would stand by him no matter what. Because these other important areas of his life were doing well, they balanced out the crisis in his career. Soon after suffering probably the greatest embarrassment of his life, he was optimistic and looking forward to his next chance to speak in public.

How can you protect yourself from massive loss of energy? The rest of this week's study offers protection and more. Here's how you can replenish your energy. Middle-aged men especially need to understand the importance of balance in life. Imbalance is a major cause of mid-life crisis; when career expectations aren't realized, too many people lose vision and hope for the future.

 Check the areas in your life that balance you by marking every area that's present and working for you.

❏ Family   ❏ Recreational time   ❏ Relationship with Jesus
❏ Marriage   ❏ Spiritual disciplines   ❏ Exercise and fitness
❏ Career   ❏ Other: _____

If you did not check more than two, you need more balance in your life. We'll study more about how that can happen the rest of this week.

 Write this week's memory verse below. Say it three times after you write it.

_____

_____

 Pray that God will give you wisdom, understanding, knowledge, and courage to balance your expectations with reality.

Day 2
Identify Priorities

Imagine your life as a large, lush vegetable garden. (I know this may sound strange at first, but trust me—the word picture will help you better understand these concepts that have been of tremendous benefit to me and thousands of others.) Each type of vegetable represents one part of your life. For instance, the carrots are your relationship with your mate. The cucumbers are your role as a parent to your children. The lettuce is your career, whatever that may be. The green beans are the members of your extended family. The tomatoes are your friendships. Then add on your hobbies, your volunteer work, your home-owner responsibilities, etc.

Now, what I'm about to say may seem so obvious that you're tempted to skip to the next subhead, but stay with me. Far too many of us understand this intellectually but act oblivious to the obvious: *You won't have a very satisfying garden unless you plant several different vegetables.* And once you plant them, you need to nurture them carefully if you're eventually going to enjoy their taste. If you overwater or overfertilize some parts and neglect others altogether, the result can be one sick garden.

I've discovered that we usually need at least five "healthy vegetables" to keep up our vigor and love for life, even in the face of crises.

 To help you find the five most important parts of your own garden, take a few minutes right now to think about the main parts of your life. Complete the following sentences with your top five responses.

I am a _____

I am a _____

I am a _____

I am a _____

I am a _____

As I ask people to do this all over the country, the most common answers include:

I'm a spouse.	I'm a son or daughter.
I'm a parent.	I'm a [name of vocation].
I'm a friend.	I'm a [name of avocation].
I'm a spiritual person.	I'm a man or woman [a physical being].

Take this a step further. Who are you in Christ Jesus?

 Read the following Scriptures and underline phrases that describe who you are in Christ.

Yet to all who received him, to those who believed in his name, he gave the right to become children of God (John 1:12).

Consequently, you are no longer foreigners and aliens, but fellow citizens with God's people and members of God's household (Ephesians 2:19).

Don't you know that you yourselves are God's temple and that God's Spirit lives in you? (1 Corinthians 3:16).

But you are a chosen people, a royal priesthood, a holy nation, a people belonging to God (1 Peter 2:9).

Why have I asked you to identify five top areas, and to consider several phrases that describe who you are in Christ? It's a principle called diversification. A wise investor spreads his money—diversifies—over a number of different investments. That way, if any one or two of them is in the pits, his overall results can be helped by those that are doing better. If he held only one investment, on the other hand, and it took a nose-dive, he could be wiped out.

If we focus most of our energy and effort on just one or two areas of life—our career and a hobby, for example—and something goes wrong there, we can be dumped emotionally, spiritually, and physically. But if we have five priority areas and a problem develops in one or two of them—like giving a speech that goes poorly and wondering if we'll ever be invited to do it again—our health in the other areas can lift our spirits and restore our energy.

If you're completely wrapped up in one aspect of life and that area crumbles, you can feel as low as Gene, the small-business owner who committed suicide. How sad to think of all the men and women who can identify with his depression brought on by a career crisis! If you relate to his dilemma at all, it's time to diversify, to give some attention to the other key areas of your life.

Why do I suggest you list *only* five key areas? While life offers many good things, I've discovered there are only a few best, most important things. Those are the vegetables that both deserve and require my most careful attention.

Life is filled with *good ideas* and *God ideas.* The right priorities of our lives are the God ideas. If your life becomes so busy with just good ideas, good things to do and be, then you will miss out on the important God ideas in your life.

The necessity of focusing on our top priorities can be illustrated visually. (I've actually done this demonstration before seminar audiences.) Take two large jars of the same size. One is filled almost to the top with uncooked rice. Each grain of rice represents one of the many good things we could make a part of our lives. The other jar is filled almost to the top with whole walnuts still in the shell. There are a lot fewer of them, and they represent the top-priority areas of our lives.

If you try to pour the walnuts into the jar that's already nearly full of rice, you'll manage to get in only a few nuts. However, if you pour the rice into the jar that's virtually full of walnuts, all the rice will fit! Before your very eyes, the rice will fill in the many spaces under, around, and on top of the walnuts.

Here's the point: If we fill our lives and give the majority of our time and energy to countless good and worthy things (the rice), we won't have much room left for what is truly important. But if we devote ourselves first to those things that deserve top priority (walnuts), we'll find we're able to enjoy the many other good things as well. They come as bonus energy boosters.

If your life becomes so busy with good ideas, you will miss out on the important God ideas in your life.

The top priorities of life—the God ideas—need to fill your life right now. Write a prayer asking God for the wisdom and discernment to set the right priorities—to live for the God ideas in life.

_____

_____

Day 3
Compare Expectations Against Reality

Yesterday you named five key areas of your life—ways you identify yourself. By identifying these "I ams" as top priorities, you've admitted these are important to you. And if they're important to you, they are areas in which you want to do well. They encompass your "high hopes." Those great expectations provide the happiest moments of our lives. They also lead to our greatest disappointments, when expectations don't jibe with reality. And that gulf between expectations and reality means crisis.

What is the next step in keeping your emotional and mental energy high, in surviving life's crises? Slow down and perform a reality check. How do your expectations compare to your life's realities? What is the condition of your garden? How is each part doing? The effective gardener has to inspect all areas of the garden daily.

Another helpful way to picture this is to imagine that each of those top five areas of your life has its own thermostat. You might set the temperature at a comfortable 72 degrees in, say, the area of your marriage. In other words, you develop a set of nice, comfortable, satisfying expectations. Everything seems to go fine for a while. Before long, however, you start to notice that your home isn't as warm as you had expected. In fact, it's downright cold, and you reach for a sweater.

What's the problem? You're racing through each busy day without taking time to check the *thermometer* on the wall. And the reality of your marriage isn't meeting your present expectations. Remembering where you set the thermostat isn't enough. You also need to look at the thermometer to see the actual temperature, which may be down around 60 degrees. The gap between the temperature you expect and the real temperature is a crisis that will drain energy from you every day. And that loss of strength will go on day after day as long as you're unaware of the problem.

 How exciting, dynamic, satisfying is your marriage relationship right now? Mark the thermometer on the next page to indicate where you feel your marriage relationship is now. Circle the temperature you expect the marriage to be at and check where you believe your spouse would put the temperature of your marriage right now.

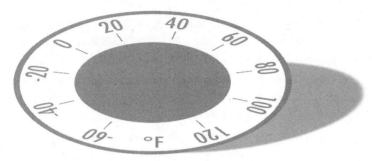

There's a theory that helps explain this predicament and our need to "check the temperature." It says the human brain is always trying—always working—to close the gap between expectation and reality.[1] To match the two up, the brain labors feverishly to somehow reconcile them. If this theory is true, then it's obvious that the further our reality is from our expectations, the harder the brain has to work to bring them together, and the greater the energy drain. In a crisis, when expectations and reality are very different, you can actually watch the strength drain out of a person.

Jesus describes this process as counting the cost before building a tower (see Luke 14:28-30). The tower could represent any goal or end result you are seeking to reach. The cost represents your expectation of what it will take to reach that goal or end result. If you expect the tower to cost a thousand dollars and it ended up costing twice that much, you would be facing a crisis.

 Below are five towers. Label each with one of the top five priorities you have for your life. Shade each tower up to the level that that area is meeting your expectations. For example, if one tower was your career and you shade it about 90 percent full, then that means that 90 percent of your career expectations are being presently met.

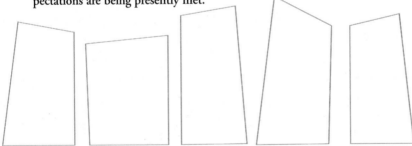

Part of the process of checking reality against expectations may send you back to look at the way you've prioritized the parts of your life. Is your home life causing you stress—because you're spending too much time at the office and therefore distancing yourself from your spouse or children? If so, look at your priorities. When it comes down to the wire, is your job more important than your family?

Years ago I was forced to check my priorities—expectations against reality. Like a lot of other people, I had gotten caught up in my career. Through church-related work, I was "doing good"—helping others. I could point with pride to how well I was providing for my family. Fine. Great. Just one problem: In the process I was neglecting the emotional and relational needs of my wife and children, who should

The gap between the temperature you expect and the real temperature is a crisis that will drain energy from you every day.

have held a much higher priority than my job. (If you'd asked me, I would have said they were my first priority. I would have said I wanted to be a good husband and father. But in reality? Well ...)

I was finally forced to deal with the situation when our son Michael was born. Besides the extra work that's inevitable when another child comes along, Michael provided added stress, as he was born with severe, life-threatening medical problems.

Now, who do you suppose was suffering the greatest loss of energy during this period? That's right, my wife, Norma. She reasonably expected her husband to be at her side, offering emotional support and also extra help with the older kids while she cared for Michael. But I was back at the office, absorbed in my job, imposing a reality far different from what she expected and needed.

This problem went on for some time, but gradually I became aware of what was happening and how my focus was almost exclusively on my work. Then I determined that I had to back off from my work somewhat and give more time and energy to my family. I had to find a better balance in the top areas of my life. And, with some effort, that's what I did.

Mind you, it's not that I started to improve my balance because I was some maturing husband or father. Instead, Norma quietly confronted me one day and stated that either I help her or she would have a complete nervous breakdown.

 How would God have you rank the priority areas of your life. List God's priorities for your life in the order you sense He would put them.

1. _____

2. _____

3. _____

4. _____

5. _____

To this day, I'll say to Michael—who is now a healthy adult—"You brought me back to our family." Much to my surprise, I also found that I could still be effective in my work even while I made my loved ones a higher priority. In some ways, rearranging my priorities made me even more effective on the job.

I could give you example after example from my own experience of the need to check expectations against reality. Another that stands out in my mind is the physical area of my life. My expectations are that I'm a trim, healthy 50-something man with a long life ahead of me. Now for a little reality: As I said earlier, the men in the Smalley family have a tendency to develop heart trouble. A little more reality: A few years back a donut would have been the best symbol to represent my body.

When I compared my thermostat to the thermometer in my physical life, I saw they were far apart. And that, in turn, led me to the next step we all need to take to

Our priorities and expectations in life must line up with God's Word.

get and keep our garden healthy, our lives in balance, and our energy high. We will explore that step tomorrow.

Just as all of our priorities must line up with God's Word, so must our expectations. Ultimately, we come to the realization that we can never set right priorities or live up to our own expectations, least of all God's expectations of us, without the power and strength of God working in and through us.

 We have covered much ground in the past three days. So sit still for a moment. Slowly read Psalm 37. Then write down at two or three things you have gained from this week's study.

_____

_____

Close with Philippians 4:13 as your prayer, "I can do everything through him who gives me strength."

---

[1]Irene Goldenberg and Herbert Goldenberg, *Family Therapy: An Overview* (Pacific Grove, Calif.: Brooks, Cole, 1980, 1985), 152-159.

Day 4
Align Expectations with Reality

One of the biggest energy-draining experiences most adults stumble through is a strained marriage. I think back over the number of times Norma and I have been bent out of shape. It's amazing how the tone of our relationship could get so dark so fast. One hour, things would be great, and then instantly we'd be locked in an angry argument over some earth-shaking situations like "Oh, no, you didn't say that! You said you wanted to stop and eat there, so my mouth has been watering to taste their specialty. How dare you change your mind!"

 Where is your marriage right now? Put your assessment on each line with an x and then put a check mark where you believe your spouse would mark the statement.

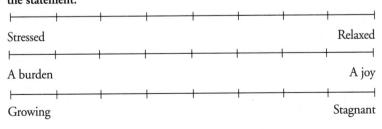

Stressed	Relaxed

A burden	A joy

Growing	Stagnant

We were in our camper driving out of Prescott, Arizona, one morning. I wanted breakfast at this certain restaurant where Norma had agreed to stop, but as we got close, she remembered this other place and asked if we could eat there instead. We quickly found ourselves locked in a three-hour battle, and all kinds of things came out that had nothing to do with eating breakfast. The "discussion" created a gap between our marital expectations and reality, to say the least. After we ate at some restaurant neither of us liked, we got back in the camper and decided to reexamine the marriage area of our respective "gardens."

I was wiped out, feeling like a failure and as if all our progress in being a loving couple had been washed away in one three-hour torrential downpour. We were never going to make it. In the middle of this type of crisis, my personality tends to see only the negatives. But Norma tends to put things in a more realistic perspective. I remember her saying, "Just look at all the things that go great between us, and this is only a small speck in the scope of all the years we've been married." That knack of pulling our expectations and reality closer together gives me more energy to continue the discussion.

We took a closer look at expectations and reality. Were expectations unrealistic? Was reality as bad as it seemed? As for reality, Norma had helped clarify that our whole relationship had not flooded away. She helped me take some of my own advice: *Avoid extreme thoughts.* Chicken Little, the sky is not falling.

As for expectations, we decided that some of my expectations about our marriage—that we would always be at peace—were just not practical or realistic. No couple can live each day without some disagreements or even major conflicts. Conflicts are inevitable and can even be healthy, as you'll see later in this study. Even if a couple can't work things out for a few days, that's OK. So I had to develop new expectations, ones that were more pragmatic.

 Forever-love does not see doom in every gap between expectations and reality. List your top three expectations you have for your marriage.

1. _____

2. _____

3. _____

List the top three expectations you perceive your spouse has for your marriage.

1. _____

2. _____

3. _____

Forever-love does not see doom in every gap between expectations and reality.

Go back over your lists and circle any unrealistic expectations that either of you have. What can you do to make your expectations more realistic?

Here's what happened to Norma and me.

Driving down the highway, we both evaluated our marriage and began making a list of things we expected to receive and what we believed would be acceptable for a mutually satisfying relationship. It's amazing how just talking and agreeing on those marital basics has increased our levels of energy and love for life and each other.

Are you willing to sit down and share your expectations with you spouse? Are you open to listening and relearning new, more pragmatic expectations for each other?

If you are willing to do this, set a time and date this week when you will sit down with your spouse and share about expectations.

It's the gap between what we expect and what we get that drains our energy. When our experience is close to what we anticipated, we're stronger and more content. That bolsters our ability to keep on loving. But unless we talk about those things and bring our expectations to the surface, our mate may not know our wishes, and we may find ourselves facing an energy-sapping gap between our desires and our reality.

God does have an expectation for your marriage relationship. It's called "forever-love" or as we see it described in the Bible—*agape*—or unconditional, accepting love. Read 1 Corinthians 13 and look over your list of expectations one more time. Complete these sentences:

The expectation I have that most closely conforms to *agape* is:

_____

_____

The biggest gap between my expectation and *agape* is:

_____

_____

If you discover on inspection that your expectations and experience don't match up well in a particular area of your life, you need to determine whether you should try to change the expectations or the reality (or both). In my own life, I've often found that when I took the time to look at them, my expectations were unrealistic and had to be adjusted. What I wanted just wasn't entirely reasonable. But other times, I've seen that there were things I could do to improve my reality and raise it closer to my desires.

When your expectations in a certain area involve other people, a good way to make sure those expectations align with reality is to talk them over with all those concerned. This can be difficult and even a little scary if you're not in the habit of speaking with them candidly. It also seems to be human nature to simply expect that

God has an expectation for your marriage; it's called forever-love.

somehow our loved ones can read our minds and know what we want.

There are some simple ways to have *agape* love in a marriage. Many wives, for example, long to hear their husbands say "I love you" more often. Yet many of those same wives will go for years without telling their husbands that's what they would like. Rather than get upset with their husbands, those women can either lower their expectations or—much better—talk over their need to hear those three magic words with their men. The result can be a richer reality, a stronger marriage, better ability to weather life's crises, and more joy and energy for the whole family.

In my own family, we decided a number of years ago to write a family constitution that would spell out what was reasonably expected of everyone. (You can read more in-depth about this idea later in week 8.) In the process of writing our constitution, we had to talk through all the expectations each of us had that we each thought made up a mutually satisfying family. By the time we were done and started putting it into practice, we were all happier, because we all knew what was expected of us and that we were generally doing a good job of meeting those expectations. It wasn't perfect, but talking things through and getting our expectations out in the open was a big step in the right direction.

Describe one way in your marriage or family that you clearly define expectations for one another.

_____

_____

_____

As you begin to understand God's expectation of your marriage and for you, His Spirit will reveal and convict you of areas that require change. Remember, you cannot change each other. But, God gives you the power to change. God also works in the lives of others in ways you cannot to grow and change them. Write a prayer asking the Lord to change your expectations and the expectations of others in your family to be more realistic and in line with His forever-love in your marriage and family.

_____

_____

_____

You cannot change your spouse, but God gives you the power to change.

Day 5
The Best Ways to Change

Before we end this week's study, I'd like to draw your attention to four simple ways I've found effective to help me "stay the course" of lasting change.

1. I like to read several of the best recommended books on the subject at hand. That begins with Scripture and also includes books and magazines.

Let's look at some key passages on marriage and family. Look up three from the list below and write a key thought that strikes you as important for you right now. Later, you will want to study these Scriptures in detail.

THE BIBLE	KEY THOUGHTS
Ephesians 5:22-6:4	_____
Deuteronomy 6:1-9	_____
Exodus 20:1-17	_____
1 Corinthians 13	_____
Colossians 3:18-21	_____
Hebrews 13:4-8	_____
Romans 12:9-21	_____

Keep growing and going.

Check the marriage and family section of your Christian book store for the latest resources. Also subscribe to a good Christian family magazine like *Home Life, Journey,* and *Stand Firm.*[1]

2. I find a professional or two in town and discuss the issue with them. I simply explain my goals and ask them to assist me in changing.

Check the box by those people around you who may be professionals that you can learn from.

❑ Pastor   ❑ Teacher   ❑ Counselor
❑ Christian couple that I look up to in their marriage.
❑ Other: _____

3. I gather three of four other people who have the same goal, and we meet regularly to give mutual support and, most important, accountability. For instance, I'm just finishing up a few months with a weight plan. It's the weekly weigh-in that keeps me losing weight. The others in the session are all supportive, which makes it easier to experience lasting change.

List people you might partner with in an accountability or home group.

_____

_____

4. I seek the strength I receive as I look to God in faith.

Are you and your wife praying together? That can become a tremendous time of power and prayer. However, the expectation to pray together must be realistic and mutually agreed upon. I encourage you to reach out to your spouse to find a time and way to pray together. Your Couple Time might be a place to start.

 If you are willing to begin having or to continue a prayer time with your spouse, write a prayer that asks God for the power, strength, and wisdom to grow spiritually together.

_____

_____

Each of these four resources has given me the ability to keep going and growing. They help me close the gap between expectations and reality. If you choose to take the steps described this week, you'll do two things: You'll maintain more of your inner strength in the midst of potential and actual crises. And when the inevitable crises do hit—expectations and reality will never totally align in this world—your balanced life will protect you from utter devastation. When a crisis strikes in one area, the health in the other key parts of your identity will provide balance that can soon restore your energy and _joie de vivre_.

 Pray, thanking God for inspiring within you and your spouse the desire to set realistic expectations together.

_____

[1]For information on _Home Life, Journey,_ and _Stand Firm,_ call 1-800-458-2772.

Couple Time

For you to complete
My top priorities and expectations in marriage are:

_____

_____

One important way biblical love [*agape*] needs to grow in our marriage is:

_____

_____

One insight I received about marriage from Scripture that can help our marriage grow spiritually is:

_____

_____

One way I need to change my expectations of my spouse to be more realistic is:

_____

For you to share with your spouse
1. Sit face to face and share how you both completed the above sentences. Concentrate on understanding your spouse's point of view.

2. Use this time to pray together. If you have not done this in the past, simply pray the Lord's Prayer together out loud for each other. Here's an example:

> Our Father, which art in heaven, hallowed be thy name. Thy kingdom come, thy will be done in [name of spouse] life, as it is in heaven. Give [spouse's name] this day his/her daily bread. And forgive [spouse's name] as he/she forgives others. And lead [spouse's name] not into temptation but deliver [spouse's name] from evil: For thine is the kingdom, and the power, and the glory in [spouse's name] for ever. Amen. (based on Matthew 6: 9-13, KJV).

3. Begin working together on a realistic set of expectations for each other. Share together what each of you wrote on day 4, page 72.

Avoiding Hurt Is My Responsibility

A couple of years ago, Norma and I were in Hawaii with some of our staff members to do a seminar. Norma was excited about being there—the beach, the sun, the rest and relaxation. I always enjoy going there, too, whether to speak or just to have fun, so we both started off in a good frame of mind. Then I did it again—something I had done all too often in our married life.

We had arrived on a Saturday, and now it was Monday morning. We woke up early, around 6:00 a.m., and as I started to get going, I was thinking, *Hey, we're all alone, and we haven't had a good discussion for a long time. We've both been so busy. Now would be a great time!*

So I looked at Norma and said, "What do you say we work for an hour or so on our marriage goals for the coming year?" I assumed she would love the idea.

Instead, however, she answered, "No, I don't feel like doing that today."

Well, the word *no* is not one of my favorite expressions, so I persisted.

Again she replied, "No, I really don't want to do that this morning."

Now her refusal started to get to me. I thought, *Wait a minute! I'm in the business of working on marriages, and we ought to be making sure our own is tuned up just the way it should be.* So I tried again. "Let's just get started on our goals," I said. "We can talk about them at length later, when we get home."

Norma still wasn't interested, and at that point I got a little upset. So what did I, the marriage counselor and seminar speaker, do? To my embarrassment now, I pushed right ahead against her will. We had our talk, all right, but it was obvious the whole time that we weren't really working on our relationship goals.

Why didn't I recognize that I was doing a wrong thing? Frankly, I'm not sure.

Whatever I was thinking, after a couple of strained hours of that discussion, Norma's displeasure was unmistakable. She's really open and honest with me about everything, which I love, though this time it hurt.

"This is just great!" she said. "This is the day that Terry [one of our staff members] is going to ask Janna to marry him. It's supposed to be a happy, festive day."

That remark made me realize that I had wiped her out emotionally with our forced conversation. *Sure, Gary Smalley,* I thought, *why did you have to push it this far?* I knew she would walk out of that room, and the staff and our kids would take one look at her and then ask me, "Now what did you do to her?"

Sure enough, shortly after she left for breakfast without me, the story was out, and my son Greg came to me first and said, "Dad, I can't believe you did this! We're both counselors, right? ..." and so on. One of the other wives also came and said, "Way to wreck our whole day!"

You can imagine how the rest of my day went. Norma and I weren't really speaking. I tried to be nice to her, to joke and warm things up a little, but nothing worked. She just wasn't ready to respond.

That night, Terry put up a big banner on his balcony asking Janna to marry him. It could be seen a long way off, from outside the hotel, and Janna saw it and said *yes*. So we were all excited and in a good mood, including Norma. I thought, *All right. She's getting warmer. There's hope for me yet. I only have four more days until my marriage seminar.*

A little later the whole staff spontaneously went out for ice cream. We were in high spirits, and I announced to everyone in the ice-cream parlor, "Hey, this couple just got engaged!"

All the people cheered, and the manager said, "All right! Free ice cream for you folks!"

After the ice cream was served and our group had finished eating, I was at the cash register trying to pay, not sure the manager had meant to give us all free food. But she ignored me for the moment and looked instead at Terry and Janna. "Listen," she told them, "I don't really know you, but I'd like to give you some marriage advice. There's this television infomercial running right now by a guy named Gary Smalley. He's selling this video series on marriage, and I got it, and it's really been helpful. I think it would help you guys, too. You ought to get it before you get married."

At that point, Janna looked at me, I looked at her, and I knew she was thinking, *Gary set this up.* So before she could say a word, I shook my head and told her, "No, I swear I didn't do a thing." Janna turned to the manager and said, "Do you know who that is—trying to pay you?"

"No," the woman answered. "Should I?"

"It's Gary Smalley," Janna said.

The woman looked at me closely for a few seconds, and then her face broke into a giant smile. She ran around the counter and gave me a big hug. It was a nice scene. But the clincher came as we were leaving, when Norma leaned in close with her arm around me and said, "You ought to order those tapes."

That day was a turning point in my life. The disaster helped Norma and me see an unhealthy pattern in our lives and our relationship: We didn't clearly understand the importance of personal boundaries. Today, I can see clearly that I was wrong to force Norma to discuss something she wasn't prepared to talk about that morning. I made a big mistake. But so did she. And the pattern we lived out that morning is repeated in home after home across the country.

My mistake was to barge into Norma's life without her permission. If you're a "Gary," in this chapter I'll give you a method that can help keep you from doing the same thing to your spouse or others.

True love never demands its own way but searches for ways of enriching the other person.

Norma's mistake was letting me barge in. For the "Normas" out there, I'll give practical advice for keeping others from storming into your life.

This week we will learn together that:
- every person is a separate and unique person, worthy of two kinds of respect: from others and from ourselves;
- true love never demands its own way but searches for ways of enriching the other person;
- we can learn a process for asking permission before entering someone's "space" and then being willing to accept the answer;
- love does not always "give in" to every request, especially to intimidation; and,
- we can develop skills that exhibit daily that we "love our neighbor as ourselves."

Love does not always "give in" to every request.

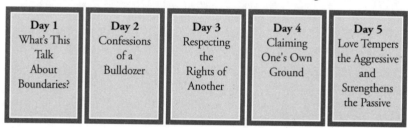

Day 1 What's This Talk About Boundaries?	**Day 2** Confessions of a Bulldozer	**Day 3** Respecting the Rights of Another	**Day 4** Claiming One's Own Ground	**Day 5** Love Tempers the Aggressive and Strengthens the Passive

This is such a vital and important week of study for you. Learning about boundaries will greatly enhance your marriage relationship. I am praying that God will give you insight and wisdom in understanding these important marriage principles.

I invite you to memorize and meditate on these Scriptures this week:

> Each of us should please his neighbor for his good, to build him up (Romans 15:2).

> "And the second [commandment] is like it: 'Love your neighbor as yourself' " (Matthew 22:39).

Day 1

What's This Talk About Boundaries?

Let me answer that question by asking another: "Do you know where you end and 'others' begin?" The question doesn't have to do with physical bodies or skin. It has to do with your emotional being. Think of yourself as having an invisible property line around you. Imagine that a land surveyor marked off where you start and end with stakes. Inside the property line is everything that makes up who you are—your personality, your likes and dislikes, your goals and dreams, the various parts that make up your life—like the garden I talked about last week. That garden has a property line around it, but because it's invisible, others may not know where it is—they may not know if they're about to cross it, or if they have crossed it—unless you tell them where the line is.

Inside the set of boundaries below, write two or three areas of your marriage that are always safe to discuss. Outside the boundary lines write two or three areas that are usually "off limits" to discuss.

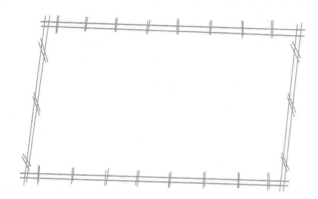

Most of us want others to respect our property lines and not enter our gardens without our OK. I call this concept "No visitors without my permission." In short, we want people to respect who we are and see us as separate from them, but also as a loving part of them. We want them to respect the thoughts and values we have chosen that reflect our most personal selves, the part of us that is unique and special, like a fingerprint.

The Scripture talks about this as being part of the same body—connected but separate. In 1 Corinthians 12, we read about the body of Christ being comprised of separate and important parts just like the human body. Each part is unique and important.

 Read the following Scripture and underline the phrases that talk about being part of and connected with others. Circle the phrases that refer to us being uniquely individual and distinct from others.

The body is a unit, though it is made up of many parts; and though all its parts are many, they form one body. So it is with Christ. For we were all baptized by one Spirit into one body— whether Jews or Greeks, slave or free—and we were all given the one Spirit to drink.

Now the body is not made up of one part but of many. If the foot should say, "Because I am not a hand, I do not belong to the body," it would not for that reason cease to be part of the body. And if the ear should say, "Because I am not an eye, I do not belong to the body," it would not for that reason cease to be part of the body. If the whole body were an eye, where would the sense of hearing be? If the whole body were an ear, where would the sense of smell be? But in fact God has arranged the parts in the body, every one of them, just as he wanted them to be. If they were all one part, where would the body be? As it is, there are many parts, but one body.

"No visitors without my permission."

The eye cannot say to the hand, "I don't need you!" And the head cannot say to the feet, "I don't need you!" On the contrary, those parts of the body that seem to be weaker are indispensable, and the parts that are unpresentable are treated with special modesty, while our presentable parts need no special treatment. But God has combined the members of the body and has given greater honor to the parts that lacked it, so that there should be no division in the body, but that its parts should have equal concern for each other. If one part suffers, every part suffers with it; if one part is honored, every part rejoices with it. Now you are the body of Christ, and each of you a part of it (1 Corinthians 12:12-27).

Oneness in marriage does not mean one mate dominates the other.

As you have discovered, the Bible recognizes our individual worth while affirming our need to be in relationship with one another. Now, let's focus on our individual need to have boundaries, uniqueness, and individual identity in marriage.

To reduce misunderstanding here, know that I'm not suggesting a husband and wife should fence out each other or their children. I'm not talking about erecting a barrier so that others can't get close. I certainly support the enriching idea that a man and a woman can become "one flesh" after marriage. But oneness does not mean one mate dominates the other or that the stronger controls the weaker. I'm also not suggesting that a shy person should use this concept to keep others at arm's length.

What I am suggesting is that each of us, married or single, is a separate and unique person—worthy of two kinds of respect.

1. Respect from others. Others should treat us as separate people with our own likes and dislikes, feelings, hopes, and tastes. Other people should not cross our property lines unless they're invited to do so.

What personal boundaries do you have that are most often violated by others? List them.

_____

_____

2. Respect from ourselves. We need to feel strong and whole enough to tell others when they are trespassing—trampling on our gardens.

Check the ways you most desire to be treated. I want others to ...
- ❑ Listen attentively
- ❑ Avoid put-downs
- ❑ Affirm and encourage me
- ❑ Avoid pushing in on topics that are sensitive
- ❑ Seek to communicate *with* instead of *at* me

This works both ways. Circle the ways you show respect for another person's boundaries.

In the coming days, you will discover how not to bulldoze someone, particularly your spouse, and how to claim your ground for your own boundaries.

 Write a prayer asking God to reveal to you ways to show respect to others and also to receive respect.

_____

_____

Day 2

Confessions of a Bulldozer

As I said earlier, the way I treated Norma that day in Hawaii illustrates a tendency I've had throughout my life. With my wife, my children, and my friends, I've often rammed my way into their lives, many times without regard for their feelings, and usually without even realizing what I was doing. I now see that my behavior was a classic example of a major way in which people are robbed of their contentment. True love never demands its own way but searches for ways of enriching the other.

 First Corinthians 13:5 reads, "Love does not insist on its own way." (RSV) How do you measure up to that standard of *agape*—God's love, forever-love? Put an x on the line where you are.

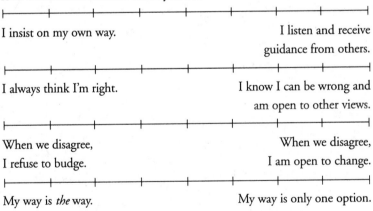

I insist on my own way.	I listen and receive guidance from others.
I always think I'm right.	I know I can be wrong and am open to other views.
When we disagree, I refuse to budge.	When we disagree, I am open to change.
My way is *the* way.	My way is only one option.

Are you open to guidance, suggestions, other options, and reform? My efforts at reform have not only made life easier for Norma; they have opened up my "lighter heart." I carry less guilt for having "ruined a day." I see that we're both responsible for our love and satisfaction. I see a way to reduce the frequency of our conflicts.

Though I use the word *bulldozer* to describe my own mode of operation, don't think that all boundary violators are as easy to recognize as a bright yellow earth mover. Some people are masters at "moving in" with subtle guilt trips: maybe a spouse's, "If you loved me you would … "; or a child's, "All the other parents are … "

Soon after I gained new understanding about boundaries, I sent a letter to all three of our children trying to explain the dramatic changes that were occurring in me. Here's what they read:

Dear (Kari, Greg, and Michael),

I woke up this morning thinking of you and thought I would send you a quick note about a very important lesson I've been learning as I prepare for my new video series.

You came to mind for two reasons. One is that without any choice of yours, you were born into our family. As I see more clearly the way I was raised, I can understand why I treated you and the other family members the way I did some of the time. There were many, many times that I was like a tank smashing down the "important and sometimes fragile property line" around you without asking if I could visit inside your life.

When you were younger, there were times I would "bulldoze" into your life even if for some reason you had asked me not to come in. In one sense, I could make you feel like "Well, I'm coming in because I'm your father." I did the same thing with your mom and your siblings. But something happened yesterday to allow me to see these things I've done more clearly than I ever have. I now know that the way I was raised and my personality contribute to a lot of what I did.

If I could live my life over again, I would change a lot of things, but the one thing I would work on most is controlling what I say to others. I have crashed over people's property lines on so many occasions that I couldn't count them. When I think of the little and major things I said to you over the years and the things I have uttered to so many people, it's scary.

The second reason I wanted to write you is that even though you will probably never do these things to people because of your maturity and loving nature, I just wanted to warn you that some of the things you may say to your classmates or others may come back to haunt you later in life. People are too precious to jump their property lines without permission. It may really hurt them, and many times we never know until years later.

Love, Dad

 Underline anything in this letter which you may need to say to your spouse or another family member like a child or parent. Circle anything you need to act upon immediately.

Making Love Last Forever

Bulldozing is another way to talk about control in relationships. The first step to take in dealing with control is to surrender. Identify an area of your life or your marriage relationship that you are still trying to control?

_____

_____

 Now that you have faced the issue, are you willing to surrender that area of control to the Lord? Read Romans 12:1-2.

> I urge you, brothers, in view of God's mercy, to offer your bodies as living sacrifices, holy and pleasing to God—this is your spiritual act of worship. Do not conform any longer to the pattern of this world, but be transformed by the renewing of your mind. Then you will be able to test and approve what God's will is—his good, pleasing and perfect will.

Write a prayer of surrender.
Jesus, the area of my life or marriage that I will stop controlling and will surrender to you today is _____.

Ask for permission to enter someone else's "space," and be willing to accept the answer you are given.

Day 3
Respecting the Rights of Another

This whole idea sounds a little like our country's Declaration of Independence, doesn't it? Our founding fathers laid down the truth there that "all men are created equal, that they are endowed by their Creator with certain inalienable rights," among which is "the pursuit of happiness."

With that God-given right to pursue happiness in mind, how should a person—especially a rather aggressive personality like me—approach others when there's something he or she wants? It's basically a matter of asking for permission before entering someone else's "space," and then being willing to accept the answer you're given, even if it's not the one you wanted. (It may seem obvious, but for many it's not practiced.) This is the thing I'm learning to do—the one thing that has most changed how I deal with people and has most improved my relationships.

Do you ask permission of another person before you enter his or her space? Mark an x on each line to indicate where you are .

I barge in.   I ask permission.

I am insensitive.   I am sensitive to where he/she is.

I talk first.   I listen first.

 James 1:19 gives this admonition, "Everyone should be quick to listen, slow to speak and slow to become angry." Underline the part of the verse you do best. Circle the part that needs the most improvement in your life.

Asking permission is critical, but so is the ability to hear a *no* or *not now* with grace. When Norma says *not now,* I need to respect myself enough to feel she is not rejecting me. What does this mean? It means anger levels need to be low; we need to be constantly working through the principles presented in previous weeks. If anger levels are low, we're best able to see a particular conversation as an incident unto itself; we're not dragging in excessive baggage from previous encounters.

Here's the approach I've learned to use when I want to talk about something or do anything with Norma. I'll walk up to her and "knock" at her imaginary gate. I'll say something like, "Could we talk about next week's schedule tonight?" or "I want to go out tonight. What about you?" It can be any subject, feeling, or need I wish to address.

She's free to respond, "No, I don't want to talk about it right now. Maybe later."

Then I'll say, "OK, when?"

She might answer, "I would love to talk about it later this evening. Or how about tomorrow?"

And I'll conclude, "Good. That's great." Then we go on to something else.

 Imagine yourself approaching your mate and asking permission to enter his or her territory. Write the dialogue that would take place.

You say: _____

Your spouse says: _____

You say: _____

Your spouse says: _____

You say: _____

Your spouse says: _____

"Everyone should be quick to listen, slow to speak and slow to become angry" (James 1:19).

If you need more room, use the side margin to write the rest of your dialogue with your spouse.

Believe me, my ability to operate this way and respect Norma's wishes—her uniqueness—is a big difference in my life. (I don't want to misrepresent Norma: If it truly is an urgent matter that must be discussed now, she'll respect the issue and talk immediately.)

My gentler approach has also helped us deal with three or four particular subject areas that we don't talk about often because it's so difficult. You and your spouse probably have similar subjects, the kind that get you heated up every time they're broached. It used to be that way when I wanted to discuss something explosive. We would just launch into the subject and hope for the best, and many times we ended up in a hurtful argument. Now we both ask for permission to bring up those topics, and we feel much more comfortable, safe, and loved.

 Name two subjects that are difficult for you and your spouse to discuss.

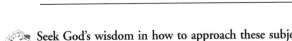

_____

_____

 Seek God's wisdom in how to approach these subjects. Repeat this week's memory verses–Romans 15:2 and Luke 22:9–as part of your prayer to God.

One final and very down-to-earth illustration of how to use this approach in a healthy way: Jim and Suzette, a couple from our support group and close friends of ours, were having lunch with us and practicing this concept one day. Suzette said to Jim, "May I talk to you about something?" (Notice she's asking for his permission respectfully.)

Jim immediately responded, "Well, I've got a video camera security system on my property today." But he continued, "What do you want to talk about?" (He wants to know more before he grants permission.)

"Just one thing," she answered.

"What is it? I want to know what you want to talk about before I decide to let you inside my gate."

"All right," she said, "I want to talk about what you're eating for lunch today."

"OK, come on in and we'll discuss it," he told her, inviting her to come through his elaborate security system. (Remember, Norma and I are good friends with them, and they felt safe enough with us to have a discussion like this in front of us. I recognize that some couples can't imagine discussing a sensitive marital problem in front of others. But we've been doing it for so long, it's now second nature, and it has been extremely helpful.)

Suzette went on, "I know we've talked about this before, but when you order your favorite kind of spaghetti at this restaurant, by six o'clock at night you really have an unusual odor."

A gentle approach will help you deal with the difficult subjects you don't talk about often.

"What do you mean?" he said, surprised.

"Well, this garlic gets in your system, and you really ... ahh ... smell. It's embarrassing to me when we go to basketball games or other public events. I'm very aware of it, so I find myself trying to keep you away from other people so they don't notice it."

Jim accepted that graciously if reluctantly and said, "All right, I won't order that today. If it really bothers you, I'll have something else." (Notice his sensitivity to her feelings and her uniqueness.)

Then Suzette decided to push her luck. "While I'm inside your garden," she continued, "may I talk about just one other thing?"

Now, realize he could have said no to that request. He could have said, "I really don't feel like two in one hour. Maybe later." But he answered, "All right, go ahead."

"OK, one other thing," she said. "When we go to that high-school basketball game tonight, would you not yell at the officials and the fans from the other school? It really embarrasses me when you pick out a fan and start haggling with him."

"But I'm a coach," he protested. "I know how to work referees, so I do that. It's part of the game."

"Well, it really embarrasses me," she repeated, standing her ground. "You're a community leader, so other people are watching you. And it makes me feel like I want to wilt."

"All right," he said, choosing to be gracious again. "I'll try to be more aware of yelling tonight."

Here again, Jim had the freedom to decide. He could have said, "When I go to a game, I love to yell. That's just me. I can't help it, though I'll try not to be rude." But he had invited her comments, he was in a generous mood, and he gave her what she wanted. For her part, Suzette had respected his property line, asked for permission to speak, and then stated her case clearly. That's a healthy personal property line at work.

 List the issues you want to ask permission to discuss with your spouse in the coming week.

_____

_____

 Be sensitive to his or her schedule and demands. Try what I have suggested at an appropriate time with one or more of the issues you listed above. In preparation for that time, write a prayer asking God for wisdom and the right words to say.

_____

_____

Day 4
Claiming One's Own Ground

Early that morning in Hawaii—the disastrous day that woke Norma and me up to the reality of our border disputes—I was not the only person who made a mistake. Norma had a choice in how she responded to me. She and many people like her tend to blame their circumstances or others for their discontent with life. Each of us can and should take responsibility for how we allow others to "visit" us inside our "gardens" without permission. The Normas of the world need to understand that love does not always "give in" to every request, especially to intimidation.

Some people have the mistaken notion that love means to be enslaved, completely surrendered and dependent upon another person. There's a difference between being a servant and being a slave. First Corinthians 7:23 says, "You were bought at a price; do not become slaves of men." Forever-love can never meet all the needs of another person. Forever-love is never called to be a slave. If we have surrendered totally to Jesus Christ, we cannot be another person's slave.

 In Romans 12:9-21, the apostle Paul gives us a list of qualities and actions that defines forever-love as a serving, not an enslaving, force in our relationships. Check the qualities and actions present in your marriage. Underline those that need attention in your marriage right now.

- ❑ Sincerity
- ❑ Devoted to each other
- ❑ Share joy and hope
- ❑ Faithful in prayer
- ❑ A blessing to others
- ❑ Do not take revenge
- ❑ Overcome evil with good
- ❑ Do what is right
- ❑ Share with people in need
- ❑ Keep spiritual fervor

- ❑ Hate what is evil
- ❑ Honor each other above self
- ❑ Patient in difficulty
- ❑ Live in harmony
- ❑ Not proud nor conceited
- ❑ Do not repay evil for evil
- ❑ Rejoice with others
- ❑ Live at peace with each other
- ❑ Comfort and grieve with others
- ❑ Serve the Lord

Compare your response with that of your spouse. Talk about similarities and differences, especially those qualities and actions that require attention in your marriage.

Gaining Strength

As a human being in relationship to another human being, you are not a genie or slave with the motto: *Your wish is my command.* You have the ability and responsibility to say *no* if someone bulldozes over you. Allowing that bulldozer to tear down your fence and trees can cause resentment. You'll feel trampled and squeezed. (Think back to the "can of anger," where a dangerous substance was compressed, pressurized.) That unhappiness and unresolved anger you'll blame on the bulldozer. But wait.

You have the ability and responsibility to say no *if someone bulldozes over you.*

Have you let the bulldozer on your property without as much as a warning sign? Are you responsible for warning others and then lovingly standing your ground?

But, you say, *saying no will cause an unhappiness of its own. "Making waves" is so uncomfortable.*

Yes, bulldozers have a way of making it difficult to hold your ground. But let me give some advice:

Work through old, unresolved anger. I repeat, *if anger levels are low, we're able to see, and deal with, one incident at a time.* You don't need to escalate a minor boundary infraction into World War III proportions. But that's what can happen when you've let someone squeeze you in for so long that one day you finally blow—pointing a weapon at someone and screaming "Get off my land!" That's what happens when you let a bulldozer's "few choice words" set off a minefield of emotion.

 Complete these sentences:

It's most difficult for me to say *no* to my spouse when:

_____

My boundaries are violated most often when:

_____

The way I most often violate my spouse's boundaries is:

_____

One thing I will do to stand firm in love is:

_____

At the beginning of this week we said respect for others is half the boundary issue; respect for self is the other critical ingredient. As you claim your ground, speak in love. Speak with respect for yourself and the other person. Be reasonable but firm. And watch as a new self-respect counters your dis-ease.

 Self-respect begins with accepting your position and identity in Jesus Christ as a child of God, a new creation in Him. Pray these sentence prayers completing each statement.

In Jesus, I am _____ .

In Jesus, my spouse is _____ .

I thank you for creating each of us as unique in your creation. May we grow in our love for you and our love and respect for each other.

If anger levels are low, we're able to see, and deal with, one incident at a time.

Day 5

Love Tempers the Aggressive and Strengthens the Passive

How can you tell if the imaginary line around your life isn't being respected as it needs to be? This is one area where your emotions may be a pretty good guide. For instance, have you been really angry in the last month, an anger that lasted more than a couple of days? Have you been frustrated over a period of time? Have you felt used or abused? Have you felt suffocated in a relationship?

If you're living with any of these negative emotions, your boundary may need to be better marked. Remember, your present quality of life depends upon the choices you make. Claim your ground. Except in cases of extreme abuse, I recommend that you choose to tell others when they're trespassing.

One caution about unresolved anger. If you find that everybody's always frustrating you, your old anger may be making your boundary unnecessarily broad. Remember, anger keeps you distant from others. Love builds bridges to others.

Tough Situations

What do you do if you're in a relationship with someone who constantly bulldozes into your life without permission and just won't take any form of *no* for an answer? Obviously, that's a tough situation, and there are no easy answers. I recommend that every couple be part of a couples' support group. This might give you a safe place to discuss touchy things if your mate is willing. Professional counseling is another tool you might use for yourself or—even better—both of you together. There are so many helpful resources (agencies and counselors) available today in most cities.

Giving forever-love—*agape*—will temper aggression from you and toward you. If you express forever-love and the aggression doesn't cease, then either you have unresolved anger or you may have an abusive spouse.

In extreme cases, especially where there is any threat of physical harm, you may have to physically separate yourself from the boundary violator. This might involve calling 911 and contacting legal authorities. No one should suffer physical abuse.

Perhaps you're thinking, *I want this person's love, so I had better just leave matters alone or he or she might leave me or harm me further.* Believe me, you're not the first person to think that way. But if you choose to ignore your circumstances, I've found the problem usually gets worse, not better. It's much better to alert an offender to your property line and insist that you will no longer allow trespassing. Take a stand, and defend yourself. In the short term, the other person will probably resist and may give you a hard time. But in the long run, he or she will respect you much more. It's your only real hope for a satisfying relationship.

Love builds bridges to others.

The biblical principle is clear—"Speak the truth in love" (Ephesians 4:15). Circle the attitudes you need to work on when you speak the truth in love.

Acceptance	Be assertive	Empathy
Understanding	Attentiveness	Concern
Being calm	Listening	Affirmation

Notice the list includes "be assertive." There is a difference between being aggressive and being assertive. The assertive person stands his or her ground. The aggressive person charges into the territory of another.

 In Galatians 2:11-21, Paul disagreed with Peter. He was assertive and stood his ground without putting Peter down or being disrespectful. We can learn three valuable lessons from Paul.

❏ Paul spoke his opposition face to face with Peter. Paul didn't tell a third person about his problem. He went directly to Peter and spoke the truth.

❏ Paul spoke the truth in light of the gospel. He was concerned about his personal opinions or ideas. Truth was measured by the standard of the gospel.

❏ Paul had dealt with his ego and pride. He had been crucified with Christ. Paul's assertiveness did not rise out of his pride or ego.

Check the box beside the actions you want to incorporate into your life.

Clearly defining who we are is essential. It can make or break our love for life and the satisfaction we receive from relationships built on respect and honor. Learning this concept and beginning to respect the boundaries of my wife, children, and friends has literally changed my life, and I'm glad to say I'll never be the same.

 Briefly describe who you are in relationship to Jesus Christ.

_____

_____

_____

Keeping a "garden area" in good repair and defending it is hard work. For people with either tendency—too aggressive or too passive—the final word is *moderation*. An age-old rule of life and love is found in our second memory verse for this week: " 'Love your neighbor as yourself' " (Matthew 22:39). The two loves are intertwined in a tight strand of respect that can temper the aggressive and strengthen the passive. And make for long-lasting peace—with one's neighbor (spouse) and with oneself.

Loving ourselves isn't egotistical or prideful. When we love ourselves as God loves us, we can accept and forgive ourselves. That empowers us to let go of any anger we have been harboring against ourselves for past failure and guilt. First John 3:21 declares, "Dear friends, if our hearts do not condemn us, we have confidence before God."

" *'L*ove your neighbor as yourself' " (Matthew 22:39).

Forever-love tempers aggressiveness and strengthens our passiveness. I have introduced you to nine qualities of forever-love this week. After each quality listed below, put an *x* on the line to indicate where your marriage relationship is right now.

├───┼───┼───┼───┼───┼───┼───┤

• Forever-love respects another person's personal boundaries.

├───┼───┼───┼───┼───┼───┼───┤

Weak   Growing   Strong

• Forever-love never demands its own way but searches for ways of enriching the other.

├───┼───┼───┼───┼───┼───┼───┤

Weak   Growing   Strong

• Forever-love asks permission before entering someone's garden.

├───┼───┼───┼───┼───┼───┼───┤

Weak   Growing   Strong

• Forever-love hears *no* or *not now* with grace—not with paranoia.

├───┼───┼───┼───┼───┼───┼───┤

Weak   Growing   Strong

• Forever-love is not a genie. "Your wish" is not "my command."

├───┼───┼───┼───┼───┼───┼───┤

Weak   Growing   Strong

• Forever-love can hold its ground against intimidation.

├───┼───┼───┼───┼───┼───┼───┤

Weak   Growing   Strong

• Forever-love knows the quiet, confident strength that comes with self-respect.

├───┼───┼───┼───┼───┼───┼───┤

Weak   Growing   Strong

• Forever-love equally respects self and others.

├───┼───┼───┼───┼───┼───┼───┤

Weak   Growing   Strong

• Forever-love tempers the aggressive and strengthens the passive.

├───┼───┼───┼───┼───┼───┼───┤

Weak   Growing   Strong

 Review the qualities you marked *weak*. Pray that God will bring about growth in that area of your life. Write a brief prayer committing to God one action you will take as a result of this week's study.

_____

_____

Forever-love tempers our aggressiveness and strengthens our passiveness.

Couple Time

For you to complete

1. In what ways are you a bulldozer in your marriage relationship?

_____

_____

_____

2. How does your spouse invade your boundaries at times?

_____

_____

_____

3. What will you do to change being a bulldozer?

_____

_____

_____

4. What is one thing your spouse could avoid in crossing your boundaries?

_____

_____

For you to share with your spouse

1. Share together how you both completed the above section.

2. Ask for forgiveness in ways that you both have bulldozed each other.

3. Pray for one another thanking God for His power to forgive and change us.

Finding the Power to Keep Living

Where do we find added strength to keep loving and enjoying life when difficulties hit, when we get tired of trying, or when life turns into a boring routine? I've found one of the key truths lies in "sighting" and avoiding a deadly cluster of "icebergs" that could block our spiritual journey.

Why is the spiritual journey so important? Marriage researchers are finding a correlation between one's spiritual journey and one's satisfaction in marriage. Howard Markman and Scott Stanley report that religion has a favorable impact on marriage. They write that religious couples "are less likely to divorce … show somewhat higher levels of satisfaction … lower levels of conflict about common issues … and higher levels of commitment."[1] And in worldwide research Dr. Nick Stinnett found six characteristics common to most happy marriages and families—one being an active, shared faith in God.[2]

Though a recent Gallup poll revealed that over 90 percent of Americans believe in a God, many struggle to find a personal living faith. Most of us realize we don't have it all together and we do need some outside strength to help us keep our love from fading or to endure the pain caused by others. But often, as I did for so long, we choose some course that drives us in a different direction from developing our spiritual dimension.

Out of my depression 20 years ago, I started learning about the obstacles that kept me disconnected from a personal God. As I've gradually seen how to connect, I've become keenly aware of how vital this spiritual area of life is for anyone wanting to experience greater satisfaction in life and lasting love.

This week, I discuss *four main factors* that hindered my spiritual journey. I kept hearing that God was a God of love who could somehow give a person the ability to love others and himself. But I couldn't find them to be real for me. I seemed to need more than education and support from family and friends to keep my love for life and others alive and growing. I wanted supernatural help, but it wasn't there for me until I turned 35, when I was tired of hitting "icebergs."

New Life in Christ

The Bible tells us:

• Your heart tends to run from God and rebel against Him. The Bible calls this *sin*. "For all have sinned and fall short of the glory of God" (Romans 3:23).

• Yet God loves you and wants to save you from sin, to offer you a new life of hope. Jesus said, "I have come that you may have life, and have it to the full" (John 10:10).

• To give you this gift of salvation, God made a way through His Son, Jesus Christ. "But God demonstrates his own love for us in this: While we were still sinners, Christ died for us" (Romans 5:8).

• You receive this gift by faith alone. "For it is by grace you have been saved, through faith—and this not from yourselves, it is the gift of God—not by works, so that no one can boast" (Ephesians 2:8).

• Faith is a decision of your heart demonstrated by the actions of your life. "If you confess with your mouth, 'Jesus is Lord,' and believe in your heart that God raised him from the dead, you will be saved" (Romans 10:9).

• If you are choosing right now to believe Jesus died for your sins and to receive new life through Him, pray a prayer similar to this to thank Him for your new life: *Dear God, I know I am a sinner. I believe Jesus died to forgive me of my sins. I now accept Your offer of eternal life. Thank You for forgiving me of all my sin. Thank You for my new life. From this day forward I choose to follow You.*

If you prayed this prayer, share your decision with a Christian friend or minister. Join other believers in a local church. Grow in your new life in Christ.

In my 30s, feeling hopeless and isolated, my anger grew like mold in a damp basement. I distanced myself from my wife and kids, I didn't want to go to my job, and I was ready to quit the profession for which I had been preparing for years.

I felt as if I were floating in a sea of anger, and I kept allowing Norma and my kids to poke more and more holes in my leaky life vest. I realized I was sinking fast. I had to take some steps in a hurry and cry out for help.

It was like the time our family visited a wave-pool water park in Las Vegas; I went out in the deep end without a raft. Wave after wave came, and I finally tired. I was all by myself—the kids were already out of the water—and I decided to swim to the ladder at the side of the pool and climb out. But I couldn't make it! Every time I got close to the edge, another wave would push me away again, and I was too tired to fight it. I swallowed water, began to panic, and realized I was helpless. At that point my only thought was, I'm going to drown here in Las Vegas in front of my family! I was sure I was going down for good.

Fortunately, my family had seen what was happening. The next thing I knew, my son Greg was stretching way out, grabbing me by the arm, and pulling me toward the ladder. When I got to it, I wrapped my arms around it and hung on for dear life.

That's kind of what happened to me with God. I kept trying to reach out for some kind of satisfaction in life, but each time a wave of reality would push me back out and I was sinking. I've heard alcoholics, the addicted, and many other hurting people just as miserable as I, say this same thing. Each of us finally reached out and grabbed God's hand, which had always been there, outstretched waiting for us.

My outstretched hand came in the midst of my depression and disillusionment. I recalled a verse from the Bible, Psalm 50:15: "Call upon me [God] in the day of trouble; I will deliver you, and you will honor me." I realized that was all I could do then, and it was what I needed to do. Sinking like the *Titanic,* I cried out to God for help, asking him to somehow rescue me from the mess I was in and show me He was real. And deep in my spirit, I kept hoping He heard me. Eventually I did find a personal connection to God, and it's been so rewarding, I've never looked back.

Before I get to the four "icebergs" that kept blocking my ability to find a personal God, let me share what this week will not do. I obviously won't be addressing all the subtle meanings that you bring to this spiritual area of life. I want to present my ideas so you see how wonderful it has been for me, yet I don't want to come across as preachy or artificial and possibly cause some to further avoid its tremendous benefits. Also, I'm not trying to address all the various doctrines or great concepts about faith in God. I simply want to share the hindrances I encountered in my spiritual journey and why the lack of connection with a personal God affected my ability to love my wife, my family, and others—even myself.

Your spiritual life may be suffering because you've been wounded by someone who claimed to be a "religious person." Perhaps you've been hurt in a past church experience. Maybe you've had close friends who claimed to be spiritual but lived out hypocritical lives. I've been jerked around and hurt by a lot of "religious" people myself.

But I finally saw that I cannot let the failings and hypocrisy of others affect my personal relationship with Jesus Christ.

In the spiritual arena, I've found truths that have meant the world to me. This area has been the most enriching part of my entire life's journey. My faith has become like a powerful turbo-charged engine in an old '57 Chevy. God has become like the warmth of a fireplace after being out too long in the cold.

Before I found God to be real, I allowed myself to be spiritually hindered, even battered, by four "icebergs" that blocked my path. This week you will discover how to avoid shipwrecking your spiritual life on these icebergs. You will:

- uncover your deep need for a personal relationship with God;
- come to understand that what others believe and do are insignificant in a personal search for God;
- learn the key to maintaining love and satisfaction in life is not expecting lasting satisfaction and love to come from people but from God;
- discover that power isn't gaining a higher position at work or securing more income but is found in a relationship with God;
- develop skills that exhibit in daily life that you "love God with your whole heart, and love others as yourself."

Day 1 My Doubts	Day 2 Hypocrisy	Day 3 Expecting Too Much from People	Day 4 Expecting Too Much from My Job	Day 5 Practical Ways to Draw Closer to God

My prayer for you this week is that you will set aside all hindrances to your relationship with God through Jesus Christ. As you grow closer to Him, you will grow closer to your spouse and others. Keep this verse close to your heart this week.

> Hear, O Israel: the Lord our God, the Lord is one. Love the Lord your God with all your heart and with all your soul and with all your strength (Deuteronomy 6:4).

---

[1] Howard Markman, Scott Stanley, and Susan Blumberg, *Fighting for Your Marriage*, 285.
[2] Nick Stinnett and John DeFrain, *Secrets of Strong Families* (New York: Berkley, 1986).

Day 1
My Doubts Keep Me from God

When I was seriously questioning the existence of God back in my college days, someone challenged me to open my mind to the possibility of a personal God by asking me three humbling questions. Those questions were healthy for me because they caused me to develop my own personalized belief system.

God has become like the warmth of a fireplace after being out too long in the cold.

Here are those questions. Indicate your answer by marking an x on the line in 1 and 2, and checking the appropriate box in 3.

1. How much knowledge do you think we now have in the world out of all the knowledge that can be known?

├──┼──┼──┼──┼──┼──┼──┼──┤

0 percent   100 percent

2. How much of this knowledge do you think you know personally?

├──┼──┼──┼──┼──┼──┼──┼──┤

0 percent   100 percent

3. Do you think it's possible that a personal God could someday reveal Himself to you through the remaining knowledge you could gain? ❑ yes ❑ no

My anger kept me from God.

When I ask these questions of others, the average person admits to having only a small percentage of the available knowledge. And most then take the position that it may be possible to someday see and experience a personal God.

Again, for me, I was full of doubts about a personal God, and with my level of anger and guilt, even during my college years, there was no way I was going to "see" God. My anger kept me far from Him.

 Check the barriers that you believe most often block your personal relationship with God.

❑ Doubt   ❑ Uncertainty   ❑ Insecurity

❑ Fear   ❑ Guilt   ❑ Pride

❑ Confusion   ❑ Anger   ❑ Pain

❑ Lack of knowledge   ❑ Other: _____

The New Testament contains two interesting character portrayals of doubt. One overcame doubt and distance from God. The other never did. Let's contrast the two.

 First there is Felix, the Roman governor at Caesarea, who heard Paul's case and invited Paul to share the gospel with himself and his wife, Drusilla (Acts 24). Read Acts 24:25 and underline Felix's response to having a relationship with Jesus Christ.

> As Paul discoursed on righteousness, self-control, and the judg-
> ment to come, Felix was afraid and said, "That's enough for now!
> You may leave. When I find it convenient, I will send for you."

In contrast, consider the disciple Thomas. He also had doubts and fears. How did Thomas respond to Christ? Read John 20:5-8. Underline Thomas' response.

> But [Thomas] said to [the disciples] "Unless I see the nail marks
> in his hands, and put my finger where the nails were, and put my
> hands in his side, I will not believe it."
>
> A week later … Jesus came and stood among them … and
> said to Thomas, "Put your finger here; see my hands. Reach out
> your hand and put it into my side. Stop doubting and believe."
>
> Thomas said to him, "My Lord and my God!"

Notice that Felix's initial response was interest but that faded. On the other hand, Thomas initially doubted and then believed in Christ. What made the difference? Check what you believe made the difference for Thomas.

❑ Thomas kept seeking Christ.

❑ Thomas experienced Christ.

❑ Thomas did not let doubt make his final decision.

❑ Thomas did not let fear or personal gain determine his decision.

Like Thomas, can you identify any fear or doubts you have that stand in the way of your relationship with God? Write them below.

_____

_____

Release your doubt and begin in faith to trust God more.

I could fill an entire book with my elaborate doubts, many of which left as my anger and guilt subsided. You may not have a lot of doubts about God's existence, and you may well be on your way with your own spiritual journey, but possibly telling my version of this vital area of life will further enhance yours. From my personal experience as well as that of thousands of others, I'm convinced you can obtain the single-most-important key to lasting love, one nothing or nobody can ever take away.

 Pray, asking God to help you release your doubts and begin in faith to trust Him more in your relationship with Him and others.

Day 2
Hypocrites Keep Me from God

I didn't start attending church regularly until I was a teenager. My older brother and sister got me involved.

At the very first church I attended, the minister was asked to leave because of some moral problem. That was a harsh reminder of the truth that no one is perfect. Nonetheless, I was fairly active in this first church until I had a fist fight with one of the staff members! Shortly after that scuffle, my father passed away, leaving me in need of someone older to look up to. A new staff member with a sincere, loving nature kept me coming to church, and he proved to be genuine. I still deeply admire this man even though he, too, eventually left the church because of personal struggles. I used to wonder how this vital area of life, our faith in God, could survive with such inconsistencies among its believers.

In spite of the leaders I encountered, my faith remained alive during my college years, and then, as a graduate student, I was hired by a church to work with youth.

I was excited at the opportunity and looked forward to a satisfying, fulfilling ministry. To my dismay, however, the senior pastor never bothered to learn my name. In staff meetings he would call me "Hey, you." I thought, That's incredible! People who say they serve a God of love are supposed to be more loving. And I was "scratching my head" in wonderment a lot of the time.

My first meeting with the youth of this church knotted my stomach. The teenage leader was asked to pray before a noon meal. He rose respectfully to utter these words: "Rub-a-dub-dub, thank you for the grub. Yeah, God." Then he sat down amid giggles from the other kids. One evening a while later, that same teen admitted in a formal youth meeting that he couldn't find God as a meaningful experience. Several others in the meeting expressed their disbelief as well, along with the adult sponsors. Everyone else seemed to get into the confessional mood, so I joined them. That night after the meeting, I told my wife I would probably be asked to leave the church because I had just admitted that God was not real to me. I believed God existed; I just couldn't find him to be personal. Nothing ever came of my confession, but the experience certainly motivated me to find out what kept blocking my ability to know God.

My wife's childhood church experience also fed my growing disappointment with "religious people." In her first church, the pastor ran away with her best girlfriend's mother. The church family members were devastated, and so was the child who would become my wife.

Following graduate school, I worked for a religious organization with which I grew disenchanted. I finally left that place as a discouraged man. Despite my spiritual condition and disillusionment, I went to work—briefly—in another church. I was hired to guide the congregation in setting up a counseling center. But within months that pastor was asked to leave because of marital infidelity.

The term hypocrisy refers to being what one really is not—in most cases, pretending to be better than one really is. What's most disappointing to you about hypocrites? Check all that apply.

❏ Their attitudes   ❏ Their self-righteousness
❏ Their pride or arrogance   ❏ Their condescending ways
❏ Their denial of personal sin ❏ Other: _____

Hypocrisy is a concern throughout the New Testament. Read the following selected Scriptures and briefly summarize how we are to respond to hypocrisy.

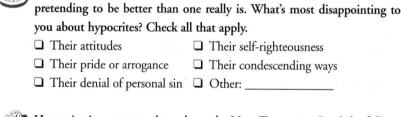

OUR RESPONSE TO HYPOCRISY

"Do not judge, or you too will be   _____
judge. For in the same way you judge   _____
others, you will be judged, and with the _____
measure you use, it will be measured   _____
to you.   _____

"Why do you look at the speck of sawdust _____
in your brother's eye and pay no _____
attention to the plank in your own eye? _____
How can you say to your brother 'Let _____
me take the speck out of your eye,' when _____
all the time there is a plank in your own _____
eye? You hypocrite, first take the plank _____
out of your own eye, and then you _____
will see clearly to remove the speck from _____
your brother's eye" (Matthew 7:1-5). _____

"The teachers of the law and the Pharisees _____
sit in Moses' seat. So you must obey them _____
and do everything they tell you. But do _____
not do what they do, for they do not _____
practice what they preach" _____
(Matthew 23:2-3). _____

Therefore, rid yourselves of all malice, and _____
all deceit, hypocrisy, envy, and slander _____
of all kind (1 Peter 2:1). _____

We are not asked to focus on what others do wrong but on what God expects of us.

It's important to realize God, not us, will deal with hypocrites. We are not asked to focus on what others do wrong but on what God expects of us. I stayed in the last church to help out for a while, and when I left there I started my own work teaching marriage seminars, along with writing books about how to stay happily married. I've since had many wonderful experiences being a member of various churches—but for more than 15 years I've not had the opportunity again of being a staff member.

You may be wondering how I stayed on a spiritual journey with all I had experienced. I had plenty of reason for skepticism, and you may as well.

I came to realize I wasn't responsible for the wrongs of those other people. I wasn't going to let their irresponsibility rob me of my future love for life. I held on to a baseline faith in the "God of hope" (Romans 15:13). I chose to heed the advice of Scripture, "Come near to God and he will come near to you" (James 4:8). I listened when someone said, "God is still enriching the lives of those who find Him." I always wanted to know if it was possible to experience God. I no longer cared how hypocritical the "bank tellers" or the others who "deposited" at church were; I was going to keep up my own search for God's treasures and His power.

Is there someone who has kept you or is keeping you from a close relationship with God through Jesus Christ? What will you do to forgive them?

_____

_____

Write a prayer asking God to forgive you for harboring negative feelings toward Him because of other people. Thank God for His grace and love .

_____

_____

Day 3
Expecting Too Much from People Keeps Me from God

I came to see the major hindrances for me in knowing a personal God. I can best explain it by asking you to imagine a life-size baby doll in a store. Picture this doll moving and even speaking a limited vocabulary. In her back a battery pack opens up; it holds three D batteries to supply the power so she can function as she was designed to—so she can be all she was meant to be.

We're all somewhat like that doll. God made us capable of doing many good and wonderful things, but we need power to operate. God intends for us to get the main power for living—and the primary things we need in life—from Him. If we let Him, God can empower our love; it's like having all three D batteries in place. God fits. I find that many people, like me, have had this vague emptiness in their lives; they don't know what will fill it. We can feel a need to be connected to a personal God, a longing for wholeness, or a desire to gain control over our emotions and struggles.

Our spiritual problems only increase when we try to stuff things other than God into our battery packs, hoping these things will fit and empower us. I've found that if we try to gain completeness, strength, love, and joy from any substitutes for God, they don't bring a lasting fulfillment. In fact, when you look closely at negative emotions of hurt, frustration, and fear, they often come as we expect God's creation—rather than God—to "charge" our life batteries.

These substitutes generally fall into one of two categories: what we expect to get from other people (like AA batteries) and what we expect to get from our jobs (like C batteries). I tried to stuff people and my job into my battery pack for years, and all I kept getting was the very emotions I didn't want—hurt and emptiness.

 At the top of the next page are two batteries. One is labeled _Other People_ and the other is labeled _My Work_. Write in each battery the people or the things about work from which you expect to get power for living your life.

 Zechariah 4:6 says, " 'Not by might nor by power, but by my Spirit,' says the Lord Almighty." What is your real source of strength and power in life?

_____

God is our enduring source of power.

I'll never forget the day I realized that my lack of connection with God was primarily the result of my decision to remain angry. My main anger source was my expectations that people and my job would fit nicely into my battery pack; they would provide me with power, love, and satisfaction. Unfortunately expectations bring the hurt and frustration leading to anger. People and the things our jobs can bring are great batteries, just the wrong size for us.

On this particular day, I was casually reading a section of Scripture and my eyes stopped at a verse that screamed: *If you remain angry with anyone, you'll lose your ability to walk in the light of God* and thus the ability to know the love of God (see 1 John 2:9-10). Very angry people seem to be spiritually blind and unable to draw near to God.

 Briefly describe a time in your life you felt distant from God. Identify what was between you and God—another person, your anger, an issue, etc.

_____

_____

When we rely on one person or group of folks to meet our needs for love, purpose, excitement, fulfillment, ego gratification … you know what happens? They eventually let us down because they are human. Their love often proves to be conditional rather than without reservation. Life with even the best mate is boring at times. And no one lives forever—what then? Our kids have a will of their own and may choose words and actions that hurt us rather than fulfill us. A best friend might betray us or just move away to another part of the country in our time of deepest need.

Our supply of energy for dealing with life's daily demands depends on how closely our expectations match the reality we experience. Well, when friends and family let us down, when we've been counting on them, we can suffer a huge energy loss.

Recall the last time your expectations didn't match the reality of an experience you had with your mate. Briefly write about that experience below.

_____

_____

How did you and your mate resolve the issue?

_____

_____

People will disappoint us— God never will.

When we try to stuff other people into our battery packs, the result is usually anger when they disappoint us. (People are good at not allowing us to use them.) But if we're not trying to use them to somehow energize us—if we know the true source of power, if we know that only God gives the best things in life—we can forgive them and consequently relax our expectations of them. As we understand the limitations of people fulfilling us—they can't compare to what God can do when it comes to energize us—we can sincerely desire the best of others. That's genuine love.

So if people offend us or let us down, we can release our anger to God and allow the hurtful experience to remind us of our dependency on Him. As we do this, we find freedom—power—to help others on their own spiritual journeys. Again, that's genuine love.

To summarize this idea, one of the main blockages to our spiritual journey is expecting others to meet our deepest needs and this sets us up for being hurt and getting angry. But we tend to relax when we realize that God can meet our deepest needs. Then as we actually experience God meeting our needs and doing things that could only be described as miraculous, we gain a peace and happiness that's beyond what we had imagined gaining from other people.

I believe the key to maintaining love and satisfaction in life is—not expecting lasting satisfaction and love to come from God's creation. Keep those expectations for God alone. Allow Him to be the main-battery power-source and expect everything else to be "overflow."

That's not to say I never experience down times anymore. Like you and most others, I still have anger and other defeating feelings at times. But the difference for me is that when I experience those normal negative emotions, I find myself "rejoicing," which means returning to the source of my joy. I'm willing to admit that my anger is a result of using others for my satisfaction instead of enriching them.

Close today's study in prayer asking God to give you the power to forgive anyone who would come between you and Him.

Day 4
Expecting Too Much from My Job Keeps Me from God

 Write the top five reasons you work.

1. _____

2. _____

3. _____

4. _____

5. _____

Our work will not provide ultimate meaning to life.

If you live to work instead of working to live then you are expecting too much out of your work. Men, in particular, often find their life's purpose and meaning in tasks instead of relationships. Expecting work to give ultimate meaning to our lives is a false battery. I used to squeeze God out of my life. I was looking for fulfillment and strength in a job.

 Check the following statements that apply to you.

❑ I spend too much time at work.

❑ My spouse complains about my overworking.

❑ I use work to escape problems at home.

❑ I work a lot of overtime and weekends.

You may find you are addicted to work if you checked some of the above symptoms. Too much emphasis on work begins to squeeze God out of our lives.

Think of all the *places* we can go and the *things* we can have because of our "positions." The money we earn makes all those things possible. We may think, *If only I had a bigger house or a more modern house. If only I lived in the "right" part of town. If only I could vacation in Cancun instead of Cleveland. If only I could live in Florida, where I'd never have to shovel snow anymore.*

What is your primary work or career goal in life? Check any that apply.

❑ To make lots of money ❑ To pay my bills

❑ To retire early ❑ To buy things I want

❑ To have the lifestyle of our friends ❑ To live in a nicer home

❑ To be successful and respected ❑ To travel to exotic places

It's important to have career goals. However, expecting work to give your life meaning and purpose will lead to disappointment. Do you work to gain the necessities of life, or because you are worried about having "stuff"?

Read Matthew 6:25-34. Underline everything Jesus says about the meaning of life. Circle everything He says about God's provision.

"Therefore I tell you, do not worry about your life, what you will eat or drink; or about your body, what you will wear. Is not life more important than food, and the body more important than clothes? Look at the birds of the air; they do not sow or reap or store away in barns, and yet your heavenly Father feeds them. Are you not much more valuable than they? Who of you by worrying can add a single hour to his life?

"And why do you worry about clothes? See how the lilies of the field grow. They do not labor or spin. Yet I tell you that not even Solomon in all his splendor was dressed like one of these. If that is how God clothes the grass of the field, which is here today and tomorrow is thrown into the fire, will he not much more clothe you, O you of little faith? So do not worry, saying, 'What shall we eat?' or, 'What shall we drink?' or, 'What shall we wear?' For the pagans run after all these things, and your heavenly Father knows that you need them. But seek first his kingdom and his righteousness, and all these things will be given you as well. Therefore do not worry about tomorrow, for tomorrow will worry about itself. Each day has enough trouble of its own" (Matthew 6:25-34).

*T*rying to get more "stuff" is bound to disappoint us.

Trying to get more "stuff" like a bigger home or more expensive car is bound to disappoint us. When you get right down to it, all homes are just wood, bricks, and mortar. Vacations, as great as they are, are only temporary breaks from the demands of daily living. And Florida, as warm and beautiful as it is, also gets hurricanes and is the land of large roaches.

No matter where we are, we face the challenges and difficulties that are universal to humankind. No matter how big our house, the folks inside have all the failings of the human race. When you stop to think about it, can any home or other location take the place of God in filling our battery pack and meeting our deepest needs? I haven't found any place that rejuvenates as He does.

We may also think, *If only I had a lot of money in the bank. If only I could drive the right car or wear the latest designer clothes. If only I had a higher-paying, more prestigious job, one where I was considered invaluable by all my superiors.*

Perhaps you've seen the bumper sticker that says "He who dies with the most toys wins." Well, I've been able to enjoy a few nice things in recent years, and while they provide pleasure for a while, they also rust, break, get stolen, or just wear out. And, according to the hundreds of people I've spoken with, when you have a sick child or a troubled marriage, the size of one's bank account doesn't bring the satisfaction one once expected. The more accurate bumper sticker would be one that says, "He who thinks that having a lot of toys brings fulfillment is already dead."

Read Matthew 6:19-21 below. Write a summary of what Jesus says in regard to earthly possessions.

"Do not store up for yourselves treasures on earth, where moth and rust destroy, and where thieves break in and steal. But store up for yourselves treasures in heaven, where moth and rust do not destroy, and where thieves do not break in and steal. For where your treasure is, there your heart will be also."

_____

_____

I know rich and poor people alike at both ends of a scale of contentment—some are very happy and some are miserable. Money doesn't seem to be the gauge for happiness. I can honestly say no amount of money has ever kept me satisfied or in love. Only if I'm allowing God to meet my needs and empower me with His love, joy, peace, and contentment every day am I truly happy regardless of my circumstances.

Our human tendency is to expect fulfillment (a personal battery charge) from friends and loved ones or from what our jobs can buy (where we live or visit and the things we own). They inevitably disappoint us, leaving us frustrated and angry.

 Close in prayer, surrendering your attitude toward your work to God. Ask God's Spirit to bring contentment to you life.

Money doesn't seem to be the gauge for happiness.

Day 5
Practical Ways I've Drawn Closer to God

I'd like to present some steps I take each day to maintain my relationship with God. It's not a rigid set of procedures, but just some ideas that help me in a practical way.

1. *I use negative emotions to remind myself God is the source of my power.* I recognize that His creation can't ultimately give me the kind of contentment only God can give. So I use my natural negative emotions to remind myself to let Him be that source of power for me.

2. Whenever I'm fearful, worried, or angry because someone or something has failed to meet my expectations, *I admit it to God.* (That's another way of saying I confess my error of seeking contentment from people or the things money can buy.) For example, if I'm angry, I say, "Lord, I'm thankful I'm angry right now. It shows me how easy it is to expect your creation to charge my battery pack. It also shows me I've been looking in the wrong place for my fulfillment, because I haven't been looking to you. I haven't been honoring you as the source of my power and life."

3. Then I tell God, "I'm going to take the time right now to pull that non-God thing out of my battery pack." In other words, *I make a conscious decision that I'm going to stop relying on people or my job for fulfillment. I'm not going to keep expecting them to provide my happiness, contentment, and love.*

4. Next, I say to God, "I now invite you to take full possession of my battery pack." *I realign myself with God, acknowledging only He will never disappoint me.* I start looking to Him, and Him alone, as my source of strength and joy. And when I'm aware of how I've "missed his mark" by acting in a not-loving way, I seek His forgiveness. That keeps our relationship open.

5. Finally (this is the hardest part), *I tell God, "I honor you and your ways that are beyond my knowledge. I'm willing to wait until you 'charge my battery.'"* I know it may take a while before I'm content with what you provide rather than secretly expecting my spouse, my house, or my job to meet my needs. But I want You to be the source of my life, the source of my strength, my power to love others as I should."

I've found praying this way consistently and sincerely, God has been faithful in revealing himself to me. If we're putting anyone or anything other than God into our battery pack, expecting people or jobs or things to energize us and make us happy, we're going to be disappointed—and often. Those people and things simply can't take His place. **The reality is always going to be less than our expectations.**

Review this process and check the boxes by the steps you will try this week. Circle the box by the step that will be most difficult for you.

❏ Use negative emotions to remind myself God is the source of my power.

❏ Admit my fear, worry, or anger to God.

❏ Stop relying on people or my job to provide my happiness, contentment, and love.

❏ Realign myself with God, acknowledging only He will never disappoint me.

❏ Tell God, "I honor you and your ways that are beyond my knowledge. I'm willing to wait on You."

Can you imagine what it would be like to have two people in a marriage relying mainly on God to fill their "happiness pack"? Then they would both try to outdo the other in meeting one another's needs. They would be following what Jesus called the greatest commandments: *Love God with all your heart, and secondly, love others as you value yourself* (see Matthew 22:37-39). I don't know of anything better.

Along with the process I have shared with you, there are other practical ways you might grow closer to God. From the list below, check the ways you will incorporate into your life in the coming weeks.

❏ Humble myself   ❏ Meditate on and study God's Word

❏ Worship God   ❏ Fellowship with other Christians

❏ Spend time with God in prayer, silence, and solitude

❏ Serve Christ by serving others

Close this week's study by writing Deuteronomy 6:4 in the margin. As you write, offer it as your commitment to God—the enduring source of power.

> *"Love God with all your heart, and secondly, love others as you love yourself."*

Couple Time

For you to complete

1. Which of the four "icebergs" keeps you most often at a distance from God?
   - ❏ Doubts
   - ❏ Hypocrites
   - ❏ Expecting too much from other people
   - ❏ Expecting too much from my job

   Explain why and how you will change that.

   _____

   _____

2. Write the ways you will seek to grow closer to God in the coming weeks as an individual and as a couple.

   _____

   _____

   _____

For you to share with your spouse

1. Sit down face to face and share how you have answered the above section.

2. Take turns completing these sentences:

   I will surrender my expectations of you concerning ...

   The most important thing to me in my relationship with God is ...

   I believe Jesus Christ is ...

   Together, we could grow closer to God by ...

3. Spend time praying silently together and then spend another few minutes praying out loud, thanking God for His strength and power in your lives and marriage.

WEEK 7

Five Vital Signs of a Healthy Marriage

Are my relationships healthy? Maybe you can hear someone asking the question of a counselor. Maybe you've asked the question. What does the question mean? What does *health* mean in terms of a relationship?

Here's what I'm learning about what's healthy. It's a relationship where each person feels valued, cared for, safe, and loved. Each person is relatively content with life and is growing toward maturity.

In every relationship, especially in marriage, there are at least five generally accepted indicators, or vital signs, of the health of that relationship.[1] This week we'll take a close look at those signs. To make love last forever, marriage partners must learn how to read their relationship's vital signs.

If we can identify signs of health, we can also see symptoms of ill health that indicate "something's not right here." Let's look at some of those symptoms in the story of Jack and Sherry. At one point all their vital signs were negative. Their marriage seemed to be a terminal case.

About 10 years ago, after several years of marriage, Sherry got so fed up with the shape of things that she decided the marriage was over. "This is it!" she said. "I'm not going to put myself through these emotional ups and downs anymore!" Packing a few things, she fled the house.

"I didn't have any mamma to run home to," she explains, "so I went to our houseboat and locked myself in."

In a way that boat symbolized the root of the couple's problem. Jack's father, an alcoholic, never hung onto a job for very long. "I was hell bent to be the opposite of that," says Jack, who became a classic workaholic, toiling long hours to build a successful business and provide financial security and comfort for his own family. One of those comforts was the houseboat. He enjoyed this luxurious "toy" and others, paid for by his long days and professional preoccupation. And he assumed Sherry appreciated the boat as much as he did.

She may have enjoyed the boat and what it represented, but it did not satisfy any inner restlessness. What did Sherry want? In her mind she pictured and longed for a

110

loving marriage. Central to that image was a husband who made time for her, talked with her, and cared for her. No comfortable home or big boat could take the place of a loving husband's presence and attention.

When it came to affection, Sherry felt as if she were living in a perpetual drought. She'd get no rain for months. Then a few sprinkles would drop. *Oh, this is so refreshing!* She wanted the sprinkles to turn into a shower, but she was never too hopeful. *No, no, something is going to happen, and he'll stop again.* Those negative thoughts made it impossible to enjoy even the sprinkles. Then sure enough, she soon found herself back in an emotional drought.

Sherry's resentment built over the years. It was hard for her to express her thoughts and feelings to Jack. When she did try, he shamed her into silence. "You have everything wonderful!" he'd insist. "What are you complaining about? We've never had it so good!" And her emotional needs remained unmet, her feelings unacknowledged.

The tension and pressure built until Sherry decided she couldn't take it anymore and ran to the docked houseboat. Bob, a member of their small group, went over to talk to her. He was almost like a son to Sherry, and she had always been open with him in the group setting. When he knocked on the door and identified himself, she held her ground. "Go away! This is it. I don't want to talk."

"Sherry, I'm not going to try to change your mind," he said. "I just want to be here and make sure you're OK."

"No, I can't see you!" she maintained. "Just go away!" And that, she thought, was the end of it. Nothing more was said, and she assumed Bob had left.

Later, Sherry had to leave the houseboat use the restroom. As she left, she found Bob sitting on the dock—no coat, shivering in the seven degree weather. Sherry couldn't believe it. In her concern for Bob, she immediately forgot her need for a bathroom, dragged him inside, and gave him a blanket. They started to talk, and before long she was pouring out all her frustrations and resentments. She told him every lousy thing Jack had ever done. Bob just listened—no criticism, no defensiveness, no denial of her feelings. He simply gave her the gift of an attentive ear.

As Sherry talked, an amazing thing happened. Having someone listen and understand her frustration "uncorked" her hurtful feelings, and they seemed to drain away as she spoke. Finally, she couldn't think of any other negative things to say about Jack. She began to remember some of the good things about Jack. She felt a new appreciation for him and, without fully understanding it, a fresh hope for their marriage.

Within about an hour her feelings toward Jack and the potential for their marriage had turned around. After talking to Bob a little longer, Sherry said, "I think maybe there's hope for us after all. I'm going home to work things out."

Since then Jack and Sherry have experienced the normal relational bumps that any couple can expect. But her retreat to the houseboat was a real turning point, and I've watched their marriage continue to grow and flourish right up to the present. They're such an inspiration to me and so many others.

Before this momentous day their marriage exhibited the two most common characteristics—symptoms—of unhealthy relationships: (1) **too much distance** between

What does healthy *mean in terms of relationship?*

the partners and (2) **too much control** being exerted by one person. When both are present in the same relationship, as they were in Jack and Sherry's case, disaster is almost inevitable.

Using Jack and Sherry's example, this week we will explore:

- the need and value of each person in the relationship to feel confident to use his or her creativity and intelligence to complement the other person;
- ways to encourage others to talk, feeling what they are saying is valued;
- the importance of each person sharing his or her feelings in a safe environment;
- attitudes that exhibit daily that there is a meaningful connection between partners in the relationship; and
- how to honor and respect the other person in the relationship.

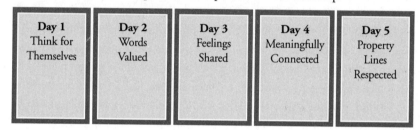

| **Day 1** Think for Themselves | **Day 2** Words Valued | **Day 3** Feelings Shared | **Day 4** Meaningfully Connected | **Day 5** Property Lines Respected |

This week we will explore in more depth the specifics of a healthy marriage. I am praying that as you share with your spouse, God's forever-love, *agape*, will fill your relationship to overflowing.

May this passage of Scripture be an inspiration to you as you share together:

> "My command is this: Love each other as I [Jesus] have loved you. Greater love has no one than this, that he lay down his life for his friends" (John 15:12).

---

[1]Irene Goldenberg and Herbert Goldenberg, *Family Therapy: An Overview*, 28-54.

Day 1

Vital Sign 1: All Feel Safe to Think for Themselves

Too much distance can occur when the husband and wife are not talking enough for both to feel "connected." One person is too often silent, unable to share deep feelings or simply closes the other person out of his or her private life. Often a couple gets too busy to stay in touch emotionally; one's job may require too much time away from home. If even one person feels this "distance," resentment can spread like a cancer.

In a situation of overcontrol, one spouse is dominating the other—choosing where the couple will live, go to church, and take vacations; making everyday decisions; and so on. The one being controlled can lose a sense of personal identity and eventually not know clearly what he or she wants or who he or she really is. This person's personal boundaries can be violated until he or she feels squeezed into a little box. And in that box anger is quickly compressed.

Unless they're recognized and understood, these problems—of distance and control—can become deeply ingrained in a marriage. That's exactly what happened with Jack and Sherry. Jack failed to understand that his controlling nature created distance between him and Sherry, who learned not to discuss her negative feelings; instead, she buried them. Until the crisis at the houseboat, neither of them recognized the warning signs of a problem potentially deadly to their marriage.

Let's turn from ill health to the vital signs of health in a relationship. We'll continue to refer to Jack and Sherry and their "new" relationship to see how several of these signs function. (I thank my friend and psychology professor Dr. Rod Cooper for his insights in this discussion.)

 Before I begin with these healthy signs, what are the healthy feelings and attitudes you believe a couple needs to have for one another in a marriage? Below is a list of feelings and attitudes. Rank the top 5 from most important (1) to least important (5).

_____ Love	_____ Respect
_____ Honesty	_____ Faithfulness
_____ Honor for one another	_____ Willingness to listen
_____ Desire for physical intimacy	_____ Understanding
_____ Kindness	_____ Caring
_____ Safety and security	_____ Forgiveness
_____ Share thoughts and feelings	_____ Other: _____

In any healthy relationship, people have the freedom to think for themselves. Think of a converse situation. If a spouse says things like, "That's a stupid idea!" or "Just do what I say and don't ask questions!" the mate soon learns that it's not safe to think for himself or herself. It's not long before that berated person learns to belittle his or her own thinking or grow resentful (or both).

Do you or your spouse ever put down one another by saying demeaning things? **What is the most demeaning put-down you have used toward your spouse?**

_____

How would you refrain from saying this or reword this in order to affirm, not put down, your spouse?

_____

_____

In a healthy relationship, people have the freedom to think for themselves.

Write the most demeaning put-down your spouse has said to you.

_____

In the case of Jack and Sherry, he made it clear that if she didn't see things his way, there must be something wrong with her. If she said he was working too many hours, he told her she was failing to appreciate the sacrifice he was making for the financial good of the family. If she claimed he was giving tennis a higher priority than time with her, he insisted she was refusing to recognize his need for recreation to relieve the pressures of his job. In short, he communicated that her thinking must be flawed.

Let's face it. Men and women often perceive things differently. Those different perceptions are not right or wrong, merely different. Scripture tells us about a way both men and women think alike, not differently. Recognizing that at times we have different perceptions, as Christian husbands and wives, how are we to think?

 Read the following Scriptures from Paul's letter to the Philippians. Briefly summarize how we are to think as Christians.

Whatever is true, whatever is noble, whatever is right, whatever is pure, whatever is lovely, whatever is admirable—if anything is excellent or praiseworthy—think about such things (Philippians 4:8).

_____
_____
_____
_____

If you have any encouragement from being united with Christ, if any comfort from his love, if any fellowship with the Spirit, if any tenderness and compassion, then make my joy complete by being like-minded, having the same love, being one in spirit and purpose. Do nothing out of selfish ambition or vain conceit, but in humility consider others better than yourselves. Each of you should look not only to your own interests, but also to the interest of others, Your attitude should be the same as that of Christ Jesus (Philippians 2:1-5).

_____
_____
_____
_____
_____
_____
_____
_____
_____
_____
_____
_____

Since both men and women who know Christ have the mind of Christ, they can both regard one another's thoughts with honor and respect.

In healthy relationships, we encourage others to think, using the mind and wisdom that Christ has given them. We want our kids to verbalize their plans, ask questions, and then learn to make their own decisions. We want our spouses to use their creativity and intelligence to complement our own. As someone has said of marriage, "If both of us think exactly alike, one of us is unnecessary."

> _Since men and women who know Christ have the mind of Christ, they can regard one another's thoughts with honor and respect._

In fact, having only one opinion or source of input greatly limits our abilities to think clearly or righteously.

 Read Proverbs 24:3-6. Summarize what these words say about the counsel of others—that includes your spouse!

By wisdom a house is built,
    and through understanding it is established;
through knowledge its rooms are filled
    with rare and beautiful treasures.
A wise man has great power,
    and a man of knowledge increases strength;
for waging war you need guidance,
    and a victory many advisers.

_____

_____

I have to admit, with embarrassment, that I was somewhat insensitive to my wife's thinking process in the early years of our marriage. I believed many stereotypes about the female "emotional" way of thinking; at times I would discount her ideas because of my desire to have everything be "perfectly logical." I foolishly assumed my way of thinking was superior.

Now, having been married for more than 30 years, I've learned not only to listen to Norma's ideas about everything, but also to draw out her thinking as much as I can. That's because I've so often seen her intuitive and logical thinking processes work wonders and keep me out of messes.

 Think of the times your spouse's counsel blessed your life, your marriage, and perhaps even saved you from a big mess. Pray, thanking God for the gift of your spouse.

> *"I've not only learned to listen to Norma's ideas, but also to draw out her thinking."*

Day 2

Vital Sign 2: All Are Encouraged to Talk and Know Their Words Will Be Valued

In a good relationship, you have not only the freedom to think, but you also are encouraged to talk, to express yourself. When you talk, the other—your spouse, parents, friends, boss, or whomever—listens with the attitude that what you try to express is greatly valued, even if the two of you disagree.

(Please understand I'm not saying it's OK to speak disrespectfully. With freedom comes responsibility, and everything we say should be honoring to those we're addressing. Even strong opinions can be stated in a way that's clear, yet respectful.)

 What does the Bible have to say about the importance of listening and hearing the other person? James 1:19 gives a clear picture of the importance of listening, "Everyone should be quick to listen, slow to speak, and slow to become angry." Put an x on the line to indicate where you are and an s on the line to indicate where you believe your spouse is.

I speak too quickly.   I listen before I speak.

I think about what I'm going to say next.   I listen carefully to my spouse.

I listen critically.   I listen to understand.

I don't look when my spouse speaks.   I look at my spouse while listening.

My anger keeps me from listening effectively.   I control my anger while listening.

God provides for us the perfect modeling of listening. The Bible affirms that God hears and answers us. "I call to God, and the Lord saves me. Evening, morning and noon I cry out in distress, and he hears my voice. … Cast your cares on the Lord and he will sustain you; for he will never let the righteous fall" (Psalm 55:16-17, 22).

Think of the ways God listens to you. Below are some of the qualities of God as He listens to us. Circle the qualities you need most as you listen to your spouse.

Allowing anything to be said	Caring	Attentive
Nurturing	Willing to answer	Loving
Always willing to listen	Empathetic	Patient

In a lot of homes, unfortunately, spouses and children are literally treated as objects to be seen and not heard. Or perhaps when they do speak, they're constantly interrupted. Or they know certain subjects are taboo and are raised only at their peril. Getting shut down like that can produce a lot of buried, destructive anger.

Whatever type of communication was used in your childhood home, that's the pattern of communication you'll tend to use as an adult. If you weren't allowed to talk as a child, you'll tend not to give your spouse or children that freedom, either. If you were encouraged to speak, you'll probably give others the same right.

Whatever type of communication was used in your childhood home, that's the pattern you'll tend to use as an adult.

⊙ Briefly describe the patterns of communication you had at home when you were growing up.

_____

_____

Describe how your current patterns of communication at home are different and similar to when you grew up.

Our family communicates differently than when I grew up by

_____

One way communication hasn't changed is

_____

Did you have a distant or controlling parent? Were you never allowed to speak candidly? Were the words "I love you" seldom heard? If you now find yourself repeating such an unhealthy pattern, I have a recommendation that has worked for many of my clients. Go to your spouse (or your kids or close friends) and say, "I wish I were talking to you more and listening to what you have to say, but I wasn't raised like that, so it doesn't come naturally to me. It's hard for me. But I want to break that habit—that generational pull. Will you help me?" When the people we love begin helping us love them more, they are usually much more tolerant of our ways and forgiving of us.

⊙ Describe one thing in communicating with your spouse that you need your spouse's help in doing.

_____

_____

When the people we love begin helping us love them more, they are more tolerant of our ways and forgiving of us.

I've asked for help a lot as a husband and dad. I've had to, because as soon as I would tell myself I would never jump on Norma or the kids and shut them down again, I would turn around and do it once more. It helped them to understand why I sometimes reacted the way I did, and it helped me to know they were holding me accountable. It also gave us a basis for asking for and extending forgiveness when I "slipped."

⊙ When was the last time you asked for help in relating from your spouse? Check one.

❏ In the last 24 hours   ❏ In the last few months
❏ In the last week   ❏ In the last year
❏ In the last month   ❏ Can't remember

If you can't remember when you last asked for help in relating from your spouse, what keeps you from asking? Write down one or two barriers that keep you from asking.

_____

_____

In Jack and Sherry's case, he learned a very unhealthy pattern from his alcoholic father; in turn, Jack was an expert at shutting down Sherry's attempts to express herself. You'll recall that his weapon of choice was shame: "How can you complain? Look at how good you've got it!" So Sherry kept silent and grew more angry and more frustrated until she had finally had enough and ran away.

The pull of our past can be broken.

Anytime I see parents controlling their children in unhealthy ways, I don't think, *What rotten people!* Instead I usually think, *I wonder what kind of parents they had?* Almost always, their negative parenting habits can be traced back to the way they were raised. Based on research presented in their book *Family Therapy: An Overview,* Irene and Herbert Goldenberg have concluded that the communication skills we learned as children tend to be the ones we use as adults. Again, it's the generational effect: *What we got as kids, we tend to give to our mates and kids.*[1]

The encouraging evidence for us today is that the pull of our past can be broken. And as I suggested above, one of the best ways to accomplish the break is by making ourselves accountable to our loved ones.

To convey acceptance of others' words, I recommend a gentle touch. Whenever you're listening to your spouse or children, remember to put an arm around them or a hand on their shoulder. That tender touch communicates that you love them, that they're important to you, and that what they're saying is valuable.

Eye contact is also vital, especially with children. When we make the effort to set aside whatever else we may be doing and look them in the eyes, they know they have our full, undivided attention. But if we're trying to talk at the same time we're doing something else, they know we're not really listening.

Body language can also convey interest and acceptance. Leaning toward the person who's speaking; occasional nods of the head—these are some of the subtle signs of active listening that encourage people to talk.

 What do you need to be doing to convey acceptance of your spouse's words more effectively? Underline the ideas I shared in the previous paragraphs that you will implement in your relationship with your spouse.

 Close today's study in prayer, asking God to heighten your level of sensitivity to your spouse's thoughts and ideas.

_____

[1] Irene Goldenberg and Herbert Goldenberg, *Family Therapy: An Overview,* 55-85.

Day 3
Vital Sign 3: All Enjoy a Sense of Safety and Value in Sharing Their Feelings

In a healthy relationship, you not only know your thinking and words will be valued, but you also have the freedom to share your feelings, knowing they will be respected. In an unhealthy situation, on the other hand, any attempt to share feelings may be met with a denigrating statement: "Oh, grow up!" "Lighten up!" "You're making a mountain out of a mole hill." "Give me a break!"

Which of the following feelings are most difficult for you to share with your spouse? Check all that apply.

❏ Love   ❏ Anger   ❏ Frustration   ❏ Insecurity
❏ Inferiority   ❏ Inadequacy   ❏ Hurt or pain   ❏ Anxiety
❏ Fear   ❏ Joy   ❏ Acceptance   ❏ Affirmation

In a healthy relationship, you have the freedom to share your feelings, knowing they will be respected.

Recently I was with a husband and wife as they packed the car for a trip during which they were leaving their high-school-aged son with some friends. They hadn't spent a lot of time away from their son in the past, and the wife expressed some feelings of regret about leaving him behind. "Who's going to make his lunch in the morning?" she said. "Who's going to fix him a snack when he gets home from football practice?"

The husband responded, "Come on, lighten up! We're only going to be gone a few days. I can't believe you're making such a big deal out of this!"

Being a friend of the couple, I put my arm around the wife's shoulder. As I looked at the man to make sure I had his attention, I asked her, "How do you feel about what he just said?"

"It makes me feel silly and like my feelings aren't valid," she said, staring at the ground.

"Would you rather not go on the trip?" he asked, embarrassed.

"No, I want to go," she replied. "But I would love it if you would just let me say what I'm feeling without criticizing."

Then I put my other arm around his shoulder and asked, "Do you hear what she's saying?"

"Yeah, I hear it," he said with a sheepish look.

Do you think he realized what he was doing when he made that harsh comment? No! He had no idea he was controlling her by belittling her feelings. He was like so many of us who fail to realize what we're doing unless it's pointed out to us.

Feelings are important. God encourages us to share our feelings with Him without judgment, fear, or belittlement. Let's explore that for a moment. Get out your Bible and turn to the Book of Psalms. Take five minutes to skim through as many psalms as you can. In the space below, write down every feeling or emotion expressed by the psalmists.

_____

_____

_____

God encourages us to share our feelings with Him without judgment, fear, or belittlement.

Do you see the wonderful breadth of emotions in the Book of Psalms? One scholar has noted that every emotion known to humanity finds expression in the Book of Psalms. If it's acceptable to tell God how we feel, surely we can accept how one another feels in marriage.

 What emotion are you uncomfortable with that your spouse expresses?

_____

Will you share that truth with your spouse in a way that accepts his or her emotion and still communicates your uncomfortable feelings?

I have had problems accepting Norma's feelings. Norma would express her feelings, and I would reply sarcastically, "I can't believe this! Here we go being sensitive again." If she would cry, I would roll my eyes in frustration and do all I could to win the argument quickly so we could get on to "more important things." For much of our married life, I didn't realize how unhealthy that kind of response was. But as I've learned, I've given her more freedom to share her feelings, and she has grown to feel safer doing so.

Because the tendency to belittle her feelings was ingrained by my background and personality, however, this will probably always be an area of struggle for me.

I tell the story in another of my books about the time Norma sheared off part of the roof of our mini motor home as she pulled into our garage after a shopping trip. If I had still been reacting like my father at that point, I could have gone ballistic the way he did one time when I had an accident with his car. In the early years of our marriage, I was capable of saying something like, "That was stupid! Weren't you looking where you were going?"

But because I had been learning and growing a little in this area, I knew Norma felt bad enough already and didn't need a lecture from me. (I also knew she had told the neighbors across the street, and they were looking to see how I was going to respond!) She needed me to understand her heart and reassure her I didn't think it was the end of the world. So I put my arms around her and told her I loved her more than campers. We even managed to get the roof fixed within a couple of hours.

Answer these questions by putting an *x* on the line in the appropriate place.
How safe do you feel sharing your feelings with your spouse?

Unsafe   Safe

How safe do you think your spouse feels sharing with you?

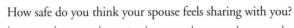

Unsafe   Safe

This freedom to share feelings is one of the clearest indicators of the health of a relationship.

 Pray, asking God to give you the courage and confidence to share your feelings with your spouse. Ask God to help you be more sensitive to the feelings expressed by your spouse and the way you respond.

The desire for connection is a basic human need.

Day 4
Vital Sign 4: All Feel Meaningfully Connected

What are the best ways of knowing if you're "connected" to the ones you love? You're connected if you regularly share your deepest feelings with one another; when you're enthusiastic about seeing one another at the end of a long day; when you enjoy being together and doing things with one another. The opposite of this is a situation where a partner is either neglectful—perhaps a workaholic—or controlling. Neglect or control creates distance rather than connection.

 Are you connected to or distant from your spouse? Circle one of the statements in each column along the fence below to indicate whether you feel connected or distant in your marriage.

CONNECTED	DISTANT
Share deepest feelings	Can't share deepest feelings
Enthusiastic about seeing each other at the end of the day.	Dread seeing each other at the end of the day.
Enjoy being together	Dislike being together
Attentive to one another	Inattentive to one another
Give one another freedom	Try to control one another

The desire for connection is a basic human need. It's so powerful that when people don't feel connected, they're far more likely to develop addictions. The pain of

empty relationships is so great that they go looking for some way to medicate the hollow feeling, to cover it over with some numbing pleasure. They get their sense of connection not from healthy relationships, but from some unhealthy addictive substance. Pam Smith, a nationally-recognized nutritionist, notes that some compulsive overeaters "eat to 'fill the gaps' in our lives. Food becomes a friend and companion who is always there no matter what. When we're lonely, eating seems to fill the emptiness. It can substitute for love, attention, and pampering."[1]

 The Bible asserts that any barriers between us have been and can be broken down by Jesus Christ. Read the following Scripture. Underline the phrases that speak most directly to your marriage.

> For he [Christ] himself is our peace, who has made the two one and has destroyed the barrier, the dividing wall of hostility, by abolishing in his flesh the law with its commandments and regulations. His purpose was to create in himself one new man out of two, thus making peace, and in this one body to reconcile both of them to God through the cross, by which he put to death their hostility. He came and preached peace to you who were far away and peace to those who were near. For through him, we both have access to the Father by one Spirit (Ephesians 2:14-18).

Think again of Jack and Sherry. Because his alcoholic father had been unable to connect with his children, Jack didn't know how to connect, either. (From my experience, it appears that alcoholism disconnects people.) And because Sherry had had a poor relationship with her dad, Jack says, "Some of the suspicions and lack of trust of me didn't come from what I was doing but from her memories of her father." So neither Sherry nor Jack knew how to connect. It's no wonder they had an unhealthy relationship for so long!

Remember, too, that unresolved anger disconnects people. It makes a person want to withdraw, not draw close. If your spouse hates his parents, he's going to have a harder time connecting with you. Hidden anger sabotages a lot of relationships, and that's one of the reasons it's so important to deal with our anger the right way, through forgiveness and pearl counting, as we've discussed previously.

 How do we build better connections with others? Look at my suggestions below. Check the ways you have connected with each other in your marriage. Add other ways to my list.

❑ Shared experiences   ❑ Meaningful touch
❑ Intimate conversations   ❑ Shared crises
❑ Other: _____   ❑ Other: _____

As Norma and I look back over our years of marriage, we both realize that one particular type of shared experience was the key to our family being so "connected." Namely, we took time for a lot of outdoor family activities. We did everything from skiing to scuba diving. But of all the things we did, the best one for emotional connecting was our camping trips.

Hidden anger sabotages a lot of relationships, and that's one reason it's so important to deal with our anger the right way.

Camping has a way of creating a crisis—hopefully minor—in every outing. We discovered, by trial and error, that any time a family experiences a common crisis, if the people can overcome the inevitable accompanying anger, they're drawn closer together after the dust settles. At the end of two weeks of mosquitoes, rain, and cold sleeping bags, folks are either more closely connected or very angry at each other! But as soon as the anger subsides and forgiveness is experienced, the shared crisis has driven everyone into close bonding.

 Write one way you and your mate have experienced meaningful connection.

_____

Let's take another look at Jack and Sherry. As part of their eventual effort to develop a more healthy sense of connection, they scheduled more activities together. Recently they went boating on a lake and stopped for a romantic picnic on a remote part of the shoreline. By the time they started back to the dock where their car and trailer were waiting, night had fallen. Suddenly, as they were driving through the water, they collided head-on with an unlighted boat. Their boat was thrown about 10 feet into the air! Miraculously, no one was hurt. But the whole day, from the romantic meal to the near tragedy in the boat, became an experience that drew them closer as they remembered and retold the story in the weeks that followed.

Just a few months later, Jack and Sherry went on a caving trip in Arkansas. As they were climbing out of the deep and long cave, Sherry slipped and fell headlong about 12 feet. She was rather seriously injured and needed two months to recover. But this experience, too, as Jack rescued her and then cared for her as she healed, multiplied their feelings of loving closeness.

I'm _not_ suggesting you have to go on dangerous outings to stay connected, but I do encourage you to plan regular activities that have the potential for minor things to go wrong. Then watch how any shared crises bring you and your mate into a deeper sense of closeness. You don't even have to go on an outing; crises and bonding can occur in your apartment or backyard. The key is to go through the crises together however and whenever they happen.

Connection is healthy. Lack of connection, or distance, is unhealthy. How connected do you feel to your spouse, your children, and other members of your family? How much distance are you putting between yourself and those you love? Just like Jack and Sherry, you can plan activities that you have discovered bring you and your loved ones into closer connection.

 Close today's study by listing two or three activities you and your spouse enjoy doing together. Plan to do at least one of these in the coming week.

_____

_____

_P_lan activities that you have discovered bring you and your loved ones into closer connection.

---

[1]Pam Smith, _The Food Trap_ (Altamonte Springs, Fla.: Creation House, 1990), 23.

Day 5

Vital Sign 5: Personal "Property Lines" of All Are Respected

The fifth vital sign of a good relationship is respect for each other's personal "property line." We discussed this in detail in an earlier week, so I won't say a lot here. But honoring and protecting others' boundaries is crucial to healthy relationships.

Let me give you a couple of new word pictures to illustrate the importance of this. One of the primary functions of physical skin is to protect a person's internal organs. If you cut it, disease and infection can get in and threaten the whole body. Now think of your mate's property line as a sort of skin around his or her personality and feelings. Violating it can cause a crack that lets in emotional infection, especially anger, that threatens every area of the person's life.

Or think of your loved one's property line as a fragile robin's egg. If you care for it and nurture it, you'll see a beautiful, healthy bird. But if you're careless and crack it, the growing bird inside may die. Respecting the property lines of your spouse means you honor that person.

For the ancient Greeks, something of *honor* called to mind something "heavy or weighty." Gold, for example, was something of honor, because it was heavy and valuable. And the word *dishonor* actually meant light-weight "mist."[1]

 The Bible tells us to honor others. Read the selected passages below and underline phrases that tell us how we are to honor and respect one another.

> Be devoted to one another in brotherly love. Honor one another above yourselves (Romans 12:10).

> Each one of you also must love his wife as he loves himself, and the wife must respect her husband (Ephesians 5:33).

> "Honor your father and mother"—which is the first commandment with a promise—"that it may go well with you and that you may enjoy long life on the earth" (Ephesians 6:2-3).

> Show proper respect to everyone: Love the brotherhood of believers, fear God, honor the king (1 Peter 2:17).

If we honor someone, that person carries weight with us; the person is valuable to us.[2] When we honor someone we give that person a highly-respected position in our lives. *Honor* goes hand in glove with *love,* a verb whose very definition is "doing worthwhile things for someone who is valuable to us."

What's the relationship between *honor* and *love?* We first honor (increase the value of) someone, and then we feel the desire to love (do worthwhile things for) the person. Love is honor put into action regardless of the cost.

If we honor someone, that person carries weight with us; the person is valuable to us.

List three ways you show honor to your spouse on a regular, consistent basis.

1. _____

2. _____

3. _____

Honor provides us with the power to stay in love. If your goodwill is flagging, take a deep breath and fill your lungs with honor.

Consider the biblical truth: " 'Where your treasure is, there your heart will be also' " (Matthew 6:21). When we highly value something, such as a job, car, friend, toy, or a coat, we enjoy taking care so as not to lose it or harm it. We enjoy "being with it." I've found as I increase the value of my mate and family, it's easier to love them. I want to be with them, and I feel as though I'm "in love." The feeling of love is simply a reflection of my level of honor for them. So how do you retrieve lost feelings of love? By choosing to increase the value that person has in your mind.

 Below is a treasure chest. In the chest are all kinds of precious gems. Label each gem with a way you treasure your spouse.

Honor provides us the ability to stay in love.

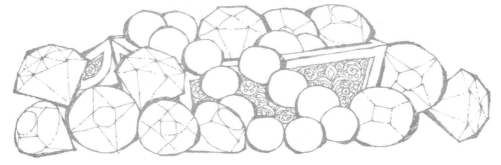

There's a little trick to honoring someone. You can feel as if you're showing honor or doing someone a favor, but your intentions can go awry if you're not listening and communicating well.

Just recently, though I had the best honoring intentions, I actually managed to communicate dishonor to my mate. Besides being the keeper of our home, Norma runs the day-to-day affairs of our business. She gets up at 5:00 each morning to accomplish everything, and I thought I saw strength draining from her because of overwork. In addition, since she was doing our financial reports manually and not using a computer, I wasn't getting some information I thought I needed.

So I figured I would kill two birds with one stone by suggesting she get some accounting help. That would lighten her workload and get me the financial data I wanted. A good idea, right? I thought so when I proposed it to her.

There was just one problem with my plan to help Norma: It wasn't what she wanted or needed. "Gary," she said, "if you think that's what would make me happy, you haven't been listening to me. I enjoy what I'm doing. I like getting involved in financial details, even if it makes for a long day. In fact, a total high for me would be if all three of our kids (who are all married now) would call a family conference and ask me to sort out their finances and set up budgets for them." She was right. I don't ever remember hearing how much she enjoys working with numbers. She really didn't want anyone else taking her jobs away.

As I said, I started that whole affair with the best intentions. But because I didn't ask Norma what she wanted and what was best for her—I just assumed I knew—I ultimately failed to honor her. Instead of giving her more power and fulfillment, my idea would have been draining energy away from her.

In one sense, however, I *was* honoring Norma. I'd made the suggestion to get help because I consider her valuable. But if I value and respect her, I need to ask what she wants and then listen carefully. I can't make decisions that affect her without first getting her input and approval. She's a unique and special person, and I prove she's these things when I listen to her and understand her.

Honor and forever-love for your mate grow best out of a healthy respect for yourself. When you have healthy regard for yourself, you more easily and energetically—with greater focus, clarity, and insight—do things that help your mate feel valued.

 Here's a real test. List 10 things you like and honor about yourself.

_____	_____
_____	_____
_____	_____
_____	_____
_____	_____

Was that easy or difficult for you? If it was difficult, you may also have difficulty showing honor and respect for others. Many of the things we've already discussed in this study will help you value yourself in a healthier way. For example, draining anger out of your life will increase your sense of self-worth. Pearl counting can always raise your awareness of personal benefits. As you work to align your expectations with reality in your life garden, you will be renewed—better able to love your mate and your children. This, in turn, honors them and makes you feel more worthwhile as a person. And as you'll see in a later week, accepting and appreciating your unique personality, as well as your mate's, is another way of valuing and honoring both of you.

Do you recall our verse for the week? Jesus tells us that we should lay down our lives for our friends. Laying down our lives involves dying to pride and egotism while treasuring, spending time with, giving honor and respect to our mates. Close in prayer asking God to show you ways in the coming week that you might honor and respect your mate even more.

[1] William F. Arndt and R. Wilbur Gingrich, eds., *A Greek-English Lexicon of the New Testament and Other Early Christian Literature* (Chicago: University of Chicago Press, 1957), 119-120.
[2] See Gary Smalley and John Trent, *The Gift of Honor* (Nashville: Thomas Nelson, 1987).

> *When you have healthy regard for yourself, you more easily and energetically do things that help your mate feel valued.*

Couple Time

For you to complete

1. List the feelings that are most comfortable for you to share with your spouse.

_____

_____

2. List the feelings most uncomfortable for you to share with your spouse.

_____

_____

3. What put-downs of your spouse will you avoid making in the future?

_____

_____

4. What do you honor and treasure most about your spouse?

_____

_____

For you to share with your spouse

1. Share with one another how you completed the above section.

2. Talk about two or three of the most meaningful experiences you have had as a couple over the years that really connected you as husband and wife.

3. Sit facing one another. Take two minutes each to tell one another all the things you appreciate and respect in the other.

4. Hug each other and pray out loud thanking God for what you value in each other.

Communicating Between Different Personalities

At most of my live marriage seminars, I ask several hundred couples to name one thing they believe could improve their marriage above everything else. Without exception, in more than 20 years and from more than three hundred thousand people, the answer has come through loud and clear: *"We need better communication!"*

The quality of our communication affects every area of every relationship we have. Review the vital signs of a healthy relationship. Effective communication is at the heart of all five. It even influences our physical health. Effective communication reduces occasions for anger to be buried inside. And, as we saw in week 2, unresolved anger can disastrously affect one's health. Learn how to be a better communicator and everyone wins.

Why such a high priority on communication? Because good communication is the key to what all of us who marry basically want—to love and be loved. We want to share our lives with someone who loves us unconditionally. We want to grow old with a mate who values us, understands us, and helps us feel safe in sharing our deepest feelings and needs. We want to make love last forever. And this type of loving relationship is most often attained by couples who have learned how to reach the deepest levels of verbal intimacy.

This week we will focus on communication in marriage. As you study, you will:

- learn about five levels of communication and evaluate communication between you and your partner;
- understand what drive-through talking is and how to develop a marriage or family constitution;
- discover how communication can be an all-you-can-eat buffet, what the salt principle is, and when to use emotional word pictures;
- develop an understanding of the four basic personality types;
- uncover how to make a commitment to self-control.

Day 1 Communicating— At What Level?	Day 2 Methods of Communication (Part 1)	Day 3 Methods of Communication (Part 2)	Day 4 Understanding Personality Types	Day 5 Tempering Your Natural Tendencies

I am praying there will be breakthroughs in communication in your marriage this week. As you learn better communication skills with one another, you will discover how to communicate at the deeper levels of forever-love.

Keep this verse in mind as you study this week:

"Instead, speaking the truth in love, we will in all things grow up into him who is the Head, that is, Christ" (Ephesians 4:13).

Day 1

Communicating—At What Level?

Marriage researchers have helped us understand there are five levels of intimacy in communication, moving from the superficial to the most meaningful. The more often a husband and wife reach and remain on the fourth and fifth levels, the more satisfying their marriage.

1. When we communicate on the first level, we speak in *clichés*: "How did your day go?" "Fine." "Give me five!" "What's happening?" Think about it. Does conversation at this level mean much? A question like "How are you?" may be more than a cliché, especially in marriage, but it's often asked just as superficially in a domestic setting as it is by a store clerk you've never met. Some couples who are afraid of conflict spend a lot of time at this "safe" level.

 The cliché that I use most with my spouse is

_____

_____.

2. At the second level of communication, we share *facts—just information*. "It looks pretty wet today, doesn't it?" "Watch out for that road construction." "Did you hear the latest about the president?" Like level one, this is pretty shallow communication, and it's still relatively safe. Not many major marital wars start this way.

 What facts do you and your spouse talk about most? Check the top two or three "factual" communications you most often have with your spouse.

❏ Children   ❏ Home.

❏ Jobs   ❏ Church

❏ Beliefs   ❏ Hobbies

❏ Friends   ❏ Other: _____

3. At the third level, we state our *opinions*. Here is where communication feels a bit more unsafe and conflict may arise. "How can anyone vote for that person? He has no experience." If we feel insecure in our marriage, we tend to steer clear of this level. Though most couples do get to this level, most of our conversation, even with family, rarely goes beyond it to the deeper levels.

When you and your spouse communicate on this level, what do you most often talk about? Check the two top topics.

❏ Politics   ❏ Community activities or affairs
❏ Religious beliefs ❏ Opinions about social issues
❏ Other: _____

4. The fourth level is when we say what we're *feeling*. "I was really hurt by what my father said on the phone last night." Opening up this way can be scary, but we can reach the deeper levels of loving and being loved only when we put ourselves at risk of having our feelings misunderstood or ridiculed. In fact, one of the healthiest questions we can ask is "What are you feeling right now?"

How comfortable are you communicating your feelings? Put an *x* to indicate where you are and an *s* where you believe your spouse to be.

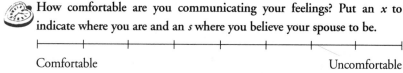

Comfortable   Uncomfortable

5. The fifth level is where we reveal our *needs*. "I just need for you to hold me for a few minutes," you might say after hearing about the serious illness of a good friend. To risk at this level of verbal intimacy, we have to feel secure in the relationship.

What are your deepest needs in your marriage? Check two or three of the deepest needs you have.

❏ Love   ❏ Sexual intimacy   ❏ Happiness
❏ Respect   ❏ Forgiveness   ❏ Openness
❏ Faithfulness ❏ Peace   ❏ Harmony
❏ Security   ❏ Honesty   ❏ Other: _____

Let's see how a couple with a strong marriage and good communication skills might work their way quickly to this fifth level. Suppose a conversation starts at the third level with the husband saying to his wife, "Hey, you're drenched! Why don't you ever remember to put your umbrella in the car?" That's an opinion that his wife should keep an umbrella handy.

She responds at the fourth level by saying, "Do you know how I feel today? I feel like somebody ran over my foot at work. It's been a tough day! And with that cute comment, you're now standing on my foot!"

Instantly he knows how his spouse feels. He can now encourage her to move to the fifth level by asking, "What do you need tonight? What would it take to make you feel as if your foot is being massaged and soothed? What can I do?"

The more often a husband and wife reach and remain on the fourth and fifth levels, the more satisfying their marriage.

She might respond by saying, "You know that movie we were planning to see? I don't feel like going tonight. I'm beat! I would love a hug, and I just want to talk and be with you. But first, I would like to be alone for a while, to relax and kind of cool down." Those are needs, and their expression is the deepest level of verbal intimacy.

If the environment is really safe and healthy, he might say, "OK, let's do that. I wanted to go to that movie, but we don't have to go tonight. We can go tomorrow. What do you think?" That's a mutually satisfying relationship, where both people's needs are expressed and they have the flexibility of give and take.

Our goal as a married couple should be to go into those fourth and fifth, more satisfying levels of communication more easily and frequently. But again, the key to deep verbal intimacy is feeling *safe* to share our feelings and needs and feeling that our feelings and needs are *valued* by our mate. Having the self-control to listen lovingly without overreacting or misunderstanding keeps the lines open. The caution I would interject is that we need to speak in love, measure our words carefully, and only make requests that we can reasonably expect our mate to respond to favorably.

Review the five levels of communication and evaluate how often you and your spouse reach levels four and five.

My spouse and I communicate
at this level ...

1. Clichés _____ percent of the time
2. Facts _____ percent of the time
3. Opinions _____ percent of the time
4. Feelings _____ percent of the time
5. Needs _____ percent of the time

Another caution is that you allow honor to regulate when and how your communication goes to the fifth level of verbal intimacy. Sharing needs that require your mate to make too great a change can be hurtful and weaken the relationship.

Ask God to give you the courage to share with your spouse at the deepest levels. Write your prayer.

_____

_____

_____

The key to deep verbal intimacy is feeling safe to share our feelings and needs and feeling that our feelings and needs are valued by our mate.

Day 2
Five Effective Methods of Communication (Part 1)

Now let's take a look at five effective communication methods that can enrich a marriage and help you move into those deeper levels of intimacy more often and with greater ease. Over the years Norma and I—and our children—have tried many communication methods, and these five I consider my favorites. To help give you the flavor of them, I've given them names or headings that relate to eating in a restaurant.

1. Drive-through Talking

Drs. Markman and Stanley report this type to be the key to overcoming the four main reasons couples divorce. For me, it's the absolute best method I've ever learned. My wife and I use it as a couple and with our family, and our company profits by it as an organization. Communications expert Dr. Dallas Demitt, of Phoenix, taught me this approach several years ago.

Have you ever really listened to your spouse? By really listening I mean concentrating on what your spouse is saying and not on what you will say next.

 Put your hand over what you just read. Summarize it on the next two lines.

_____

_____

Check what you wrote. How did you do? Were you on target?

I call this first method of communication *drive-through talking*. Drive-through talking helps you stay focused and on target in your communication. Let me explain. I've just driven to one of the fast-food restaurants and pulled up at the speaker. I'm ready to place an order for my whole family. The clerk comes on the intercom and says, "Welcome. May I take your order, please?"

"Yeah," I say, "I would like three hamburgers, a cheeseburger, three Diet Cokes, one Pepsi, three fries, and one order of onion rings." I ask my family, "Is that it, guys?"

They say, "Yeah."

The clerk comes back on the intercom and says, "We have three cheeseburgers, one hamburger, three Cokes, one Pepsi, three fries, and one onion rings."

"No," I say. "That was three *hamburgers,* one *cheeseburger,* three *Diet* Cokes, one Pepsi, three fries, and one order of onion rings."

The clerk says, "OK, I think I've got it. Three hamburgers, one cheeseburger, three Diet Cokes, one Pepsi, three orders of fries, and one onion ring."

"You've got it!" I answer. "Thank you."

"Drive through, please," he says.

> *Drive-through talking helps you stay focused and on target in your communication.*

Then I drive up to the window, get our order, check the bag, and say, "This isn't even close to what I ordered!" And I start all over again.

Have you ever had that frustrating experience at a fast-food place? We all have, I imagine. And it illustrates the best way to communicate what's on your mind. Drive-through talking is when you say something to someone, and you wait to hear it repeated back exactly the way you said it. If the other person gets it right—if he or she can tell you accurately what you just said without somehow missing your meaning—you respond, "Yes, you understand me." If it isn't right, you say, "No, that's not what I said," and you repeat your message until the individual gets it right. Once the other person reflects an understanding of what you meant to convey, you know you've communicated.

 When we use this method with Scripture, we call it meditation. To meditate on Scripture is to repeat God's Word back to Him. For example, open your Bible and read Psalm 1 out loud. Now close the Bible. In the space below, write Psalm 1 in your own words.

_____

_____

_____

_____

This method of communicating—taking the time to repeat back what we think we've heard (or what we think the real meaning was behind the words)—eliminates so many unnecessary hostile episodes. You can practice it with your mate, your kids, your coworkers, and I promise you'll be amazed by the results. You'll understand each other more clearly and feel so much better about the relationship.

 Are you using this method of communication now? If so, with whom do you practice drive-through talking? Check everyone you use this type of communication with.

❑ My spouse ❑ My colleagues at work
❑ My friends at church ❑ My children
❑ People in the community ❑ Other: _____

Did you check others, but not your spouse or children? Often we do a better job communicating with others than we do our families.

Recently I was with a couple who in more than 20 years of marriage had never tried drive-through talking. When I had them sit together and start practicing it, they were instantly pleased with the results. At first this confirming feedback might seem awkward. But try it. It's the best method I know to enrich communication—with anyone.

Often we do a better job of communicating with others than we do our families.

One form of prayer is drive-through talking. When we pray God's Word back to Him, we are confirming in His Word what God is doing and saying in our lives. Try it by yourself or with your spouse. Choose a portion of Scripture and pray it to God. Use Psalm 23, Psalm 37, Psalm 51, 1 Corinthians 13, or the Lord's Prayer in Matthew 6:9-15.

2. Marriage or Family Menu

My second favorite and effective communication technique involves listing the most important "foods" on your marriage menu. It can be like a marriage or family constitution. Sounds like a chore? Keep reading to see the rewards.

What is a marriage or family constitution? It's a written list of the most important things you and your loved ones want out of your relationship every day. It objectifies your feelings and needs, and it sets guidelines for a nation. When you read a restaurant menu, you know what the establishment is all about. You can say the same for a marriage constitution.

My wife and I wrote our constitution for our relationship, and we order our lives according to it. We feel great about it, because we each know our crucial feelings and needs—critical to intimate communication—are understood and in writing. It has evolved over the years and today lists 8 items. Yours could have 3, 5, 10 … whatever fits your situation.

A family constitution forces couples to the fourth and fifth levels of intimacy. But it's also the best method I know in training and disciplining kids. As I go into more detail about how a constitution helps make for a mutually satisfying marriage, let me show you how it works with kids as well.

First, a constitution brings a couple—or a family—into unity. There's terrific strength and consistency when you're united on a course of action you all believe in and are committed to. When a young couple writes a constitution, it's theirs, both the husband's and the wife's. When a family writes one, the kids have ownership, too. Let me illustrate this from my own family's experience.

Our kids helped write our constitution. That meant the rules it contained were truly family rules and not just a code imposed by Mom and Dad. This caused the kids to become very committed to the whole approach. And then, for more than three years, we had a meeting at our dinner table every night where we reviewed our constitution, which was printed and hanging on the wall. We would just read through it and see how we all did that day.

At that time our constitution included about a half dozen requirements for the kids, such as, "How well do you obey Mom and Dad in things, like when they tell you not to go up the street?" We had some things about cleaning their rooms, chores, manners, and honor. (If I had it to do over again, I would put honor at the top, and all the others would be subpoints to honor.)

Finally, our children agreed on three character qualities they had to have to some degree before they dated. Then, when they got to the age where they were about ready to date, they would say, "Can I date? Can I date?" Norma and I would answer, "Remember you agreed these three qualities need to be present."

A marriage or family constitution is a written list of the most important things you and your loved ones want out of your relationship every day.

And they would have to say, "Oh, yeah." Our constitution saved us a lot of arguments that way.

The three qualities our kids had to exhibit to date, in case you want to know, were: 1. Honor of God, others, and themselves; 2. Responsibility for one's actions and emotions; and 3. Self-control and the understanding of the consequences of premarital sex.

Likewise, a constitution helps keep everyone together on what the consequences will be when family rules are broken. Just as a restaurant menu lists rules such as "No shirt, no shoes, no service," so a family has rules to meet its needs.

Let's say one of your marriage constitution items is "We'll spend at least 20 minutes a day in meaningful conversation with each other." And it's your turn this week to be the initiator. But by the time you get ready for bed, you haven't fulfilled your commitment. That's when your spouse says, "You were supposed to do this before 10:00 p.m., but you forgot."

Once you're caught, the agreed-upon consequence kicks in. You can choose various penalties for violations of your constitution. Pick things that are realistic but still mildly painful if they're to be effective. For example, you might agree not to watch a favorite TV show, do extra chores, do something with your spouse that he or she enjoys but you could live without, and so on.

For the constitution to do this part of its job effectively, the key once again is flexibility. Couples in a healthy relationship feel safe to introduce any revisions. And parents especially need to be flexible.

 The Bible refers to this as making a covenant with another person. Are you willing to enter into a covenant with your spouse? Read an example of a biblical covenant in Genesis 12:2-3.

> "I will make you into a great nation and I will bless you;
> I will make your name great, and you will be a blessing.
> I will bless these who bless you,
> and whoever curses you I will curse;
> and all peoples on earth will be blessed through you."

In this covenant, God promised Abram to _____.

 List three promises you are willing to make in a covenant or constitution with your spouse.

1. _____

2. _____

3. _____

 Close today's study in prayer asking God to give you the willingness and strength to keep your promises in a marriage or family constitution or covenant.

A constitution helps keep everyone together on what the consequences will be when family rules are broken.

Day 3

Five Effective Methods of Communication (Part 2)

3. All-You-Can-Eat Buffet

A third effective communication method is what I call an *all-you-can-eat buffet*. You can use this in a marriage, but you can also use it in parenting, friendship, your relationship with God, or any other relationship. It is like giving someone a huge injection of energy—feeding someone a gigantic meal. Here's how this worked with the Smalleys. We would pick out one member of the family, and for 60 seconds all of us would barrage him or her with praise. We would say anything positive we could think of and as much as we could think of. After 60 seconds, the person was "stuffed."

To the individual being praised, it was overwhelming. You would sit there and say, "Oh, oh, OK. Thank you a lot. OK. I believe that one. Oh, that's a good one." It's fun and very enriching.

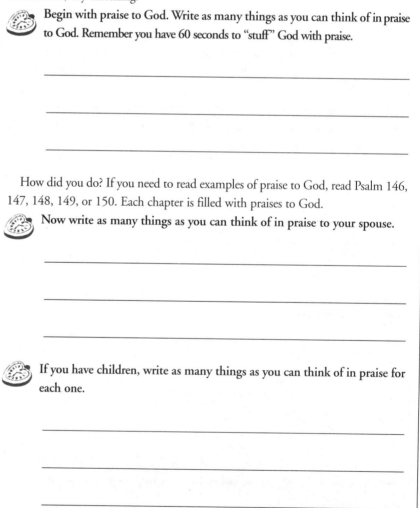

Begin with praise to God. Write as many things as you can think of in praise to God. Remember you have 60 seconds to "stuff" God with praise.

_____

_____

_____

How did you do? If you need to read examples of praise to God, read Psalm 146, 147, 148, 149, or 150. Each chapter is filled with praises to God.

Now write as many things as you can think of in praise to your spouse.

_____

_____

_____

If you have children, write as many things as you can think of in praise for each one.

_____

_____

_____

You really can't overdo genuine, meaningful praise.

I remember interviewing dozens of women years ago and asking, "How often do you need to be praised by your husband?" I heard repeatedly, "As often as he wants to praise me." Almost all women say, "I have a bottomless capacity to be praised."

From those interviews and other evidence, I've concluded that we don't need to worry about praising a person too much. Some people say, "If we praise them too much, they'll get a big head; they'll get conceited." But just the opposite is true. If people aren't praised and don't feel valuable, that's when they appear to be conceited. You really can't overdo genuine, meaningful praise, because most of us can't remember to give it as much as we should.

You cannot overdo praise to God. You cannot praise a spouse and children too much. Remember, affirmation begins with the person, not their performance. Before you praise what a person does, be certain to praise who they are—their character and integrity in Christ.

4. The Salt Principle

What I call *the salt principle* is a communication method by which you can be sure you have the full attention of the person you want to talk with. This fourth method is great when you're wanting to say, "Hello in there. Is anyone listening? Is anyone home?" I especially recommend this method to wives, as I've repeatedly heard wives complain that their husbands don't listen to them. (I've found it's naturally harder for many men to connect verbally than it is for women.)

Using the salt principle, you don't try to make your point to someone unless you have that person's full, undivided attention. To get that attention, you pique that person's interest until he or she is "thirsty."

Check the ways you and your spouse try to get one another's attention.

❑ A special look ❑ Asking for attention

❑ Demanding tone of voice ❑ The silent treatment

❑ Yelling ❑ Acting wounded or hurt

❑ Pouting ❑ Crying

❑ Other: _____

Jesus used the salt principle to get the attention of those around Him. Read John 13:2-5, 12-14 and underline the phrases that describe what got the attention of His disciples.

> The evening meal was being served ... [Jesus] got up from the meal, took off his outer clothing, and wrapped a towel around his waist. After that, he poured water into a basin and began to wash his disciples' feet, drying them with the towel that was wrapped around him. When he had finished washing their feet, he put on his clothes and returned to his place. "Do you understand what I have done for you?" he asked them. "You call me 'Teacher' and 'Lord,' and rightly so, for that is what I am. Now that I, your Lord and Teacher, have washed your feet, You also should wash one another's feet."

Don't make your point in the conversation until you have the person's full, undivided attention.

Jesus used a menial task to get the attention of His disciples and teach them a lesson about Christian living.

Consider how my wife got my attention and motivated me to listen to her one time. She had a desire, or need, she wanted to communicate to me. She wanted me to spend more time with our children. So she came up to me and said, "I talked to Greg's teacher today. I found out he's not doing well in reading and spelling. The teacher said part of his problem is that he hasn't developed his hand-eye coordination well enough. That's a real serious thing." Immediately she had salted my interest with the word *serious*. Then she said, "It could cost us a lot of money in the future."

"A lot of money in the future," I repeated, engrossed now.

"Yeah," she said, "because we would possibly have to get some tutors. So the best thing to do is to nip it now." (That's a whole can of salt.)

"What do we have to do?" I asked as I *thirsted*.

"I've been thinking about it," she continued, "and I think it would be good, if you're interested, to start playing catch with Greg regularly so he can develop that hand-eye coordination."

"Football, you mean?"

"Yeah."

I thought, *Hey, hey, hey. Saving money in the future and helping my son. Where's the football?* I started playing catch with him right away. In high school, Greg was a receiver on the football team (not just because I played catch with him, of course), and he's also a great reader, a good writer, and a good speller today. Notice that before Norma made her request that I play catch with Greg, she first got my interest.

 The salt principle can be effective in almost any relationship. Briefly share an experience when you used the salt principle to get someone's attention and motivate them to do something.

_____

_____

5. Recipe Titles

A fifth and powerful method of communication calls for the use of *emotional word pictures*. Most of us use these already. The poets among us might call them metaphors or similes.

In a relationship, word pictures might work like this. When you meet somebody who seems a little off, you might say, "That person seems one taco short of a combination plate." If you've had a really tough day at work, you might come home and tell your spouse, "I feel as if I've been run over by a steamroller." One spouse may tell the other, "I feel as if you're standing on my foot."

Those are simple word pictures that help one person quickly understand what another is thinking and feeling. Why is this method is so powerful? It helps us "step into the other person's shoes" and experience something emotionally close to what he or she feels. It can move us into and keep us in the fourth and fifth levels of intimacy.

Simple word pictures help one person quickly understand what another is thinking and feeling.

Let me give you another example. When a couple that I know would have a disagreement, he wouldn't lose his temper and yell at her; he would switch into a lecturing tone of voice that made her feel he thought she was stupid. He wasn't even aware he did it, but it bothered her to no end every time it happened.

Finally, she decided to use a word picture. The next time he spoke to her that way, she stopped the conversation and said, "Do you realize what I see when this happens? I see you gritting your teeth and speaking deliberately, as if I'm stupid and can't understand you otherwise. I feel like a little girl being lectured by her daddy."

"Really?" he said. "I had no idea I was doing that or that it made you feel that way. But now that you mention it, I can see how you could take it that way. I'm sorry." And ever since, though the wife says he occasionally needs a "you're doing it again" reminder, he has tried to be much more careful about how he speaks to her in times of conflict. Her word picture helped him see and feel clearly, in just a few words, how dishonoring his way of speaking had been.

 Think of something your spouse does that constantly irritates you. Develop a word picture to describe that. Write your word picture down and the next time the irritation arises, try your word picture out on your spouse.

_____

_____

Word pictures are powerful. Just one is worth a thousand pictureless words. More times than I can count, I've seen one word picture stop and change people like that husband. If you'd like even more examples, Dr. John Trent and I have created more than three hundred that anyone can use in any relationship.[1]

 The Bible uses powerful word pictures to communicate God's feelings and thoughts about us. I have highlighted phrases from Psalm 91:1-2. On the line beside each phrase, list every word picture it creates and what feeling that picture communicates about God's care toward you.

HOW DOES GOD CARE?

He who dwells **in the shelter of the**   _____
Most High will rest in **the shadow of**   _____
the Almighty. I will say of the Lord,   _____
"He is my **refuge** and my **fortress**, my   _____
God, in whom I trust."   _____

 The Lord's Prayer is a powerful word picture of how God desires us to pray. Pray that prayer out loud as you close today's study.

---

[1] See Gary Smalley and John Trent, *The Language of Love* (Colorado Springs: Focus on the Family, 1988, 1991).

*M*ore times than I can count, I've seen a word picture stop and change people.

Day 4
Understanding Personality Types

We're all a blend of four basic personality types, but most of us have one or two dominant styles. Our individual blends make us unique, like fingerprints. And one of the best ways to improve our relationships is to bring balance to any of our traits that we've neglectfully or subconsciously pushed to an extreme. If you're already familiar with one or more categorizations of personality types, stay with me. This week, I present a short course in how we can "take the edge off" the extremes that make us less lovable than we could be.

Many unhappy spouses are just like Sam, whom you're about to meet. They create problems for themselves because they don't see their greatest personality strengths pushed a bit too far out of balance can become their biggest problems in relationships.

A person's basic blend of personality tendencies seems to be natural or innate. But as we grow older, we can get into the habit of pushing one or more of our natural traits to an extreme that can strain our marriage and hurt others. It's just harder to love some people who push their natural strengths to the limit.

Understanding why people behave a certain way helps in working through anger or conflict. And in the same manner, better understanding of the motivations and actions that grow out of our basic personalities can help us achieve personal and marital satisfaction. Sam didn't have that basic self-understanding and self-control, and it was about to cost him his marriage.

 Before we explore the specific personality types, in the top portrait on the left write a description of yourself. Do not describe physical characteristics or tasks you can or cannot do. Rather, use words that describe attitudes and emotions. For example, *I am outgoing, a talker, enjoy being active, sensitive, and forgiving*, etc. Write a description of your spouse in the bottom portrait.

The Lion King

One day several years ago, when I was still counseling regularly, Sam called my office. When my secretary buzzed me and said there was a man on the phone who insisted on talking to me directly, I immediately had a clue as to what kind of personality we were dealing with. And when the secretary put the call through, Sam's voice came booming—even barking—over the line.

"My name is Sam, and my wife is getting ready to leave me," he said, getting right to the point. "I'm miserable and depressed. So I need to see you, and I'd like to see you *today*, if possible."

"I'm sorry," I answered, "my schedule is full for the next two weeks. But I could see you after that."

Understanding why people behave a certain way helps in working through anger or conflict.

"You don't seem to understand," he said in a commanding tone. "I *have* to see you. I'll come over after hours, I'll come to your home, or I'll meet you early, but I won't take no for an answer."

Faced with his aggressive personality and the fact that I really did have a full schedule, I decided to try an approach I had never used before. "Sam," I said, pausing, getting aggressive myself, "I have to tell you that you're one of the pushiest people I have ever talked to! I don't know why your wife is leaving you, and I certainly don't condone it, but I have a strong suspicion I know her motive!"

The phone line was silent for what seemed like a long minute as my words sank in. Finally Sam replied, "I'll call you back later," and he hung up.

A few days went by, and after he had a chance to cool down, Sam called again, saying, "No one has ever spoken to me the way you did—but it was exactly what I needed to hear. I'm too pushy with my wife and others. I'm too controlling. Would you help me overcome that tendency?"

Sam did become one of my counseling clients, and as I got to know him and his background and present circumstances, we established that his domineering behavior was just an outgrowth of his basic personality. He wasn't carrying deep-seated anger; no one had seriously violated his "property line." But he had a type of personality that I call the lion style (more about that shortly). With no understanding or even awareness of his natural temperament, he had allowed it to get out of hand and his wife was suffering the bad, sad results.

You Know the Type?

All of us have distinct personalities—not just the aggressive lions—and all of us can, without knowing it, push some of our inborn characteristics to an unhealthy extreme that can wreak havoc in a marriage.

In the late 1970s, Tim LaHaye and Florence Littauer helped me understand, through their books and lectures, that there are four basic personality types.[1] And while all of us reflect a combination of styles, one or two styles usually dominate a personality. LaHaye feels that wives tend to understand their husbands' personality styles better than husbands understand their wives'. But in the many years since I first started talking about personality differences, I've seen too many husbands and wives misunderstand their mates, causing a lot of relational damage.

Then in the mid-1980s, I gained further insight from a personality inventory— a tool for learning what your personality type is—given to me by my dear friend, Dr. John Trent. It's called *Performax*. Thanks to Dr. Trent's personal touch and advanced understanding of personality styles, we were able to write our own inventory and test it on thousands of people. In 1990, we did an entire book on the subject, titled *The Two Sides of Love*. Dr. Trent is still teaching an excellent seminar on understanding how our personality affects one's marriage and especially parenting skills.

I want to invite you and your spouse to take the inventory (see page 145). One word of caution: *Use the inventory to strengthen your relationship, not as a tool for criticism or as something to throw in your spouse's face.* Before you take the inventory, let me explain the approach.

All of us have distinct personalities, and all of us can, without knowing it, push some of our inborn characteristics to an unhealthy extreme that can wreak havoc in a marriage.

Dr. Trent and I came up with a way of describing the four personality types using four animals that capture the common traits of each style.

First come those people we call *lions*. Our friend Sam, whose story began this chapter, is a classic lion. These folks are like the king of the jungle. They're usually leaders at work, in the civic group, or at church. They're decisive, bottom-line oriented, and problem solvers. They build big buildings and organizations, and they command armies—but they're normally not intimate conversationalists.

Next come the *otters*. If you've ever seen an otter frolicking in the water, you'll know why we chose this animal to describe people who are basically fun-loving and playful. Human otters are essentially parties waiting to happen. They tend to be the entertainers and networkers (they love to talk!), and they're highly creative. They're also good at motivating others.

Then we have those who are the most sensitive and tender in the world; we call them *golden retrievers*. Just like that special breed of dog, these folks are unbelievably loving, nurturing, and loyal. They'll stick with something or someone forever. These are the people who buy all the greeting cards. I like to call them the nerve endings of our society. They're great listeners and real encouragers.

Finally, we have the *beavers*—those people who like to do things right and "by the book." These folks tend to be hard working, and they actually read instruction manuals! (Those manuals were probably written by beavers to begin with.) They're excellent at providing quality control in an office or factory, and they shine in situations that demand accuracy. They're also the bankers and accountants of this world. They like quality things, too—no junk for a beaver.

Perhaps you've already got a good idea of your basic personality type and that of your mate from your own previous study or from these brief descriptions. The four animals capture the four styles in a way that's easy to understand.

 Below are the four personality types. Let's take a moment and see if we can put different people we know with each animal. First is a list of biblical personalities. Where would you put each one? Write each name by one of the four animals. Next think of at least one person you know who fits each type. Add their names. Finally, put yourself with one of the animals.

Peter, Paul, Ruth, Joseph, prodigal son, Pharisees, Mary

Lion: _____

Otter: _____

Golden Retriever: _____

Beaver: _____

Four personality types:

• *lions*

• *otters*

• *golden retrievers*

• *beavers*

We can't know for certain where the biblical characters would be but here's my evaluation. Peter, Paul, and Joseph seem to be lions; Ruth and Mary may have been golden retrievers; the prodigal son seems like an otter; and the Pharisees appear to have many of the traits of beavers. How closely did we agree?

Remember, the same traits that make each type of person unique and valuable often get taken to an extreme, and that's the source of a lot of unhappiness for everyone involved. We may be born with more than one characteristic, even so, the characteristics can be controlled. Want a happily-ever-after marriage? Consciously work to become more aware of your natural tendencies. Go for a healthy balance, tempering any extreme, problem area. Focus on the strengths of your dominant characteristics and learn to cultivate the strengths of your less-dominant areas. Tomorrow we will look at how you can tame the extremes of your dominant personality trait.

Each person is a unique creation in Christ Jesus. Second Corinthians 5:17 declares, "Therefore, if anyone is in Christ, he is a new creation; the old has gone, the new has come!" The Greek word for new is *kainos* which means "completely new, unique, one-of-a-kind." While you may exhibit the dominant personality of a lion, you have traits of other personality types in you. If you know Christ, your personality mix is new and being transformed in Christ Jesus.

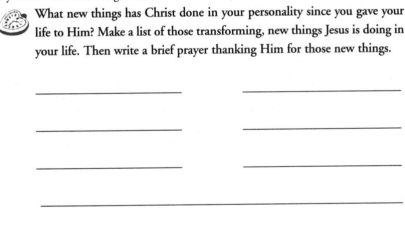 What new things has Christ done in your personality since you gave your life to Him? Make a list of those transforming, new things Jesus is doing in your life. Then write a brief prayer thanking Him for those new things.

Each person is a unique creation in Jesus Christ.

_____   _____

_____   _____

_____   _____

_____

_____

---

[1] See Tim LaHaye, *Understanding the Male Temperament* (Grand Rapids: Zondervan, 1970); and Florence Littauer, *Personality Plus*, updated and expanded (Grand Rapids: Fleming Revell, 1992).

Day 5
Tempering Your Natural Tendencies

Because I've asked more of you a couple of days, let me close this week's study with a couple of final suggestions for each personality type. If you take no other advice away from this discussion, applying these tips can make your life more pleasant and your marriage more enduring (and endearing) as you take responsibility for tempering your natural tendencies.

> **Lions:** Be softer and more gentle, and include others when making decisions.
> **Otters:** Think before you speak, and consider the consequences before you act.
> **Golden retrievers:** Practice saying *no* and making firm decisions.
> **Beavers:** Learn to relax, and don't expect others to do things just like you.

 Underline one or more of my suggestions that you will implement in your life beginning this week.

I am not suggesting you deny your dominant temperament. I've found if you try to become too different from your natural tendency—from the personality with which you were born—you ineffectively use or drain off an excessive amount of strength. But if you accept yourself as you are and work to accentuate the positive aspects of that temperament while tempering its extreme manifestation (and if those closest to you praise you for that—though we'll get to this point next week), you'll find you're constantly being energized.

New creations in Christ are constantly growing and changing—being transformed into the image of Jesus Christ. That doesn't mean we all think, act, and feel alike. Christ uses the uniqueness of each person to minister and serve with their spiritual gifts and natural talents. (See 1 Corinthians 12.)

 Affirm your growth in Christ. Read Romans 12:2. Briefly write how you are growing and maturing in Christ.

> Do not conform to the patterns of this world, but be transformed by the renewing of your mind. Then you will be able to test and approve what God's will is—his good, pleasing and perfect will.

 Pray this prayer out loud.
> *Lord Jesus, I pray for the renewing of Your Spirit to be at work always in me. Thank You for my unique personality. Mature me in Your image day by day. Amen.*

*A*ccept yourself as you are and work to accentuate the positive aspects of your personality while tempering the extreme aspects.

Personality Inventory

How to Take and Score the Inventory

1. For each temperament type, circle the positive traits (in the left column) that sound the most like you are at home. Do not score yourself as you behave at work. (If you want to evaluate your "at work" tendencies, take the test again later, with that environment—or any other—in mind.) For now, ignore the right-hand column.

2. For each temperament, add up the number of circled traits (left column) and then double that number. This is your "score."

LION TEMPERAMENT CHARACTERISTICS

Likes authority	Too direct or demanding
Takes charge	Pushy; can step in front of others
Determined	Overbearing
Confident	Cocky
Firm	Unyielding
Enterprising	Takes big risks
Competitive	Cold blooded
Enjoys challenges	Avoids relations
Problem solver	Too busy
Productive	Overlooks feelings; do it now!
Bold	Insensitive
Purposeful; goal driven	Imbalanced; workaholic
Decision maker	Unthoughtful of others' wishes
Adventurous	Impulsive
Strong willed	Stubborn
Independent; self-reliant	Avoids people; avoids seeking help
Controlling	Bossy; overbearing
Persistent	Inflexible
Action oriented	Unyielding

"Let's do it now!"

Lion score (double the number circled):_____

OTTER TEMPERAMENT CHARACTERISTICS

Enthusiastic	Overbearing
Takes risks	Dangerous and foolish
Visionary	Day dreamer
Motivator	Manipulator
Energetic	Impatient
Very verbal	Attacks under pressure
Promoter	Exaggerates
Friendly; mixes easily	Shallow relationships

Enjoys popularity	Too showy
Fun loving	Too flippant; not serious
Likes variety	Too scattered
Spontaneous	Not focused
Enjoys change	Lacks follow-through
Creative; goes for new ideas	Too unrealistic; avoids details
Group oriented	Bored with "process"
Optimistic	Doesn't see details
Initiator	Pushy
Infectious laughter	Obnoxious
Inspirational	Phony

"Trust me! It'll work out!"

Otter score (double the number circled):_____

GOLDEN RETRIEVER TEMPERAMENT CHARACTERISTICS

Sensitive feelings	Easily hurt
Loyal	Misses opportunities
Calm; even keeled	Lacks enthusiasm
Nondemanding	Weakling; pushover
Avoids confrontations	Misses honest intimacy
Enjoys routine	Stays in rut
Dislikes change	Not spontaneous
Warm and relational	Fewer deep friends
Gives in	Codependent
Accommodating	Indecisive
Cautious humor	Overly cautious
Adaptable	Loses identity
Sympathetic	Holds on to others' hurts
Thoughtful	Can be taken advantage of
Nurturing	Ears get smashed
Patient	Crowded out by others
Tolerant	Weaker convictions
Good listener	Attracted to hurting people
Peace maker	Holds personal hurts inside

"Let's keep things the way they are."

Golden retriever score (double the number circled):_____

BEAVER TEMPERAMENT CHARACTERISTICS

Reads all instructions	Afraid to break rules
Accurate	Too critical
Consistent	Lacks spontaneity
Controlled	Too serious

Reserved	Stuffy
Predictable	Lacks variety
Practical	Not adventurous
Orderly	Rigid
Factual	Stubborn
Conscientious	Inflexible
Perfectionistic	Controlling
Discerning	Negative on new opportunities
Detailed	Rarely finishes a project
Analytical	Loses overview
Inquisitive	Smothering
Precise	Strict
Persistent	Pushy
Scheduled	Boring
Sensitive	Stubborn

"How was it done in the past?"

Beaver score (double the number circled):_____

3. Graph your temperament "mix" by marking your score for each temperament
on the graph with a large dot. If you want, draw a line to connect the dots.

Lion	Otter	Golden Retriever	Beaver
40			40
35			35
30			30
25			25
20			20
15			15
10			10
5			5
0			0

How did you do? Remember, this isn't a pass-fail test. This evaluation simply
shows your tendencies and traits. As you look at your charted score, you may see a
blend of all four categories. That's fine. Or you may see two scores significantly higher than the others. Or you may have one category head and shoulders above the other
three. No one pattern is "correct."

4. Note the right-column extreme for each of your circled characteristics. This
might be how your positive trait is perceived by your family or friends.

(Special thanks to Dr. John Trent and Dr. Rod Cooper for their help in working on this inventory.)

Couple Time

For you to complete

One thing God wants me to do as a result of this week's study is:

_____

_____

For you to share with your spouse

1. Share with each other the three promises you are willing to make in covenant or constitution with your spouse (see page 135). Use drive-through talking. Repeat what you think your mate is saying and continue repeating until you hear a "Yes, you understand me."

2. Sit face-to-face and share your lists of praises on page 136. Try the 60-second praise exercise with each other.

3. Share together the word picture about something your spouse does that irritates each of you on day 3, page 139.

4. Share the spouse portraits you completed on page 140.

5. Discuss what each of you learned from your personality inventories.

6. Share one thing God is doing to grow you in Christ Jesus. Pray together, thanking God for how He is transforming you into Christ's image.

WEEK 9

Energizing and Understanding Your Mate

I trust some of my readers remember that old love song with one unforgettable line: "You say to-ma-toe, and I say to-mat-oe." That simple phrase can describe the wonderful—and yet maddening—differences between you and your mate. When you were courting, those fascinating qualities may have intrigued you, attracted you. But now, after living in the same house for 20 years—even 2 years—fascination has turned to frustration; intriguing characteristics are now idiosyncrasies. You may appreciate the more drastic word picture that titled a best-selling book: *Men Are from Mars, Women Are from Venus.*

If you and your spouse are so very different from each other, how do you maintain your energy for love? That's what we'll discuss this week. Again, an understanding of the issues is the basis for a breakthrough in the relationship.

To illustrate differences between Norma and me—differences that go beyond our natural, dominant temperaments—let me walk you through a moving experience we had not long ago.

We were out driving together on a Sunday afternoon, and we both started extolling the virtues of another state thousands of miles from our home in Phoenix. After a bit, she said, "Why don't we just move there? I mean, why are we staying here in Arizona when we both love it so much over there?"

"Great idea!" I said.

So far, so good; we were in agreement on the general idea. But then a lot of the basic differences between us started to come into play. The moment we said we would like to move, I was ready to pack my bags, load the pickup, and hit the highway! I get going in a hurry when I decide to do something. In fact, within two months of that day, I was already living in the Midwest.

Norma, on the other hand, moves more slowly and cautiously. Before she does anything, she thinks of all the ramifications and makes a plan to cover every detail. It took another eight months to close down our business, sell the house, take care of all the changes of address, and complete the move.

If you and your spouse are so different from each other, how do you maintain your energy for love?

Before Norma moved east, we had bought a small farm and begun remodeling the house to suit our needs and desires. She had flown out three times to check the building plans and make changes, but by the time she arrived to stay, the renovations were only about half done. I remember an exchange we had right after she moved. She walked into the farmhouse, and with great anticipation I asked, "Do you think we captured what you wanted with the kitchen?"

She took one look and said, "I don't like that. I thought I had explained how I wanted it done, and that's not it."

"Yeah," I said, "we tried to get close to what you wanted. Doesn't it look nice?"

Well, it was obvious from the look on her face that she was not pleased at all. "I have to get out of here for a while and think about this," she said.

"But you need to stay," I insisted. "We should figure this out."

"No, I have to go," she insisted. "I have to be alone." As she was getting into her car, I urged her to stay because decisions were needed the next day. I yelled my last words at her car as she was driving away: "Stay! It's safe. I'm a marriage counselor!"

Clearly, that was a time of real stress for us. With my extroverted nature, I wanted us to stay together and work out what to do. But Norma, being much more introverted, needed to get by herself to think things through. I'll say more about this extrovert-introvert difference shortly.

The story goes on. One afternoon as we were walking around our small farm (we'd moved in and the remodeling was almost complete), she said, "Wouldn't it be great someday to have animals out here—chickens and turkeys and maybe a little lamb?"

"That's a terrific idea," I told her. "Why don't we go get them now?"

"Can we?" she asked.

"Sure," I said with confidence. "There are farmers around here that sell animals—I think. Let's go!"

We impulsively hopped in the pickup, making no provision for carrying animals home. I assumed the farmers would have boxes—or something. So we found a place; bought a few turkeys, chickens, guineas, and a cute baby goat, and put them in a makeshift pen in the rear of the pickup. Actually, we had to put the goat in the cab with us; Norma held it all the way home. And, of course, on our way back, Norma named all the animals.

To say the least, we didn't know how to keep or protect our "pets." As soon as we got home, the goat escaped. Norma felt bad about the loss of her new friend, but I just shrugged: "He'll come back when he's hungry, won't he?" Too soon every animal we bought had escaped from the barn or the chicken pen. Most we recaptured.

But then we discovered we had neighbors—foxes, coyotes, and wild dogs—who suddenly made their presence known. They quickly started picking off our birds; if the birds didn't get up in a tree for the night, they were gone by morning. Norma was pretty upset by this. But I took it in stride. "Oh, that's too bad for those precious little animals. I guess we'll have to build a pen."

I recall the day we were walking our new dogs in the woods. Unleashed and roaming nearby, they came back to us dragging this turkey carcass. "That's Carl!" Norma exclaimed.

150

"Oh, that's Carl," I repeated with considerably less grief.

Fortunately, some of our animals have survived up to the present. Norma loves them. I tolerate them. We're different that way and—as the whole story illustrates—in many other ways, too. It shows the uniqueness of our personalities, our extrovert-introvert tendencies, and the major distinctions of being male or female. Once we were married for several years, those and other distinctions irritated both of us. But gradually, with new understanding, we learned to appreciate the other's uniqueness.

As you study this week, you will:

- develop an understanding of some of the basic differences in men and women;
- learn to value your spouse by looking for attributes and actions to praise;
- cultivate an attitude of acceptance for your spouse's differences in the areas of personality, birth order, personal history, extrovert/introvert, and gender;
- strengthen your commitment to the marriage relationship;
- begin to understand a woman's intuitive sense.

Day 1 Your Maddening Mate	Day 2 Have You Had Your Spouse Boosters?	Day 3 In Pursuit of Praise	Day 4 Drawing Closer, Not Apart	Day 5 Accessing a Wife's Marriage Manual

> *"Love must be sincere. ... Honor one another above yourselves" (Romans 12:9-10).*

I pray that this week you will grow significantly in understanding your spouse. I encourage you to learn this Scripture passage as a foundation for understanding one another in marriage.

"Love must be sincere. Hate what is evil; cling to what is good. Be devoted to one another in brotherly love. Honor one another above yourselves" (Romans 12:9-10).

Day 1
Your Maddening Mate

Part of my goal in this week's study is to have you see your mate's maddening differences from a new and positive perspective. Impossible, you say? Consider this light-hearted story of a church secretary and a rich Texan. Watch how quickly her view changes.

The Texan called the church office in the middle of the week and said to the secretary, "Hello. I'd like to talk to the head hog of the trough."

"Excuse me?" the secretary said, annoyed.

"You heard me, Ma'am," the Texan said. "I want to talk to the head hog of the trough."

"Are you referring to our senior minister?" the secretary asked.

"That's what you call him," he said. "But I call him the head hog of the trough."

"Well, sir," the secretary said stiffly, "I'm sorry, but he's out of the building right now. May I take a message?"

"Yeah," he said, "I visited your church last Sunday, and I was real impressed. I see that you're having a building fund drive, and I'd like to give a million-dollar gift if I could."

The secretary hesitated and then answered, "Sir, I think I hear that big old pig coming down the hall right now." Her whole perspective on the Texan changed when she suddenly saw some value in him.

You may not see it yet, but there is great value in your mate's uniqueness. That's because natural tendencies that may be fundamentally different from your own can enrich you and your marriage.

 List differences between men and women you have observed over the years.

_____

_____

Differences between men and women, husbands and wives, do not make one superior or inferior to the other.

Differences between men and women, husbands and wives, do not make one superior or inferior to the other. Rather, God desires that we understand our differences and draw closer to one another—not apart.

Galatians 3:28 stresses the fact that 'There is neither … male or female, for you are all one in Christ Jesus." Jesus emphasized the importance of husbands and wives becoming one flesh.

> "Haven't you read," [Jesus] replied, "that at the beginning the
> Creator 'made them male and female,' and said, 'For this reason
> a man will leave his father and mother and be united to his wife,
> and the two will become one flesh' ? " (Matthew 19:4-5).

 List ways you and your spouse have become one over the years.

_____

_____

Becoming one does not mean we give up our personal tendencies and traits. Each mate remains a unique creation. Becoming one involves an intricate blending of each partner's tendencies and traits into one spirit that glorifies God.

 Write a prayer thanking God for both the differences and the oneness you have in marriage.

_____

_____

Day 2
Have You Had Your Spouse Boosters?

As you learn to *understand* various differences between you and your spouse, you can spark appreciation for qualities he or she has that you lack. Verbalize that appreciation, and you can bring out the best in your spouse. Try praising your spouse and see what happens. Praise is like a shot of adrenaline that energizes a person. It's gives a quick, 60-second boost to any relationship. Dr. John Gottman says that long-lasting "in-love" marriages enjoy a regular dose of five positive experiences to one negative.[1] Praise brings a very positive experience to any marriage.

How do you energize, motivate—bring out the best in—your mate? Give the gift of praise. Think about it. When someone praises you for some attribute, like being a thoughtful person, doesn't that instantly give you a lift and make you feel better about yourself? When you're praised for some action, like cooking a delicious meal, doesn't that make you want to do more of the same? It takes only a few words to praise your mate, only a few seconds of time, but the impact can be monumental.

 List two or three attributes or actions you praise God for in your spouse.

_____

_____

When was the last time you praised your spouse? _____

The opposite of *praise* is *criticism*. Think about what criticism does to you. If you're like most people I talk with, criticism drills a hole in your emotions and through that hole your strength flows out. Along with it goes most of your motivation to try to do better. Remember the concept covered in week 5: *The further we are from what we had expected in any area of life, the more strength we lose.* Criticism causes us to feel that we've let someone down. We haven't met that person's expectations or our own, because we expected ourselves to be acceptable to the other.

 Check some of the negative actions or attitudes you find yourself having in your marriage.
- ❏ Being judgmental
- ❏ Being negative
- ❏ Quickly responding *no* before listening and considering *yes*
- ❏ Thinking the worst instead of the best
- ❏ Thinking something won't work rather than focusing on the possibilities
- ❏ Being critical
- ❏ Other: _____

> *Long-lasting in-love marriages enjoy a regular dose of five positive experiences to one negative experience.*

Criticism isn't always blatant; it can be subtle, as with the wife who wakes each morning and right off gives her husband a honey-do list ("honey, do this; honey, do that"), no hugs, no smile, not even a *good morning*. No *thank you* in the evening. She's telling him each day: "I'm not happy unless you're performing. I'm not happy even when you're performing." You can imagine how that implied criticism and lack of love and appreciation makes that guy feel.

 The Bible warns us about our tongues. Proverbs contains many passages telling us about the care we need to give our tongues. Read the selected passages and match them with the type of words we are to use.

1. _____ Truthful lips endure forever, but a lying tongue lasts only a moment (Proverbs 12:19).

2. _____ The tongue that brings healing is a tree of life, but a deceitful tongue crushes the spirit (Proverbs 15:4)

3. _____ A gentle answer turns away wrath, but a harsh word stirs up anger (Proverbs 15:1).

4. _____ The tongue of the wise commends knowledge, but the mouth of the fool gushes folly (Proverbs 15:2).

5. _____ A fool spurns his father's discipline, but whoever needs correction shows prudence (Proverbs 15:5).

6. _____ The tongue has the power of life and death, and those who love it will eat its fruit (Proverbs 18:21).

a. Comforting words
b. Gentle words
c. Corrective words
d. Powerful words
e. Wise words
f. Truthful words

 We can offer praise and affirmation that gives life or criticism and negativism which fosters death. Put an *x* on the line to indicate where you see yourself on the continuum between bringing life and death to your marriage.

In our marriage my tongue brings _____.

                          Life   Death

Praise energizes because it helps to meet two of our most basic human needs: (1) a deep need to feel significant—to feel that we matter, that we're important somehow, that we're needed; and (2) a great need to feel secure in our closest relationships, to feel that no matter what happens, we belong to each other and will be there for the other.

(Answers: 1. f.; 2. a.; 3. b.; 4. e.; 5. c.; 6. d.)

We can offer praise and affirmation that gives life or criticism and negativism which fosters death.

Praise begins with praising God. Once we praise Him, we are ready to affirm and encourage others. If you find yourself being negative and lacking praise, how has your praise of God been? Complete each sentence and look up the Scripture cited for further ideas.

I praise God for _____

_____

(Psalms 147–150; Revelation 5:9-13)

I praise and affirm my spouse for _____

_____

(Romans 12:9-10)

I praise and affirm my family members for _____

_____

(Romans 15:7)

Accepting and affirming others brings glory to God in Jesus Christ.

Accepting and affirming others brings glory to God in Jesus Christ according to Romans 15:7: "Accept one another, then, just as Christ accepted you, in order to bring praise to God." Praise for God opens us up to His praise and acceptance growing in us for others.

We can give the gift of praise at any time. Don't worry that your spouse will get tired of being praised. When I ask seminar audiences, "How many of you would like to be praised more often by your spouses?" everyone in the room raises a hand. It's just something we can never get enough of.

 Write a prayer praising God both for His nature and for the spouse He has given you.

_____

_____

_____

_____

[1] John Gottman, *Why Marriages Succeed or Fail* (New York: Simon & Schuster, 1994), 29.

Day 3
In Pursuit of Praise

Let's look today at five areas that make each of us unique. In each area, look for natural things to praise and energize each other.

In Praise of Personality Differences

Last week, we labeled the four basic personality types as *lion, otter, golden retriever,* and *beaver.* I trust you took the self-test and identified which one (or maybe two) of the four is your dominant type. Maybe your spouse also took the test.

We all need to be appreciated and affirmed for our inherent strengths: if a lion, for decisiveness; if an otter, for spontaneity; if a golden retriever, for being kind and steady; if a beaver, for being careful and detailed. Pointing out your mate's uniqueness in this area and expressing appreciation will give him or her a real power boost.

Even if your spouse's dominant type is the same as yours, the degree of dominance and the overall mix of all four types will vary between any two people.

In Praise of Birth-Order Differences

Research shows that your place in the birth order of your family has a great deal to do with how you live with and relate to others. If you were the firstborn of several children, for example, you probably tend to be a leader-type, because you learned to take charge of the other kids. Secondborns are usually somewhat competitive and insecure, because they had to prove themselves—measure up to big brother or sister. On the positive side, middleborn children are good negotiators and adaptable; they often feel little need to "control." And third or lastborn children are often very sociable, knowing how to deal with people.

 Can you see birth-order influences in you and your spouse? How are they similar or different?

_____

_____

Look for a birth-order characteristic in your spouse to praise. Try it—discover its effect in energizing your mate.

This discussion hardly scratches the surface. If you'd like to know more about this subject, I recommend *The Birth Order Book,* by Dr. Kevin Leman.[1] I warn against using these categorizations as a weapon against your mate. Look for the positives.

In Praise of Personal-History Differences

We all have a unique personal history. That means you. It means your spouse. Was your spouse raised by just one parent? Raised with several brothers and sisters, only sisters, or only brothers? Was your spouse abused? Raised in a tough home? Rejected

We all need to be appreciated and affirmed for our inherent strengths.

as a child? All these things made a lasting impact and contributed to the person your spouse is. And his or her history is different from yours. How can these differences draw you together?

Again, honor and communication are key starting points. Talk about your pasts—events, feelings, resulting needs. Look for positives to praise. How does your spouse's past enrich your relationship?

You can also take the hardships your mate endured and together "count pearls." As you see more clearly what your mate learned from past hurts and how those hurts matured him or her, you can reinforce the resulting good through praise.

 In the box below, write a brief personal history using a one-word outline from birth until now. Take a few moments to share this with your spouse.

*H*onor and communication are key starting points in confronting your differences.

In Praise of Extrovert-Introvert Differences

As you may have noticed in the opening story of this week's study, Norma has a lot of introvert in her, though she's fairly balanced, while I'm an off-the-chart extrovert. Whichever you are, you need for your spouse to know that, appreciate it, and praise you for it (and vice versa).

Extroverts like to be with people. Even if I've been with others all day, I still like to be with people at night, because I get energy from interacting with them. But if introverts have been with others all day, they'll often need some time alone at night. They've had enough of people for one day. A lot of times Norma will come home at the end of a workday (I work out of our house now, while she runs the business office), and I'll want to spend time with her right away. "No, just give me a little time by myself first," she'll say. I used to be bothered by that until I understood this basic difference between us. She's much more steady than I, and part of that trait comes from her desire to be alone and process things by herself. She doesn't have to run from thing to thing or person to person. I'm much more spontaneous, and I like to tell her, "Honey, I love it that you naturally calm me down."

 Mark yourself with an *x* and your spouse with an *s* on the line indicating the degree you tend to be an introvert or an extrovert.

Introvert   Extrovert

In Praise of Gender Differences

Not every man and every woman will fall neatly into the categories I'll cover in this section, but from both the present research and my own observations, the majority certainly do. In fact, I find the generalizations to be true 70 or 80 percent of the time, so if you're a skeptic, I ask that you humor my generalized statements "men do this and women do that." It's amazing how our nation is enjoying all the new information about gender differences, and that's because it rings true.

There are many studies and books on these differences. I'd like to summarize five of my favorites from my own study and observations. As you increase your understanding of your complementary strengths, you'll have more ammunition with which to praise your mate. Look for the positive; discover the value of variety!

Difference 1:
Men Love to Share Facts—Women Love to Express Feelings

Men, even in close friendships, tend to be into gathering and expressing facts. Women in the same sort of relationship tend to be better at and more interested in sharing their feelings. This is no rigid rule, remember. Both genders can and do share feelings and facts, but the scale seems to be tipped in favor of facts for men and emotions for women.

Remember, men, we are healthier when we become better communicators. Thank God for your wife. When's the last time you paused and thanked her for wanting to talk about emotions?

Difference 2:
Men Tend to Be Independent—Women Tend to Be Interdependent

A second big gender difference is that men tend to be independent, while women are more interdependent. This shows up clearly in the way young boys and girls play and disagree.

Have you ever wondered why it takes millions of sperm and only one egg to make a baby? Maybe it's because not one of those little surfers will stop and ask for directions!

Difference 3:
Men Connect by Doing Things Together—Women Connect by Talking Together

This third difference—*men connect by doing things together; women connect by talking together*—is closely related to the first two: *facts/feelings and independence/interdependence.* A fascinating aspect of this difference is the way the two sexes define the word *intimacy.* Over the last few decades, women have played the major role in defining intimacy for our culture, with the result that many men have concluded it's just not for them. That definition always includes "talking and touching"—that's what women want when they say they want more intimacy.

What's the male definition of *intimacy* according to the latest research? *Doing something with another person.*[2] There doesn't have to be any talking at all. A couple may just be watching TV together, but the man will think that's getting close or being intimate, while the wife is sitting there thinking, *When are we going to say something?*

As you understand your complementary strengths, you'll have more ammunition with which to praise your mate.

Most men like just being with someone else. But they tend to avoid togetherness if the woman is critical or insists on communicating the entire time, because that's not their idea of intimacy.

Difference 4:
Men Tend to Compete—Women Tend to Cooperate

This difference is very important to understand, because it can help explain why a male may all of a sudden start an argument over something the wife had no idea would lead to a fight.

Why do males tend to be competitive, while females tend to be more cooperative? You can see this in the kind of pets the two sexes like. Most men prefer dogs to cats. Think about it; dogs don't engage us in a contest of wills; most dogs are loyal, obedient, and easy to train. They come when you call them. We men want to win and feel we're in charge.

Difference 5:
Men Tend to Be Controlling—Women Tend to Remain Agreeable to Stay Connected

This gender difference is closely connected to difference 4—competition/cooperation. You see, most men think that a "boss" of anything is a winner; a wife challenging a husband can be a threat to a man's need to feel like a winner. But I separate out this controlling/agreeable difference, as it hits right at the heart of a man's deepest need—feeling significant.

Men usually like to be in control. Research has shown, for example, that when men and women talk, the conversation *"follows the style of the men alone. ... "*When women and men talk to each other, both make adjustments, but the women make more.[3] As we've seen, women desire verbal communication—to create intimacy—and many will let the man lead—to preserve the connection and keep conversation going.

Below is a summary of my observations. Even though the columns are labeled *Men* and *Women*, evaluate how you and your spouse fit this description. Place your and your spouse's initials by the characteristics that apply. Consider each one carefully before you initial it.

MEN	WOMEN
___ Share facts	___ Express feelings
___ Independent	___ Interdependent
___ Connect by doing	___ Connect by talking
___ Compete	___ Cooperate
___ Control	___ Remain agreeable

Compare your evaluation with your mate's evaluation. Do you agree? Close today's study in praise to God for creating you as male and female—different in so many wonderful ways.

---

[1] Kevin Leman, *The Birth Order Book* (Grand Rapids: Fleming Revell, 1985).
[2] Bernie Zilbergeld, *The New Male Sexuality* (New York: HarperCollins, 1992).
[3] Deborah Tannen, *You Just Don't Understand* (New York: William Morrow, 1990), 236-237.

God created us as male and female—different in so many wonderful ways.

Day 4
Drawing Closer, Not Apart

Clearly, there are many potential differences between a husband and wife, and we tend to be attracted to our counterpart. Some of those differences are general in nature; others are male-female distinctions that usually hold true (though "any randomly chosen woman might do better at a 'male' skill than a man, and vice versa").[1] Men and women can be critical of one another because of these differences, or we can learn to praise the other for his or her unique and complementary characteristics. In doing so, we can energize the other and strengthen our marriage.

Men, when was the last time you looked your wife in the eyes and said, "I appreciate so much your emphasis on relationships and all you do to build ours up. The things you do to make our house into a home and the time you give to the kids—you're terrific"?

Women, when is the last time you looked your husband in the eyes and said, "I really appreciate the way you're always doing your best for our family. Your dedication and hard work mean a lot to me?"

 How can your mate's differences help you in every area of your life, and especially in your marriage? Briefly write about some of the areas your mate has helped to enrich you and your relationship.

_____

_____

Let me share a few of the advantages Norma has brought to me.

Help with my job. Norma has kept me out of more conflicts than I care to think about with coworkers. She has also helped me restore relationships that were broken. When we were first married, she "tutored" me when I was trying to learn how to talk with and relate to other adults in my first job. With her "woman's intuition," she has also helped me understand coworkers and evaluate potential employees for our business, and I'm constantly amazed at how accurate her perceptions are. So I praise her for all these things.

 One way my mate helps with my work is …

_____

Help with self-confidence. Norma has continually told me, "Yes, you can do it!" When I was stuck in an unfulfilling job, she encouraged me, "You're not using your talents. Just look what you could do!" She has also used her personality, her introvert tendencies, and her energy to help make my dreams come true and boost my confidence that I can reach my goals. Over and over I've tried to get her to pursue dreams of her own, and her reply is "Helping you and the others in our company to be successful is my dream!" For these things I praise her as well.

One way my mate helps with my self-confidence is …

_____

Help with personal finances. I have a friend who is president of a large chain of banks. He told me that he sees men as being primarily responsible for couples falling into deep financial trouble. Men tend to buy the big things, he says, and women tend to buy the things that keep the families running smoothly. My wife has always been the one to keep us "down to earth" with money. She questions everything I do if it has any potential of weakening the family or threatening our security. Before we met with a financial advisor, she told me, "I'll go, but I'm going to 'sniff him out' and hear what he has to say before I'll go along with his idea." Again, that's one of her strengths, and I also praise her for that.

 One way my mate helps with our finances is …

_____

You can do the same type of thing with your spouse. Think of the many ways your mate enriches various areas of your life. Then praise him or her for each one.

As you get ready to go to sleep each night, ask yourself, *How many times have I praised my mate today? How many times have I praised my kids?* We don't often think about it, but I guarantee that every person in your life would love to be praised more and criticized less.

Praise is such a great gift from God, and it's so easy to give! So look at the things that make your spouse and others unique, and develop the habit of praising them for those very things. It will bring out the best in them. It will energize them instantly—and you, too! And that's what makes love last.

 As Christians, both you and your spouse are growing and being changed into Christ's image. That growth will help both of you understand and appreciate your differences and praise God for who you are. Are you willing to praise God and thank Him for what He is doing in your marriage? Complete these sentences.

One difference between me and my mate that I praise God for is …

_____

One thing I see God doing in our marriage that I praise Him for is …

_____

This coming week, I will praise my spouse by …

_____

If you both sincerely desire to grow closer together, begin by focusing on your relationship with God. As each of you grow closer to Him by praying, worshiping, studying the Bible, and praying together, you will be drawn closer to each other. James writes, "Come near to God and he will come near to you. Wash your hands,

> *Praise is such a great gift from God, and it's so easy to give!*

you sinners, and purify your hearts, you double-minded. … Therefore confess your sins to each other and pray for each other so that you may be healed. The prayer of a righteous man is powerful and effective" (James 4:8, 5:16). As you pray and confess your sins together, your hearts will be drawn closer to God and one another.

Below is a triangle representing how growing closer to God brings us closer to each other. Put an *x* on the line between you and God to indicate where you are right now. Put an x on the line between your spouse and God to indicate where you think he or she is right now. Check the lines where each of you wants to be. Notice how the distance apart from each other decreases as you move closer to God.

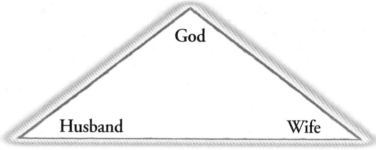

The distance between husband and wife decreases as they move closer to God.

Start right now praying about any differences between you that are causing problems. Ask God to change you and your spouse in positive ways that you might grow closer to Him and to each other.

---
[1]Sharon Begley, "Gray Matters," *Newsweek,* 27 March 1995, 54.

Day 5
Accessing a Wife's Marriage Manual

In my workshops, one thing I discuss is how husbands and wives can access a wife's marriage manual. Today's topic may change your marriage more than any we've dealt with this week.

Wives might be wondering how to get more in touch with their marriage manuals. Assuming you're in the emotionally and psychologically "normal" range, I'll help you get into it with these few spurring questions: What would it take to improve your marriage? What's one thing that brings you the most happiness or strength when your husband does it? How could he do it even better? If you could wave a wand over your marriage, what would you want your husband to change or improve, knowing it would change (and knowing he would not be upset with you for "waving the wand")?

Some husbands reading this section may be feeling very uneasy. I would have in the early years of my marriage. I used to think that Norma had too many ideas about how our marriage should improve. I reasoned that many of her thoughts about us were purely selfish ideas designed to benefit her and certainly not me. But now that I've been married more than 30 years and been in contact with well over 40,000 wives and I've never found a wife who couldn't read from her God-given manual. I'm very relaxed about asking these questions of my wife or any other woman. I can't count the number of times a wife has said to me, "If my husband only knew how much I would do for him if he would just help me to feel secure and valued in our relationship!" When wives feel like queens, they usually relax and overdo themselves in finding ways to make their husbands feel fulfilled. But, again, they won't do this as well if there's too much anger in their hearts toward their husbands or others.

With that background in mind, let's look at 11 possible ways to draw out a wife's built-in marriage manual.

❏ 1. Use Three Tried and Tested Questions

For years I've asked three questions in my marriage counseling and seminars. They do a good job of drawing out valuable parts of a woman's marriage manual.

A. On a scale from 0 (terrible) to 10 (perfection), what kind of relationship do we both want? Maybe the two of you would be satisfied with being at seven or eight most of the time. It's important for both the husband and wife to respond to this first question, which sharpens the print in her manual.

B. On the same scale (0-10), where are we today in our marriage relationship, on the average and with everything thrown in? This second question opens the cover to her "book." Nearly every woman has a more accurate answer to this question than her husband, with the man usually rating the marriage a few points higher than the woman.

C. What would it take to move our relationship from where it is now (question B) closer to where we want it to be (question A)? This last question is where the words jump out. Almost always, answers involve the kinds of things we're looking at in this book—more security, more affection, less anger, and so on.

These three questions have continually allowed couples to shorten the time it takes to improve their relationship. As a man and husband, it took me some time to get used to the idea that my wife had a better ability to read our marriage status. Frankly, it used to intimidate me. And at times it irritated me. But today, I've stopped fighting reality. It amazes me how accurate wives are at seeing the condition of their marriages. Instead of resisting this idea, I've found it tremendously helpful to husbands who take the time to listen and understand what women have to say about improving relationships. I'm not saying that all women are perfect or that any are 100 percent right all the time. I'm saying that they seem to be right most of the time.

❏ 2. Make Sure She Feels as Safe as Possible

Wives may appear at times to be selfish, whining, nagging, overbearing, or demanding, but I've discovered that almost always, they're expressing a need within the

It amazes me how accurate wives are at seeing the condition of their marriages.

relationship that's not being adequately met. If a woman feels safe, secure, loved, and honored in her marriage, she will find it far easier to get in touch with her needs and her intuitive sense of how things are going.

❏ 3. Simply Ask How the Relationship Can Be Improved

Sometimes a straightforward question is the best approach: "What can we do better?" or "What do you think makes for a great marriage?"

Once the question is asked, the husband needs to listen carefully and respectfully. According to Dr. Howard Markman, the main factor in shutting down a relationship is a husband clamming up—closing himself off and distancing himself emotionally from his wife.[1] But asking "How can we improve things between us?" goes in the opposite, healthful direction, strengthening the connection and allowing the wife to access her marriage manual.

❏ 4. Don't Argue When She Starts to Read Out of Her Manual

One woman said, "It's very important, while my husband is listening to me, that he not react or think I'm being critical."

Her comment points to a double "pain" in which many women find themselves. On the one hand, she wants her man to be concerned about the health of the relationship and work with her to make it better. If he's not interested, she feels the hurt. On the other hand, if she says anything about how things can be improved, he may take it as personal criticism and get defensive, and things can easily grow worse rather than advancing. If this happens repeatedly, a woman can close her manual because she no longer feels safe enough to keep it open.

If you're a husband with an overbearing personality, your aggressiveness or demanding approach can be intimidating, making your wife hesitant to read even a sentence out of her marriage manual. Think of that manual as having a latch with a lock on it. If she doesn't feel safe, she may take only the first step of unlocking it, but still may not unlatch it. She may be very sensitive about this, so how much she reveals depends a lot on how safe you make her feel. And most of the time, arguing with her to open it and read it on demand will double lock it.

If you're a wife, you may be saying, "I could never share my marriage manual with my husband, because he would blast me. I could suffer for months, even years, if I suggested anything about wanting our relationship to improve." If you're living with a man who has a strong personality, and especially if he has some perfectionistic tendencies as well, the only way you might be able to get his attention in reading your manual is by hitting him alongside his head with a big stick (figuratively speaking, of course).

❏ 5. Get the Support of a Loving Team

When you're in a loving, supportive group of three or four couples, you may feel safer in revealing your marriage manual. It's like going to a counselor, where you feel safe expressing your feelings and opinions. You may even get to see some of the fine print.

"How can we improve things between us?"

A small support group is so important to a marriage that in my video series I have called participation one of four "musts" of a great marriage. (The others? Things we're covering in this book: (1) honor; (2) daily resolution of anger; and (3) the monitoring of the wife's marriage manual.)

❑ 6. Allow Her to Read from Her Manual at the Time When She Feels Most Able to Share

A wife may, for example, feel safer or more in the mood to share when the two of you are out on a dinner date. Men, ask her when and where is best for her.

I learned the importance of this the hard way. When I discovered Norma had this built-in marriage manual, I used to demand she read it to me when I wanted so I could grow and we could have an improved marriage. That was not only heavy irony, but it shut her down from time to time and made her close her book completely.

❑ 7. Discover New Communication Resources

For some couples, having the wife write out some sections of her manual is very helpful; it also serves to give a lasting record of what's going on inside her. Try out the various methods described in the week on communication, and then regularly use those that work best for you and your spouse. Learn to use and reuse the method called "drive-through communication." Take extra time to understand it and try it, because the couples I've worked with find that method to be at the top of the list.

Maybe your best method will be using word pictures, such as, "Read me the fine print under the section on improving our sexual relationship." Word pictures are an effective and powerful way to get a point across; you can get your mate to understand you and feel your feelings instantly.[2]

❑ 8. Ask Other Women to Share Their Marriage Manuals with You

This might be your mother or grandmother, your sister, your wife's sister, or maybe even a female friend of your family. I've done this myself for years, asking women in groups or individually what they think makes for a great marriage. Some women will feel safer articulating their manuals to someone who is not their spouse. After all, we have few reasons if any to criticize what they say, because they're not talking specifically about us. And if one or more of these women knows your wife well, it's amazing what you can learn. When I take the time to explain to a wife that I'm trying to improve my marriage, most have not only tried to help me, but they usually get excited about seeing a man doing something specific to enrich his relationship.

If your wife doesn't feel good about you reading some other woman's manual, her concern is usually filed under the "security" section in her manual. Whenever I find a wife who is somewhat jealous of her husband becoming too friendly with another woman, especially talking about improving their marriage, it usually has something to do with how secure she feels in her husband's love and value for her. If a conflict should come from your friendliness with other women, use the conflict to find out what it would take for her to feel more secure and loved. Listen to her, and look at

Word pictures are an effective and powerful way to get a point across.

your own motives. This can be a great opportunity to reestablish your life-long commitment by assuring her of your love and devotion "till death do us part."

Also, once again, if your wife has too much unresolved anger stored in her heart, then no matter what you say or do, she probably will not become more secure in your love. Her anger needs to drain somewhat before your relationship can improve.

❑ 9. Use Reverse Role Playing

The psychiatrist who wrote the best-selling book *Passive Men, Wild Women* said reverse role playing is the best method he has ever found to help husbands make lasting changes for the better.[3]

This is something you can do by yourself in your living room or office. Picture your wife in the room with you, sitting in one of the empty chairs, and ask her what it would take to improve your relationship. Then, if you can, even though you might feel silly, go over and sit in the empty chair where you pictured her, and talk back to yourself as you think she would. Next, move back to where you started and see yourself listening and responding. If you "get inside her mind" and start saying the things you imagine she would say, you'll be amazed at the insights that come.

❑ 10. Ask Her What You Do for Her That Gives Her Energy and What Takes Energy Away

What discourages her, and what gives her hope? This is another way to pull out the fine print in a woman's marriage manual. (We'll discuss this point at greater length in a later week's study.)

❑ 11. Analyze the Main Points of Criticism You've Heard from Your Wife Over the Years

These may have to do with you, the house, the kids, her job or yours, the general state of her life, or whatever. Think of two or three that have persisted for some time, write them down, and look at what they actually reflect.

Norma has criticized some of my manners for most of our married life. What does that tell me about her marriage manual? Well, most women easily and tightly connect to their husbands and become a part of them. The way we look and act can become a reflection on them. So when we bite our nails in public or make loud body noises at home, it can subtly disconnect them from us. It makes them feel, for that moment at least, that they are not a part of us. They can even feel devalued.

Women are very concerned with their husbands' reputations. They usually want their men to be respected and successful. So when we do something embarrassing in public, they're afraid we're going to be humiliated, and they along with us.

This kind of analysis of a wife's criticisms can add a lot to a husband's understanding of her marriage manual.

 We've covered 11 ways to draw out a wife's intuitive sense of what's best and enriching for your marriage. Go back and read the headings. Place a check in the box by those you currently do. Place an x in the box by those you plan to implement.

Draw out a wife's intuitive sense of what's best and enriching for your marriage.

A Word of Caution to Wives

Women who read their marriage manuals to their husbands too often—who are constantly reciting without a request—can become tiresome. The Bible says, "A quarrelsome wife is like a constant dripping on a rainy day" (Proverbs 27:15). They're like a dripping faucet; like a desert sun that beats down on you all day long; or like being trapped in a locked room with someone who just won't quit jabbering. That's the way their husbands can perceive them. King Solomon suggested in two places that it is "Better to live on a corner of the roof than share a house with a quarrelsome wife" (Proverbs 21:9; 25:24).

Holding the readings to once a week, once a month, maybe even once a year for some manual chapters is sometimes enough to have a great impact on your marriage. An interesting manual is something your man wants to read. But if he's forced to read it (listen to it), then no matter how good it is, he's going to get tired of it, stop listening, and move on to something else. Remember, "The wise woman builds her house, but with her own hands the foolish one tears hers down" (Proverbs 14:1).

Wives, how can you tell if you're overdoing it? Well, when you say something that may help improve your relationship but that could be perceived as critical, do your husband's eyes get that "vacant house" look (you can tell some lights are on but no one's home)? Does he know everything you're going to say as soon as you get the first three words out? While you're talking, does he play raisin and shrivel up before your eyes? In a typical day, how many times are you critical, and how many times do you praise him? Keep track for a few days, and if the ratio isn't seven praises or more for every negative comment, you're being too critical and maybe reading too often. (The same holds true for your husband. If he overdoes it with criticism, you may stop reading your manual to him altogether.)

Wives, appreciate and praise any and all steps he takes in the right direction. In six months or a year, if you get discouraged, think back and consider how far you've come. Occasionally remind yourself that your husband is not your all-sufficient, perfect god (or parent). And remember that your ultimate happiness comes from finding peace based on your internal well-being, not on outward circumstances.

Close this week's study in prayer. Thank God for creating women with a built-in marriage manual. Husbands, seek God's guidance as to when to open and read your wife's manual. Wives, seek God's guidance as to when to share your manual with your husband.

Your ultimate happiness comes from finding peace based on your internal well-being, not on outward circumstances.

---

[1] Howard Markman, Scott Stanley, and Susan Blumberg, *Fighting for Your Marriage* (San Francisco: Jossey-Bass, 1994), 22.
[2] For 300 sample word pictures, see Gary Smalley and John Trent, *The Language of Love* (Colorado Springs: Focus on the Family, 1988, 1991).
[3] Pierre Mornell, M.D., *Passive Men, Wild Women* (New York: Simon & Schuster, 1979).

Couple Time

For you to complete

Repeat Romans 12:9-10, the verses for the week. Write the key phrase in those verses that God has used to speak to you this week.

_____

What would God have you do as a result of today's study?

_____

_____

For you to share with your spouse

1. Look over the list of actions and attitudes you find yourself having in your marriage (day 2, page 153). Discuss how each of you marked this list.

2. Turn to one of the lists that you made during the week to praise your mate. Share your praise list with your spouse.

3. This week you have considered many differences between husbands and wives. Share with your spouse one difference between the two of you that you wish to pray about. Pray together about that difference.

4. Review the 11 possible ways to draw out a wife's built-in marriage manual. Discuss how this material relates to your marriage.

WEEK 10

Conflict: The Doorway to Intimacy

The idea that conflict is healthy may sound like a cruel joke if you're feeling overwhelmed by the negativity in your relationship. But in a sense, a marriage lives and dies by what you might loosely call its arguments, by how well disagreements and grievances are aired. The key is how you argue—whether your style escalates tension or leads to a feeling of resolution.

—John Gottman[1]

Dr. Howard Markman claims that resolving conflicts is the key area for staying in love and staying married. His 20 years of research indicate if couples learned to work out their conflicts, the overall divorce rate could be cut by more than 50 percent.[2] Just think of it! For years the divorce rate has been hovering at about one-out-of-two marriages. That sad statistic could be reduced to one-out-of-four—if only couples would learn effective methods of conflict resolution. And one of those saved could be yours! (I have wanted to write a book about the importance of staying together in marriage. I've never written it because other authors have already done it.)[3]

Most of us dislike and try to avoid conflicts, especially with our spouses. For peace lovers, this week's study has both bad and good news. The bad news is that we're always going to have conflicts. Our valued individuality—including our personality and gender differences—make them inevitable. But the good news is that we not only can reduce our conflicts, but we can also *use them to move into deeper intimacy in any relationship*.

This week you will discover:

- how to use conflict to draw closer to your spouse;
- six primary causes of conflict;
- what a *circle of conflict* is;
- what does and does not work in conflict resolution;
- how conflict reveals feelings and needs;
- how conflict provides opportunities to express affection.

Day 1 Marital Conflict Is Inevitable	Day 2 Why Most Conflicts Occur	Day 3 The Circle of Conflict	Day 4 Door Slammers and Pearls	Day 5 Conflicts: Opportunities to Express Affection

I am praying that this week you will learn as a couple to handle your conflict so it is not only resolved but also will lead to a deeper relationship in your marriage.

As you study and share this week, keep Proverbs 15:1 in your heart: "A gentle answer turns away wrath, but a harsh word stirs up anger."

---

[1]John Gottman, *Why Marriages Succeed or Fail* (New York: Simon & Schuster, 1994), 173.
[2]Howard Markman, Scott Stanley, and Susan Blumberg, *Fighting for Your Marriage*, 38ff.
[3]See Howard Markman, Scott Stanley, and Susan Blumberg, *Fighting for Your Marriage;* Judith Wallerstein and Sandra Blakeslee, *The Good Marriage;* Judith Wallerstein and Sandra Blakeslee, *Second Chances;* John Gottman, *Why Marriages Fail;* Michele Weiner-Davis, *Divorce Busting;* Diane Medved, *The Case Against Divorce.*

Day 1
Marital Conflict Is Inevitable

Marital conflict is inevitable. What are some of the most sensitive conflict areas in your marriage that seem to keep recurring? Check all that apply.

❑ Finances ❑ Discipline of children ❑ Work
❑ Meals ❑ Scheduling ❑ In-laws
❑ Church activity ❑ Sexual intimacy ❑ Other: _____

Conflict does not have to drive couples apart. In fact, conflict can lead to a closer relationship. Briefly describe a time when a conflict with your mate led to deeper intimacy. Try to identify what happened that made that intimacy possible.

_____

_____

_____

To illustrate how conflicts can lead to deeper intimacy, let me relate (with permission) a story about my daughter, Kari, and son-in-law, Roger. It was very typical of young married couples. Roger heard that his mom and dad were coming to visit. He was pretty excited about that, because he loves to eat. He especially loves a big breakfast, and his mom used to cook him one every day. She's that kind of loving mother, and he was the baby of the family, too. I know how that goes, since I was the baby of my family. But then I got married and found out wives don't always wait on you the way your mother did. Well, Roger has learned the same lesson. But also like me, he sometimes says things that have the opposite effect of what he intended.

So, thinking as a male can, when he heard his folks were coming, Roger said, "Finally, I can have one of those big breakfasts again!" He will admit that this comment was in praise of his mother, but that it also was meant as an editorial comment about Kari not cooking him breakfast. Maybe she'd get and take the hint. That made sense to him, but it didn't sit well with Kari. Instantly—wham—conflict! Kari went silent.

 Wait a moment! Let's interrupt the story.
• **What did Roger do to create a conflict situation?**

_____

• **How did Kari respond?**

_____

When conflict arises in your marriage, how do you and your mate usually respond? Check the box in the first column that best describes how you usually respond. Put an *x* in the box in the second column to indicate how you think your spouse usually responds.

❑ ❑ Yell   ❑ ❑ Compromise   ❑ ❑ Get quiet
❑ ❑ Get angry   ❑ ❑ Express feelings   ❑ ❑ Get even
❑ ❑ Become aggressive   ❑ ❑ Withdraw   ❑ ❑ Try to win

Fortunately Roger is a sensitive and loving husband. He doesn't want to offend Kari. He wants to make sure everything is going great. This happened before their first child, our grandson Michael Thomas, was born, and already Roger was concerned about providing a healthy family atmosphere. So he opened the door offered by that conflict and asked, "Kari, how did my comment make you feel?" That was level four of intimate communication, which we discussed in an earlier week.

Now, as I've already mentioned, word pictures are great for expressing your feelings. Roger and Kari have developed their own word-picture method that conveys instantly how they're feeling. Their method uses fruit imagery, and it goes like this: If something happens but it's not a big deal, she'll say, "You just hit me with a raisin." If it's a little bigger deal, she'll say he hit her with an orange. If it's bigger still, she'll say it was a cantaloupe. But this time she said, "You just hit me with a 25-pound watermelon—wham—and drove me right into the ground." And he instantly entered into her feelings.

Seeing his desire to work things out, she went on to explain that his comment had made her feel inadequate and not as good as his mom. She thought, *What about all the great dinners I make? How come he isn't saying, "Wow, your dinners are just wonderful! Your dinners blow my mom's dinners away"?*

*M*aritial conflict can lead to a closer relationship.

Making Love Last Forever

Roger had a different view. He wasn't saying he had a problem with her dinners. He was saying, "I'm not getting breakfast."

Back to Kari's perspective: *It's pretty hard to make a big breakfast when you're a teacher and getting up at six (before he gets up) just to be ready for work on time.* And what he said, thinking it was going to motivate her to want to make his breakfast, was not the way to get things done. (I think she had even mentioned to him before they married, "I don't do breakfast," but I guess that's the kind of thing you overlook at the time when you're just starting to grow in love.)

What came out of this conflict? He knew how she felt, he reinforced how much he loved her, and he found out one important way to avoid conflict in the future.

 Circle your feelings after a time when a conflict between you and your spouse resulted in both of you learning something valuable for the future.

Loving	Forgiving	Relieved	Satisfied
Happy	Peaceful	Thankful	Other:_____

This incident with Roger and Kari is an example of using conflict as a doorway to intimacy, of getting past opinions to feelings. When conflict is used this way, we don't need to be afraid of it; it actually becomes a good thing that moves the relationship forward.

 Are you able to move beyond opinion and other obstacles in your marital conflicts to feelings and intimacy? Here is a list of things you need to get beyond when you have conflict. Check the ones that most often get in the way of intimacy.

❑ Expressing my opinions
❑ Having to win the argument
❑ Making certain I am understood
❑ Bringing up problems and conflicts from the past
❑ Projecting blame or being blamed for the problem
❑ Raising our voices and one or both of us ending up yelling
❑ Other: _____

The only way conflict can become a doorway to intimacy is when both mates decide that the obstacles will be set aside for the sake of the marriage. That decision usually comes when both people are not angry. And the willingness to move beyond the obstacles has to be brought up by one of the partners in the midst of a conflict.

Scripture gives us insight into how we are to handle anger in conflict. We covered some in week 2. This would be a good time to review the key points in week 2.

 The important biblical principle foundational to conflict resolution is a willingness to forgive. Read the following passages and summarize the teachings presented about forgiveness.

"For if you forgive men when they sin against you, your heavenly Father will also forgive you. But if you do not forgive men their sins, your Father will not forgive your sins" (Matthew 6:14-15).

Conflict can be a doorway to intimacy when both mates decide that the obstacles will be set aside for the sake of the marriage.

Making Love Last Forever

Be kind and compassionate to one another, forgiving each other,
just as in Christ God forgave you (Ephesians 4:32).

_____

_____

A willingness to forgive lays the foundation for conflict resolution. But wait, what happens if a person continues to make the same mistakes? Jesus tells us to forgive 70 times 7; in other words, infinitely (see Matthew 18:21).

 Write a prayer asking Jesus for the willingness to forgive.

_____

_____

Conflict happens when there are power and control problems in the home.

We need to have disagreements. That doesn't mean we look for fights. Should we keep fighting just to enjoy the deeper intimacy of "making up"? By no means.

But when conflicts do occur, they can bring benefits (produce pearls) if we use them in the right way. With that hope in mind, we'll take a closer look tomorrow at the anatomy of a conflict, beginning with why they happen in the first place.

Day 2
Why Most Conflicts Occur

Conflicts occur for a number of reasons. Part of the following list of primary causes comes from Dr. Carol Rubin, a clinical instructor at Harvard Medical School, and her co-author, Dr. Jeffrey Rubin, a professor of psychology at Tufts University.[1]

1. Power and Control
Conflicts happen because there are power and control problems in the home. Who is going to make the decisions? Who's the boss? When there is vying for authority—boom! Conflict. It happens when we least expect it.

 Complete each sentence by placing an *x* on the line below each one.
I am …

├───┼───┼───┼───┼───┼───┼───┤

Controlling   Accepting

├───┼───┼───┼───┼───┼───┼───┤

My spouse is …

├───┼───┼───┼───┼───┼───┼───┤

Controlling   Accepting

Evaluate where your marks fall. Are either of them toward "Controlling"? Or, are they at opposite ends of the lines? When one person tries to smother the other with too much control, or doesn't let the other think or feel independently, conflict smolders or erupts.

2. Insecurity

Someone feeling insecure or unsafe in a relationship causes arguments. If you think your mate is drifting and creating distance, for instance, you're likely to feel insecure, and conflict is a natural result.

 Complete the sentence by placing an *x* on the line below.
In our marriage, I feel …

Secure   Insecure

Some personalities hold things in for a long time, and then they explode. It might be because they don't feel safe to bring those things up when they first are perceived as a problem. In time the unresolved anger explodes, "out of the blue."

3. Differences in Values

Conflicts arise out of differences in values. He thinks it's OK to drink alcohol at every meal, and she can't stand it. She thinks it's fine to tell people someone's not home when a call comes in, and he thinks that's lying. He wants to attend church every Sunday, and she likes to go only at Christmas and Easter.

 Complete the sentence by placing an *x* on the line below.
In our marriage, our values …

Are close   Are very different

It's important to remember not all differences can be eliminated. In such cases, it's healthy to say to each other, "We'll never agree on this issue, but I still love you. I hope we can learn more about each other's feelings and needs through this conflict."

4. Competition

Conflict can grow out of competition. Some people can't stand to lose at anything, even in a "casual" game of checkers. Or perhaps the husband is bothered by the fact that his wife earns more than he does, and he's determined to outdo her in that area.

Complete the sentence by placing an *x* on the lines below each one.
In our marriage, I …

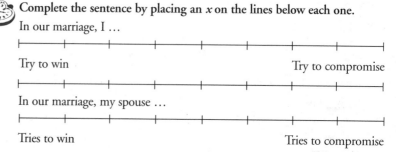

Try to win   Try to compromise

In our marriage, my spouse …

Tries to win   Tries to compromise

5. Personal Differences

Couples fight over normal male-female differences and normal personality differences. We can count on those two areas to bring a continual flow of conflict. That's why I took weeks 8 and 9 to show how to understand each other and then use that understanding to make love last rather than to tear the relationship apart.

 Complete the sentence by placing an *x* on the line below.
Our differences …

Cause conflict   Are accepted

6. Misunderstood Feelings and Unmet Needs

I believe this is the major reason for conflict—when one (or more likely both) spouses have unmet needs. Dr. Stephen Covey says this in a different way. He claims that all conflicts are caused by unfulfilled expectations in "roles and goals."[2] One spouse may think, *That's not what you're supposed to do in our relationship. I fix the car, and you fix the meals.* Or one may say to the other, "I've always wanted to go on in my education. You knew that. We'll just have to go without that new couch until I finish." We expect others to know our needs and feelings, in fact, even if we haven't mentioned them.

 Complete the sentence by placing an *x* on the line below.
In our marriage we …

Share feelings   Don't share feelings

It's been extremely helpful to me to understand that whenever I'm in conflict with someone, one or two things are occurring: Someone's feelings aren't being valued and understood or someone's needs are not being valued and met.

Knowing and meeting your mate's (and children's) needs is a basic part of intimacy, and it's also important that your needs are understood and you're reasonably sure they'll be met. (That's why the first part of this study is so vital; it gives us a plan for handling our feelings and needs, including those that cannot possibly be met by a mate.) But needs unnecessarily go unmet when we get too busy—when spouse and kids aren't getting enough time with us or there's just not enough conversation.

List two or three important needs you have in your marriage.

_____

_____

List two or three important needs your spouse has in your marriage.

_____

_____

*K*nowing and meeting your mate's needs is a basic part of intimacy.

These six causes of conflict are rooted in the heart. The Bible identifies some heart issues at the core of conflict.

 Read the following Scripture from James 4:1-10. Underline one or two areas that are heart problems for you.

What causes fights and quarrels among you? Don't they come from your desires that battle within you? You want something but don't get it. You kill and covet, but you cannot have what you want. You quarrel and fight. You do not have, because you do not ask God. When you ask, you do not receive, because you ask with wrong motives, that you may spend what you get on your pleasures.

You adulterous people, don't you know that friendship with the world is hatred toward God? Anyone who chooses to be a friend of the world becomes an enemy of God. Or do you think Scripture says without reason that the spirit he caused to live within us envies immensely? But he gives us more grace. That is why Scripture says:

"God opposes the proud
but gives grace to the humble."

Submit yourselves, then, to God. Resist the devil and he will flee from you. Come near to God and he will come near to you. Wash your hands, you sinners, and purify your hearts, you double-minded. Grieve, mourn and wail. Change your laughter to mourning and your joy to gloom. Humble yourselves before the Lord, and he will lift you up.

 Check which of the causes of conflict most often surfaces in your marriage?

❏ Power and control ❏ Insecurity

❏ Differences in value ❏ Competition

❏ Personal differences ❏ Misunderstood feelings and unmet needs

What would God have you do as a result of today's study?

_____

_____

Pray to the Lord and ask for direction to confront the cause of conflict in your marriage.

---

[1]Carol Rubin and Jeffrey Rubin, *When Families Fight: How to Handle Conflict with Those You Love* (New York: Ballantine, 1989), 39-60.
[2]Stephen R. Covey, *The Seven Habits of Highly Effective People*, audio version (New York: Simon & Schuster Sound Ideas, 1989).

"Submit yourselves to God. … Come near to God and he will come near to you" (James 4:7-8).

Day 3
The Circle of Conflict

Growing out of one or more of the causes we studied yesterday, conflict tends to go in a circle. Let me show you what I mean with a typical example. A wife with a "perfectionist" personality needs a certain measure of neatness and order in her home, but her "carefree" husband couldn't care less. So the woman might say something like, "I am so frustrated around this house! Look at this mess! Nobody ever picks up anything!"

But the husband, who may be clueless, placing less value in or having less need for neatness, may say, "Yeah, you know what? If you would just get better organized around here, you wouldn't be so frustrated." Or he may ask, "You need more energy? Are you still taking those vitamins we spent all that money for?" "Are you getting your rest?" Or simply, "What's the big deal?" Mr. Fix-it offers solutions and opinions but finds it hard to get down to discussing feelings or needs.

As a pattern, this couple may easily exchange clichés and facts, but when they get to opinions, *wham,* tension flares based on disagreement. If they're like a lot of couples (maybe most), they may go silent for a while or escalate to a hotter conflict. They don't enjoy conflict. One spouse may not feel safe enough to get to the deeper levels—expressing feelings or needs. One may have little hope that expressing feelings will make any change. One may express needs inappropriately, in a rage. One, again, may be clueless that feelings and unmet needs have anything to do with the problem.

For any number of reasons, the couple moves back to clichés, because that's safe. Then they share some facts, followed by opinions again, and *boom*—back to conflict. They circle in those three areas and never go to the deep levels of communication where disagreements can lead to a closer, more intimate bond—deeper intimacy.

Conflict tends to circle in the higher levels of communication, never going to the deeper levels where disagreement can lead to a closer, more intimate bond.

List two or three "starters" you and your spouse use in conflict that need to be avoided in the future. I'll start you off with a list you can check. Then you can add your own.

❑ "You never _____" or "You always _____."
❑ "You just don't understand."
❑ "You don't care how I think or feel."
❑ "You just go and do whatever you want no matter what we decide."
❑ "Remember when you _____?"

Now list your own pet conflict starters:

_____

_____

_____

We're not doomed to an endless cycle of *unresolved* conflict. But if we're stuck on a merry-go-round, we will need to take the risk of stepping out of old patterns.

A key biblical concept here is *repentance*. To repent means "to go in the opposite direction." In other words, you repent of what you are doing wrong. You do the right. And you don't return to the circles of conflict. Second Corinthians 7:10 says, "Godly sorrow brings repentance that leads to salvation and leaves no regret, but worldly sorrow brings death." Paul continues to write that certain attitudes and feelings were a part of the sorrow and repentance: "See what this godly sorrow has produced in you: what earnestness, what eagerness to clear yourselves, what indignation, what alarm, what longing, what concern, what readiness to see justice done. At every point, you have proved yourselves to be innocent in this matter" (2 Corinthians 7:11).

 Describe a feeling, attitude, or verbal cliché you use in conflict in your marriage.

_____

_____

 If you wish to repent and let go of it, check the responses you will have in the future when that temptation to provoke conflict arises in you.

- ❏ Earnestness to repent
- ❏ Sorrow at hurting another person
- ❏ Eagerness to clear yourself of sin
- ❏ Indignation at your own wrongful attitude or behavior
- ❏ Alarm that you are entering into a circle of conflict
- ❏ Longing to do what is right
- ❏ Readiness for doing what is just
- ❏ Desire to be innocent and pure

 Pray asking God to give you a willingness to repent (go in the opposite direction) when you find yourself entering into a circle of conflict.

Day 4
Door Slammers and Pearls

For a marriage to grow as a result of conflict—for healing to occur after conflict—we need to learn to move toward resolution. But some patterns just don't do the job as well as we'd like.

What doesn't work for healing resolution?

1. For starters, *withdrawing* into yourself. I used to do this because it's what I often saw my father do. If you withdraw, however, you don't get your needs met, your spouse's needs don't get met, and your relationship suffers. So withdrawing is not the solution.

Repent *means to go in the opposite direction.*

2. *Yielding—giving in*—isn't a satisfactory pattern either. While one person wins and therefore peace prevails for a season, the other person loses, and ultimately, the relationship also loses. If both partners don't win, the relationship is weakened.

3. A third pattern? You could be the winner—the opposite of yielding. But again, one of you ends up a loser, so the relationship loses. How about *compromise?* Isn't that healthy? Sometimes you just don't have time to resolve the issue right then, so you each settle for half a loaf. But remember that compromise is only a temporary solution, because it's still a win-lose situation for both of you and for your relationship. Postponing is OK, but if you don't get back to the dispute, you lose a doorway to a deeper intimacy that we'll discuss in a minute.

 Look over the list of patterns. Write down which one of the three you and your mate try most often that does not work.

_____

Door Slammers

A few modes of operation predictably shut and lock the doorway to intimacy. One of the most common is the use of accusatory "you statements": *"You always do this." "You never remember that." "As far as I'm concerned, you'll never change."* They immediately put the other person on the defensive. If you want to draw closer, the key is to use "I statements"—"I feel … " or "I need …"

 Change the following "you statement" into an "I statement."
"You're always late! I can't believe it. Why do you do this? You'll never change!"

"I _____

_____

If the husband is late for dinner, the wife might say, "I feel uneasy, or uncomfortable, when that happens, because I don't know where you are. I'm concerned about you when you don't call …" The "you statement" will only make him want to run away or fight back.

Sarcasm, disrespect, and screaming are all door slammers, too. Denying the conflict isn't the solution, but neither is a temper tantrum.

"Studies of the family by Murray Straus have shown that individuals who vent their anger tend, over time, to produce more and more anger and to vent it more and more vigorously until they finally resort to physical violence. … Venting anger almost invariably gets the other person angry too, and then you are going to need more and more anger to continue the fight."[1]

Kindness, respect, and calmness, on the other hand, are keys that open the door. Exactly what works best for you and your spouse is something you can work out on your own. Such keys will improve all your conversations, but they'll be especially valuable during times of conflict.

"You statements" shut the doorway to intimacy, immediately putting the other person on the defensive.

Key Lists

My son Greg and I have developed a set of keys to the doorway of intimacy in connection with his doctoral studies in psychology. I'll show you our list of 14 suggestions that have worked for us and many others. Then I'll give you a similar list by Dr. Harriet Lerner, who is one of the leaders in the field of conflict resolution. From these two lists, you and your spouse can make your own list of rules. If "rules" seems too harsh a word, think in terms of "keys to intimacy."

The Smalley "Fighting Rules"

1. First clarify what the actual conflict is. Make sure that you *understand* your partner's feelings and needs as clearly as you can before proceeding to a resolution. *Listening* is vital here!

2. Stick to the issue at hand. Don't dredge up past hurts or problems, whether real or perceived. But if you tend to veer off the issue, you might want to see if there is any other key factor in this conflict, such as fatigue, low estrogen, low blood sugar, stress, work problems, or spiritual or emotional issues.

3. Maintain as much tender physical contact as possible (like holding hands).

4. Avoid sarcasm.

5. Avoid "you" statements. Use the words "I feel" or "I think." No past or future predictions ("You always …" "You won't ever …").

6. Don't use "hysterical" statements or exaggerations. ("This will never work out." "You're just like your father.")

7. Resolve any hurt feelings before continuing the conflict discussion. ("I shouldn't have said that. Will you forgive me?")

8. Don't resort to name calling. Don't allow the conflict to escalate your tempers. If this happens, agree to continue the discussion later.

9. Avoid power statements and actions. For example: "I quit!" "You sleep on the couch tonight!" "You're killing me!" "I hate you!"

10. Don't use the silent treatment.

11. Keep your arguments as private as possible to avoid embarrassment.

12. Use the "drive-through talking" method of communication when arguing (repeat back what you think the other person is saying). This is key!

13. Resolve your conflicts with win-win solutions. Both agree with the solution or outcome of the argument.

14. Above all, strive to reflect honor in all your words and actions during the resolution of your conflicts.

 Look over this list. Circle the numbers of the three or more rules that you would like to see implemented in your marriage. Underline the three rules you and your spouse are best at keeping.

On the following page is another helpful list. Rate yourself on a scale of 1 to 5 on this list. Give yourself 5 if you always keep this rule and 1 if you never keep it.

Making Love Last Forever

Dr. Harriet Lerner's Key Rules

Rating

_____ 1. Do speak up when an issue is important to you.

_____ 2. Don't strike while the iron is hot. (Watch your timing.)

_____ 3. Do take time to think about the problem and to clarify your position.

_____ 4. Don't use "below-the-belt" tactics.

_____ 5. Do speak in "I" language.

_____ 6. Don't make vague requests.

_____ 7. Do try to appreciate the fact that people are different.

_____ 8. Don't participate in intellectual arguments that go nowhere.

_____ 9. Do recognize that each person is responsible for his/her own behavior.

_____ 10. Don't tell another person what he or she thinks or feels or "should" think or feel.

_____ 11. Do try to avoid speaking through a third party (someone speaking for you and you're not there to clarify).

_____ 12. Don't expect change to come from hit-and-run confrontations.[2]

 How many 5s do you have? How many 1s? Circle the number by the rule that you want to implement in your marriage.

> *The underlying rule for a long, happy marriage: Keep anger levels low every day!*

Master Key

When it comes to conflict resolution, everything I say here is based on an underlying rule for a long, happy marriage: *Keep anger levels low every day!*

Doing that calls for communication—primarily at the deepest level, where one talks about feelings and needs. It calls for openness and for forgiveness—a desire for the relationship to be the best it can be.

Scripture is full of wisdom. You may be familiar with the passage about anger: " 'In your anger, do not sin': Do not let the sun go down while you are still angry" (Ephesians 4:26). That is a commentary of sorts on an even older line of poetry:

"In your anger do not sin;

when you are on your beds,

search your hearts and be silent" [be at peace] (Psalm 4:4).

If anger and its symptoms of distance and control are underlying themes of your marriage, I suggest you "search your hearts" and go back to the issues I addressed in part 1 (but also keep reading). If marital conflicts ever resort to violence, see a marriage counselor to work through underlying issues.

Pearls from Conflict

The disputes—disagreements—in your marriage will never vanish. But there are pearls to be found in those disputes. That's one word picture. Another I used above: *Conflicts can be doorways to intimacy.* Here's how. (I give special thanks to Dr. Gary Oliver for his insights and research in this area.)

Conflict is a doorway into intimacy because it's a way to discover who a person is. As soon as we hit the wall and are in conflict, we have to open a door so we can walk through it to find out what the other person feels and needs. Instead of reverting to silence or clichés, we can adopt an attitude that says, "I'm kind of glad we're having this conflict, because it'll result in both of us knowing more about each other and loving each other more."

Conflict is one of the best ways to take us beyond *feelings* all the way to *needs*.

One of the best ways I know to meet another person's needs is by developing your own *love language*. This works only if your relationship is fairly healthy to begin with; if it's not, you might not be willing to give this a try. But if things are going reasonably well, this can be great.

As I've already mentioned, normal conflicts can reveal that my feelings or my needs are not being understood or valued. As we work through a conflict—discovering deep feelings and needs—we can develop a love language based on the alphabet of that new knowledge.

Or think again in terms of pearls: Over years of marriage, this love language becomes like a necklace, made from the pearls hunted and found after conflicts, in answer to the question "What can I do to show you I love you?"

As a result of conflict, over time, create a love language. Here's how. You and your spouse should each list 5 to 10 practical and specific things you would like to have the other person do for you—things you believe will really meet your needs. You agree: "This makes me feel as if you love me. I have a need, and when you do this, it meets that need." Your mate doing one of these for you (or vice versa) expresses love and honor.

Complete these lists:

Five things I would like my spouse to do for me that will meet my needs:

_____   _____
_____   _____
_____

Five things I need to do to meet my spouse's needs:

_____   _____
_____   _____
_____

Write this list out and post it where it will serve as a daily reminder. It might be in your closet if you don't want everybody in the world to see it. Or you can put it on your refrigerator. But put it in a place where you can be reminded every day.

I'll give more specific examples of what might be on your love-language list in week 12, where we discuss the energizing concept of "marital banking."

Before I go on, I pause one more time to address any skeptical reader. *Wait*, you say, *you don't know my husband. He knows how I feel, he knows what I need, he just doesn't give a rip about anything but himself.*

Whoa! If that's your view of life, I make several reminders and suggestions. First, consider this question: *Are you sure?* Have you really talked about underlying priorities? Have you listened to your mate's feelings and needs? Have you *clearly* expressed yours? Can you see baby steps of progress that you can praise?

 Write a prayer asking God to help you find pearls in the conflicts you may encounter in your marriage.

_____

_____

---

[1] David and Vera Mace, *How to Have a Happy Marriage* (Nashville: Abingdon, 1977), 112.
[2] Harriet G. Lerner, *The Dance of Anger* (New York: Harper & Row, 1985), 199-201.

Day 5
Conflicts: Opportunities to Express Affection

Conflicts can open a doorway to intimacy by surfacing feelings and needs. But it also provides an opportunity to express physical and emotional affection. We all need to be hugged. We all need to be loved on.

To illustrate this point, let me give an example of how not to do it. A young husband told me about a conflict he and his wife had before they married. She invited him to dinner at her place, where she baked lasagna. He got to the dinner table, she served the lasagna—which turned out to be as hard as a brick. So he said, trying to inject a little levity into the situation, "Do you serve chain saws with this?"

As you might imagine, she immediately got up, and ran down the hall, crying. He called after her, "And another thing, enough of this sensitivity stuff!"

Believe it or not, he proposed to her later that same night, and she said *yes*. (Was she blind or what?) But at the moment, this was a big conflict that instantly brought her feelings and needs to the surface.

What could the young man have done at that point to help the situation? He could have maintained his pride and ignored the conflict. Would that have been wise?

 Pride can get in the way of conflict resolution. Take a moment to read these Proverbs. Summarize what they say about pride.

<u>ABOUT PRIDE</u>

Pride only breeds quarrels, but wisdom   _____
is found in those who take advice   _____
(Proverbs 13:10).   _____

Pride goes before destruction, a haughty spirit before a fall (Proverbs 16:18).

_____

_____

A man's pride brings him low, but a man of lowly spirit gains honor (Proverbs 29:23).

_____

_____

_____

He could have put his arm around her, held her, and said, "I can't believe I say things like that. I don't know how I learned to be so sarcastic, but I don't want to hurt you. Will you forgive me?" She might need some time to warm up (or cool down). But his contrite spirit and gentle touch would have started the healing and resolving process.

Norma and I use this practical step-by-step method for conflict resolution every time we get into a big disagreement over some major issue, such as where to live, buying a car, or changing churches. Our approach involves making two lists. Let me explain.

Suppose our disagreement is about how to parent our children, which was often the case in years gone by. I was a tolerant father in the sense of not having a lot of rules, because that's the way I was raised. Norma, on the other hand, wanted a little more order in the home. As the kids grew older, I would also start pushing them to get out and do various activities. But Norma would say, "I don't think they're old enough. They're not ready yet."

I remember the time she expressed her concern with a great word picture. "You know how this makes me feel?" she said. "I feel like I'm the mother bird in a nest up in the tree. We've got these three little birds in here. And papa bird flies in now and then and says, 'Hey, why don't you guys get out and do some things? It would be boring to me to be in a nest all the time. You've got to jump out and enjoy yourself.' But I know how mature their feathers and bones are. I know where all the cats in the neighborhood are. And if you push our chicks out now, they're going to hit the ground and get hurt or gobbled up in a hurry."

Whenever we got into a big conflict like that, we would pull out a blank sheet of typewriter paper and draw a line down the middle, dividing it in half. At the top, on one side of the line, we would write, "All the Reasons We Should Do This." At the top on the other side, we would write, "All the Reasons We Shouldn't Do This."

In listing reasons, we would start by gathering all the facts. Then we would go deeper and find the feelings involved. We'd say, "Well, I feel this about that idea." Finally, we'd get to the level of needs: "I have a need, and if we do that, it will mess with my need."

Before long, we would have 18 to 20 reasons on one side of the paper, and maybe 15 to 18 on the other. Having it all down on paper—both the pros and the cons—and knowing we were both heard and valued, usually helped us resolve our conflict. We didn't have to win or lose. Maybe it was Norma's idea that we went with, or maybe it was mine. But I never felt I was compromising or giving in. I always felt it was the right thing to do. As soon as all the facts are on one piece of paper, it was

Conflict provides an opportunity to express physical and emotional affection.

pretty obvious what ought to happen. The facts won or lost, not us. This method objectified the conflict and took it further out of the emotional range.

Sometimes, however, if we were still deadlocked on an important issue or if the kids didn't like the outcome, we would need to take this method one step further. We would then rank each statement on both sides of the line. We would ask the question of each statement, "Is that a factor that will have long-lasting effects?" If we believed it would affect us for more than 10 years, we'd put an "L" (for *long-lasting*) beside the statement. If we believed there was only a temporary effect, we'd put a "T" (for *temporary*) beside the statement. When we were finished marking each item, pro and con, we'd add up the "L" and "T" marks and see which side won. This analysis seemed to resolve the issue every time, even with the kids involved.

 Would this work for you and your spouse? Briefly describe how you might adapt this process to your marriage.

Summary

Remember the bad news at the beginning of the week? *Conflicts are inevitable in any relationship.* But the good news overrides the bad: I challenge you to see any disagreements with your spouse as a doorway to intimacy. Let conflicts be that doorway into a better understanding of how you both feel and what you each need.

In the last of his *Chronicles of Narnia* series (*The Last Battle*), C. S. Lewis describes his characters facing a battle to end all battles. But at a strategic point they walked through a doorway into a stable; some people claimed the stable held a life-threatening creature. But once through that doorway, they discovered "In reality they stood on grass, the deep blue sky was overhead, and the air which blew gently on their faces was that of a day in early summer."[1] Walking through that door had taken them to a heavenly kingdom. And once there, they could continue to go "further up and further in,"[2] making increasingly awesome—wonderful—new discoveries that they couldn't have fathomed before they had walked through that seemingly threatening door.

That's how it can be in a marriage. Those conflicts have the potential for drawing you and your spouse closer and closer to each other. There's not a monster behind your conflicts. It's a matter of opening the door to intimacy—not closing it, slamming it, or locking it.

 Pray, thanking God for your spouse and the gift of marriage. Seek God's direction as you and your spouse determine how you will resolve conflict in your marriage.

Let conflicts be the doorway into a better understanding of how you and your mate feel and what you each need.

---

[1]C.S. Lewis, *The Last Battle* (New York: Macmillan, Collier, 1956; 1970), 136.
[2]Ibid., 161.

Couple Time

For you to complete

The area of conflict that most affects our marriage is:

_____

One way I can help us break the circle of conflict is:

_____

One door slammer I must avoid is:

_____

One technique I learned in conflict resolution is:

_____

The most important thing I need to repent of in our marriage is:

_____

The most important way for me to express affection for my spouse is:

_____

For you to share with your spouse

1. Share with each other how you completed the section above.

2. Share with each other how you filled in the responses on day 2.

3. Discuss together the following questions:
   - How can we lessen some areas of conflict?
   - What specific steps can we suggest to each other for growing closer together in the midst of conflict?
   - How can each of us more honestly share and meet our needs with each other?

4. Each of you pray out loud thanking and praising God for the other.

Was That as Good for You as It Was for Me?

Before Dennis and Lois even sat down in my counseling office, I knew what we were going to be talking about. There's a certain hesitation, a betraying look of sheepishness, that clearly signals when a couple needs to discuss one of the most difficult and embarrassing topics in marriage. Dennis and Lois had problems in their sexual relationship, a situation that isn't uncommon, even in couples that look as if they have it all. Like Dennis and Lois—one handsome, intense couple. I guessed them to be in their early 30s. Lois was attractive in her jeans and oversized sweater. Dennis was in khakis and a gold shirt from an exclusive country club.

"Where should we begin?" I asked, watching them try to get comfortable.

"I'll start," Dennis volunteered. He took a deep breath, then said, "I haven't had sex in so long, I forget how it goes!"

Lois burst into tears. After half a minute or so, she regained her composure enough to say, "That's not true. Dennis tends to exaggerate when he's angry."

"Tell me about it," I said.

"We've been married for 11 years," she said, "and sex was really good for both of us in the beginning."

"Would you agree, Dennis?" I asked.

"Yeah," he replied, "and that's part of the problem. I know how good it can be, but it's just not that way anymore."

"Go on, Lois," I said.

"I guess the best way to put it is that we began to feel two very different levels of need for sex," Lois said sadly, looking at the floor. "I was always tired, fighting depression, feeling like a fat, old cow. And Dennis, even with his long hours at the office, still seemed to want sex a lot—or at least a lot more than I did. For a while I tried to keep up with him, but I found I was getting angry at his attitude. I felt he was being demanding and extremely selfish about the whole thing.

"The more we fought about it, the more we distanced ourselves from each other. Even now, when we do have sex, it's not very satisfying for either one of us, but it's particularly unsatisfying for me. I'm just lying there, letting him have his fun."

Silence hung in the air for a few moments before I asked Dennis for his view of their dilemma.

"She's got it pretty straight," Dennis agreed. "I guess I sound like a big heel when I hear how she tells the story. But you know how a man gets. We go so long without sex, and I feel like I'm gonna burst!"

His anger had taken him as far from Lois as he could get. In a matter of moments, this husband and wife who had sat down together were at the opposite ends of my couch.

Dennis and Lois were going through experiences common to a couple married 11 years. Things change. People change. Dennis and Lois had changed. The more they could understand those changes, the better their chances of improving their life together, including their sexual relationship. I used much of the material in this week's study in counseling sessions with Dennis and Lois. We spent several sessions together and their sexual relationship started to improve before we ever talked directly about that aspect of their marriage.

Nothing in marriage is more misunderstood than the sexual union.

Nothing in marriage is more misunderstood than the sexual union. It's more than the physical act that sexually unites a couple. And probably the most important thing Dennis and Lois learned is that a sexual relationship is a mirror of an entire marital relationship. They weren't struggling with a sexual problem as much as they were with relational issues that were diminishing their sexual enjoyment. They needed to see sex in the larger context of their whole marriage. There are actually four areas of the sexual relationship that need to be developed in concert with one another if a couple is to achieve maximum satisfaction. As Dennis and Lois concentrated on other areas of their relationship first, their sexual life improved.

As you study this week, you will:
- develop a knowledge of the basic differences in how you view sex as a couple;
- understand that verbal and emotional intimacy are vital to sexual satisfaction;
- learn how physical and sexual intimacy are vital to sexual satisfaction;
- develop an attitude of cooperation in improving sexual intimacy;
- uncover how to develop an attitude of commitment to one another in order to improve your marriage relationship.

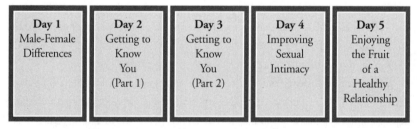

Day 1 Male-Female Differences	**Day 2** Getting to Know You (Part 1)	**Day 3** Getting to Know You (Part 2)	**Day 4** Improving Sexual Intimacy	**Day 5** Enjoying the Fruit of a Healthy Relationship

I am praying that you will discover in your marriage the joy and truth of God's intention for marriage:

"For this reason a man will leave his father and mother and be united to his wife, and they will become one flesh. The man and his wife were both naked, and they felt no shame" (Genesis 2:24-25).

Day 1
Male-Female Differences

In an ongoing study I've conducted with hundreds of couples over the years, I ask men and women privately and in groups how they would feel if they knew they would never again have sex with their mates. Almost all the women say, "It's really no big deal if I never have sex again with my husband." But they add quickly that it would be a big deal if they were never touched or kissed or romanced again.

When I ask men the same question, they're almost always incredulous. "Give up sex?" they say. "No way!" To ask a man to give up sex is to ask him to give up eating.

Why this huge difference between the views of men and women? It's not easy for some women to understand what testosterone does to a man. The hormone fires up a man sexually. (I know the image of the testosterone-driven male is a stereotype, but in this case it's an accurate one.) The level of testosterone drops in most men around the age of 40, but many men have been shown to have significant amounts far into their 80s!

To give wives a better idea, imagine you've just been informed by telegram that you've won the grand prize in a national contest. You and your husband will be whisked off to a tropical island for 10 days of first-class service at a four-star resort. You'll also be given $1,500 a day in spending money, unlimited luxury limousine service—in other words, the works! Naturally, you can't wait for your husband to walk in the door so you can tell him the good news.

Now imagine that when he does come home, you greet him by saying you have some wonderful news. But he responds, "Not now, dear. I'm really tired, so I think I'm going to take a nap." As he walks to the bedroom, he adds, "Don't tell anyone else the news. I want to be the first to hear it."

When I ask the women in a seminar audience how they would feel in this situation, most say they would be highly frustrated.

A man's testosterone level makes him feel as if he has won the grand prize … *almost every day!* He can't wait to "tell" you about it. But a disinterested wife responds, "Let's talk about it tomorrow." Imagine the way that makes him feel. Some husbands are so highly testosterone-loaded that they're literally trembling on the other side of the bed while you're drifting off to sleep. Perhaps that will help you understand why he gets frustrated when you put off his physical advances.

 What do you believe contributes to good sex? List what you believe makes sex satisfying for both partners.

FOR MEN	FOR WOMEN
_____	_____
_____	_____
_____	_____
_____	_____
_____	_____

How would you feel if you knew you would never again have sex with your mate?

What does Scripture say about the importance of the physical or sexual relationship in marriage? Let's explore this together. Read 1 Corinthians 7:3-5. Summarize what this passage teaches concerning a husband's and wife's responsibility in the marriage relationship.

> The husband should fulfill his marital duty to his wife, and likewise the wife to her husband. In the same way, the husband's body does not belong to him alone but also to his wife. Do not deprive each other except by mutual consent and for a time so that you may devote yourselves to prayer.

_____

_____

Sex is more than a physical act.

 What are your expectations sexually in your marriage? Make a list of two or three things you expect out of your physical relationship in marriage.

_____

_____

_____

If there is a mostly unfulfilled expectation, circle it. You will share your list later with your spouse. Begin thinking about how you will answer this question. What are you willing to do to meet your spouse's realistic expectation about sex in your marriage? Check those things you are willing to work at.

❑ Talk openly about our expectations
❑ Be willing to compromise
❑ Pray with my spouse about our differing expectations
❑ Seek counseling if necessary
❑ Other: _____

 Close in prayer thanking God for physical intimacy in marriage.

Day 2
Getting to Know You (Part 1)

Sex is more than a physical act. Good sex is the reflection of a good relationship. It's the icing on top of what's right in a marriage. Satisfying sex is admiring a trophy fish after all the skills went into catching it. I've learned that fulfilling sex has at least four separate aspects that work together—they must work together if we are to catch the "biggest ones."

Four aspects of intercourse contribute to good sex. We shall explore two of them today—verbal and emotional intercourse. As Denver psychologist Gary Oliver once said to me in terms of marriage, "All of life is foreplay."

Intercourse literally means "to get to know someone intimately." In our culture, we have reduced the word to refer only to the act of sex. Conversely, we've nearly forgotten a traditional meaning of the verb *to know*—which was "to have sexual intercourse." Biblical history starts the whole human lineage with this line: "Adam knew Eve his wife; and she conceived" (Genesis 4:1, KJV). The two words *intercourse* and *knowledge* are closely aligned.

For now, let's return to a simpler day when the word *intercourse* had a broader meaning. A conservative, small town in the middle of Pennsylvania Amish country is named Intercourse—and it's not referring to sex.

Verbal Intercourse

In earlier times, people used *intercourse* when speaking of an intimate conversation. Obviously, we have to be sensitive to our current culture, so it's not advisable to have a discussion with your next-door neighbor and then yell over the fence, "It sure was good having intercourse with you earlier today!"

But verbal intercourse is vital to a healthy sex life. It involves getting to know your mate through conversation and spending time together. This is especially significant to most women, who are amazed that men can have sex at almost any time without regard to the quality of the relationship. The women usually want to connect with their partners through verbal intimacy before they can enjoy the physical act. Knowing this, years ago I decided I'd do everything right. …

The first time Norma and I visited Hawaii, I envisioned a vacation filled with sexual passion. I knew that Norma loved to sightsee, so on one of our first days there, I invited her to drive around the island of Maui. She was thrilled.

We drove from the southern part of Maui, where our hotel was, all the way to the northern beaches. We talked, laughed, saw whales, and discovered roads and little villages that weren't even on the maps! It was a wonderful time of verbal intimacy. And as a male, I knew this might lead to sexual intimacy later on.

As we started making our way back to our hotel, however, I discovered that the gas gauge in our rental car was on *E.* I did my best to keep this information from Norma, not wanting to ruin the moment or jeopardize the rest of the day!

She began to get suspicious, however, when I started coasting down as many hills as I could. "Why are you taking the car out of gear?" she asked.

"Oh, no reason," I countered. "Just another way to have some fun!"

But the further we drove with no gas station in sight, the more nervous I got. Then I suddenly felt as if we were completely out of gas. I went to put the car in neutral again, but thanks to my nervousness, I forgot that this was a rental car, an automatic, not the stick-shift I was used to. Full-force I hit what I thought was the clutch. Unfortunately it was the brake. The car screeched to a halt in the middle of the road, throwing Norma's head right into the dashboard. (This was before the days of seatbelt laws.)

Intercourse literally means "to get to know someone intimately."

She wasn't injured, but she screamed, "Gary, what are you doing?"

I didn't have the courage to say what I was thinking, which was, *I'm ruining any chance I had for sex tonight!* Rather, I confessed the gas-tank problem, and we just sat back and laughed together. And I didn't ruin the day or night after all.

What makes a vacation like that so special? For many couples, it's the only time during the year that they carve out uninterrupted time to talk and listen to each other. Far away from phones, FAXes, and appointments, it's a rare opportunity for relaxation and getting reacquainted.

What's good for vacations is also good for life. As a couple, work at giving each other the time you need to relax, talk, and listen to each other.

Let's summarize some ways that busy couples can make time for verbal intercourse. After each idea, check how often you do this.

Busy couples need to make time for verbal intercourse.

TWELVE WAYS TO FIND TIME TO TALK TO YOUR SPOUSE

1. You're both home at the end of the day. Set aside a 15-minute period at some point to discuss—reflect on—your respective day's activities.
   ❑ Do this often   ❑ Do this sometimes   ❑ Rarely or never do this

2. Turn the TV *off* during dinner to encourage conversation. For that hour, let the answering machine take all phone calls except emergencies.
   ❑ Do this often   ❑ Do this sometimes   ❑ Rarely or never do this

3. Write a monthly date night in your schedule book that *cannot* be broken.
   ❑ Do this often   ❑ Do this sometimes   ❑ Rarely or never do this

4. If your schedule permits, get together for lunch once a week—even if you're just brown-bagging it in the park.
   ❑ Do this often   ❑ Do this sometimes   ❑ Rarely or never do this

5. As a couple, attend one of your children's sporting events. It's amazing how conversation can develop while you sit and watch or travel to and from the game.
   ❑ Do this often   ❑ Do this sometimes   ❑ Rarely or never do this

6. Take a walk together after dinner. It's a good time to talk, and exercise!
   ❑ Do this often   ❑ Do this sometimes   ❑ Rarely or never do this

7. If you are allowed flexibility in your work schedule, go in late one day—after the kids have gone to school. Enjoy time together with your spouse.
   ❑ Do this often   ❑ Do this sometimes   ❑ Rarely or never do this

8. Read a magazine article or book together that you both feel will stimulate a discussion.
   ❑ Do this often   ❑ Do this sometimes   ❑ Rarely or never do this

Making Love Last Forever

9. Use baby-sitters just to give you time alone to talk.
   ❏ Do this often   ❏ Do this sometimes   ❏ Rarely or never do this

10. Write each other little notes that begin, "I have something really amazing to talk with you about the next time we're together."
    ❏ Do this often   ❏ Do this sometimes   ❏ Rarely or never do this

11. Once or twice a year, plan a weekend getaway for just the two of you.
    ❏ Do this often   ❏ Do this sometimes   ❏ Rarely or never do this

12. Ask your best friend to hold you accountable to meet with your mate at least once a week for a meaningful conversation.
    ❏ Do this often   ❏ Do this sometimes   ❏ Rarely or never do this

Now go back over this list and circle one or two ideas that you will start working on right away.

For more ideas, ask people whom you respect how they find the time to talk as a couple. You may be surprised at their unique suggestions.

Emotional Intercourse

Sharing deep feelings with each other is emotional intercourse, and it's vital to sexual satisfaction. It's that sense of connectedness that occurs when you're both tracking on the same emotional level. This involves conversations that deal with more than facts alone. Any conversation might start with facts. Then any fact in a relationship can be connected to emotions with the question: "How does that set of facts make you feel?" This is especially significant to women. They are often most responsive to sexual intercourse when the entire relationship is open and loving—when they feel that their husband understands and values their feelings.

Dave and Vicki were struggling with this issue when Dave first came to see me. "I'll shoot straight with you, Gary," he said. "I'm not getting any sex from my wife, and I'm very frustrated."

As I listened to him explain his situation, I suggested he go back to his wife and seek to communicate his feelings through the use of an emotional word picture. "The analogy will get out on the table your deep feelings," I told him.

So that's exactly what he did. And then she responded with a powerful word picture of her own.

"Honey, we have a problem," he told her that night. "I want you to hear how I describe it."

"All right," Vicki agreed.

"When I'm away from you at work, I feel like I'm out in the desert. It's steaming hot, and I'm slowly baking. But when I get home, I feel like I've entered an oasis."

Vicki smiled and said, "Well, that's good."

"Not really," Dave went on. "You see, when I come home, you look so good to me that I want to enjoy our relationship completely."

Sharing deep feelings with each other is emotional intercourse, and it's vital to sexual satisfaction.

"Meaning what?" she asked.

"Sex," Dave answered. "We don't have sex anymore, so I feel that part of the oasis is a mirage. The beauty of the oasis doesn't all seem to exist."

He sat there for a moment in silence. As tenderly as he could, he asked her, "How can I make the mirage back into the real oasis we once had?"

Vicki had been listening, and they were connecting on an emotional level. After a minute she responded, "I'll tell you how to return to the oasis. I'll even do for you what you just did for me. I'll paint an emotional word picture to make it clear.

"I feel as if I'm one of your prized rare books from the 19th century," she began. "Early in our marriage, you would pick me up and admire me, make sure I was free from dust, polish the gold-leaf edges, and just take good care of me overall."

Dave smiled at her knowingly.

"But something has happened to that rare book," she continued. "You don't care for it the way you used to. It has become dusty sitting on the shelf. The gold leaf is covered with a tarnish that could be removed if it just had a little attention."

She was getting through to him for the first time in a long while, because he responded, "How can I give this book more of the attention it deserves?" Vicki was able to tell him what was important to her—things like saying "I love you," and even things that Dave considered unrelated, like spending time with the kids. She also remembered fondly the days when Dave used to send her flowers and cards.

The more the two of them talked on a deep emotional level, the more they were able to help each other. This communication at the deep levels of feelings and needs changed Dave and Vicki's sexual relationship into a richer, fuller, and mutually satisfying one. It's still not perfect, but then I've never met a couple for which it was.

 One of the most beautiful, emotional love pictures in all of literature can be found in the Bible. The Song of Songs is a powerful emotional word picture of the love between a husband and wife. Read the following sample test and then compose a word picture that expresses the way you feel about your spouse.

> Like a lily among thorns
>> is my darling among the maidens.
> Like an apple tree among the trees of
>> the forest is my lover among the young men.
> I delight to sit in his shade,
>> and his fruit is sweet to my taste.
> He has taken me to his banquet hall,
>> and his banner over me is love
>> (Song of Songs 2:2-4).

 Pray, asking God to guide you in becoming a better communicator verbally and emotionally with your spouse.

The more we talk on a deep emotional level with our mates, the more we are able to help each other.

Day 3
Getting to Know You (Part 2)

Physical Intercourse

Now we get to the real thing, right? Slow down. What we tend to zero in on is actually a small part of the physical relationship. When thinking of physical intercourse, think more in terms of *touching, caressing, hugging, kissing, and romancing.*

From my interviews and counseling with women, I've concluded that most women need 8 to 12 meaningful touches a day to keep their energy level high and experience a sense of connectedness with their mate—a hug, a squeeze of the hand, a pat on the shoulder, a gentle kiss. There are approximately five million touch receptors in the human body—more than two million in the hands alone. The right kind of touch releases a pleasing and healing flow of chemicals in the bodies of both the toucher and the touched. Studies have shown that people get healthier even as a result of tender attention and touch of animals—dogs and cats. Everybody wins when we touch each other in a proper way.[1]

God has made each of us to need and appreciate tender touch. And I would add that nowhere is that more important than in the marital relationship.

 The Bible tells us how powerful touching can be. Look at the following passages and underline what resulted from the power of Jesus' touch.

> They begged [Jesus] to let then touch even the edge of his cloak, and all who touched him were healed (Mark 6:56).

> People were bringing little children to Jesus to have him touch them … And he took them in his arms, put his hands on them and blessed them (Mark 10:13,16).

> Then [Jesus] went up and touched the coffin, and … said, "Young man, I say to you, get up!" The dead man sat up and began to talk. … They were all filled with awe and praised God (Luke 7:14-16).

 Jesus conveyed God's blessing through touch. As a couple, your spiritual lives can be enhanced through touch. Check which of these spiritual touches you will do with your spouse.

❑ Hold hands when we pray
❑ Touch my spouse when we worship together
❑ Hug or hold my spouse as we pray
❑ Hold hands while we study Scripture
❑ Touch my spouse when he or she is sick
❑ Other: _____

God has made each of us to need and appreciate tender touch.

I know it's difficult for some couples to talk about sexual intimacies. Some marriage experts have reported that the two hardest things for couples to talk about are death and sex. On the lighter side, that explains the shyness of a young minister who always wanted to be invited to speak outside his church. His opportunity came when a women's organization in town asked him to address their luncheon. He was eager to please. "What do you want me to talk on?" he asked.

"We would like to have you talk on sex," they said, and he said OK.

He was home working on his talk when his wife came into his study. "What are you doing?" she asked.

"I've been invited to speak to a women's group," he told her.

"Oh, what are you speaking on?" she wanted to know.

He was too embarrassed to tell the truth, so he said, "Uh … I'm speaking on, uh, sailing. I'm going to talk to them about sailing."

She got a puzzled look on her face, but she just said, "Oh, that's good," and walked away.

The next week, after the minister had given his speech, in the grocery store his wife ran into one of the meeting's organizers. The woman came up to the wife and said, "Your husband! Wonderful speaker! He knows so much about that subject!"

"Really?" the wife said. "He's only done it twice. The first time he fell off, and the second time he got sick!"

It's not just difficult for ministers to discuss this topic; it's hard for all of us. But regardless of how tough it is to talk about sex, the whole relationship will be much better if we give each other a lot of tender physical touches throughout the day.

Spiritual Intercourse

Some people sincerely wonder about an old motto: *The family that prays together, stays together.* But a few years ago Dr. Nick Stinnett conducted a highly publicized study at the University of Nebraska. After looking carefully at hundreds of families that considered themselves healthy, his research concluded that healthy families possess six common characteristics. One of those characteristics is "a shared personal faith in God."[2] And surveys taken by sociologist Andrew Greeley indicate that "frequent sex coupled with frequent prayer make for the most satisfying marriages."[3]

Spiritual intercourse may be the highest level of intimacy. A husband and wife can know each other as they both turn to and know God—heart to heart. Scripture writers repeatedly used a marriage metaphor to refer to the relationship God wants to have with those who turn to Him. And the Spirit of God has an otherworldly ability to draw two people into harmony, being "one" in spirit.

Consider this verse: "A cord of three strands is not quickly broken" (Ecclesiastes 4:12). Some writers have seen that truth as a picture of marriage: Man-woman-God bound together in a strong union. A man and wife can grow spiritually intimate as they pray together, worship God together, attend study groups or retreats together, or simply discuss spiritual lessons and insights. Spiritual intercourse involves knowing one another in the context of a shared faith. And through that faith a couple sees value and meaning to things that would otherwise be meaningless.

Spiritual intercourse may be the highest level of intimacy.

Check each of the following ways you and your spouse have spiritual intercourse. Circle those you need to add or strengthen.

- ❏ Pray
- ❏ Worship
- ❏ Witness
- ❏ Go on spiritual retreats
- ❏ Mentor another couple
- ❏ Read and study Scripture.
- ❏ Serve and minister
- ❏ Participate in discipleship training

Dennis and Lois, our case study at the beginning of this week's study, had always been of the opinion that people—even married couples—shouldn't discuss religion or politics. But after they learned about spiritual intercourse, they had one of their most lively conversations ever. Then they visited local churches, finally finding one where they felt comfortable. This was a whole new arena for them, but a vital link to their marital health and happiness—their union.

In a book chapter titled "Praying Together: Guardian of Intimacy," Carey and Pam Moore quote one couple's strong statement: "The most important goal of praying together is that it keeps our relationship as a couple intimate and close, and it keeps our hearts open before the Lord as a couple. There is a lot of unspoken accountability in our walk with the Lord and with each other."[4]

The Moores go on to say, "Daily prayer can serve as the guardian of the marriage, for the husband and wife who pray together do not pray alone. God Himself is present. ... He will ... encourage the formation of an ever-closer bond and He will lend His strength to that bond."[5]

Spend time in prayer with your spouse today. If you have never prayed together before, simply pray the Lord's prayer or Psalm 23 together to begin.

Getting to Know You

Dennis and Lois continued to go through a rigorous examination of their married life to improve each of the four areas of intercourse. Through much-needed discussions, they both came to understand the deep hurts they had inflicted on each other unintentionally. Lois was extremely sensitive about her weight, a pain Dennis had virtually ignored. Once he realized the extent of her pain, he was much more supportive. He made a point, for example, of telling her how much he loved her and how very attractive he still found her. Lois, for her part, better understood Dennis's feelings of rejection because of their sporadic sex life, and she made an effort to be more available to him. All these hurts took some time to heal, but it happened.

One problem was that Lois felt that Dennis touched her only when he was trying to initiate sex. Dennis admitted that to be true. So I asked them to touch each other but not allow it to end in consummation. This was particularly helpful to them as they learned to support each other emotionally and express affection.

The blending of these four aspects of intercourse provides the complete context for a healthier sexual relationship. They're like the four sides of a building—all are essential for a sound and lasting structure.

A healthy sexual relationship results from the blending of verbal, emotional, physical, and spiritual intercourse.

Which of these four aspects is growing the most in your marriage right now? Circle it. Underline the one that needs to grow the most.

Verbal intercourse   Emotional intercourse

Physical intercourse   Spiritual intercourse

 Close in prayer asking God's Spirit to open you up to a deeper intimacy with God and your spouse in the coming months.

---

[1] F. B. Dressler, "The Psychology of Touch," *American Journal of Psychology 6* (1984): 316.
[2] See Nick Stinnett and John DeFrain, *Secrets of Strong Families* (New York: Berkley, 1986).
[3] "Talking to God," *Newsweek* (6 January 1992), 42.
[4] Carey Moore and Pamela Rosewell Moore, *If Two Shall Agree: Praying Together as a Couple* (Grand Rapids: Chosen Books, 1992), 200.
[5] Ibid., 201.

Day 4

Improving Sexual Intimacy

Once you're establishing the verbal, emotional, physical, and spiritual connections, you can follow additional steps to improve the sexual dimension of your marriage. I'll give five suggestions that either a wife or a husband can try to enhance the physical act of sex. Then I'll offer some suggestions specific to each of the partners.

Suggestions for Both Partners

❏ 1. *Take the initiative sexually.* This is generally appreciated by your partner, especially if it's not your usual approach. The change of pace will energize your experience.

❏ 2. *Take care with your appearance.* Your spouse will value the effort you make to look attractive. I'll say more about this in the specific advice below.

❏ 3. *Take more time to enjoy the sexual experience.* Routinized sex—relegated to 10 minutes after the TV late news on Saturday night—is the kiss of death to a vibrant sex life. Don't be in a hurry. Think in terms of the four areas of intercourse we've discussed, and then take an unhurried walk through all of them. It can make a sexual evening very special.

❏ 4. *Pay attention to the atmosphere in which you'll make love.* Beyond candle light, soft music, and a fire's glow (which are all great ideas), don't overlook some basics like a locked door. Visitors aren't welcome, even if they're members of the family. This is a time for husband and wife, and no unpleasant surprises are appreciated.

❏ 5. *Express your desire.* Many couples feel that the sexual act expresses how much they are attracted to each other, and they use sex in place of verbalizing the desire to be together. But words such as "I love you," "I need you," "I'm crazy about you,"

"You look great," and "I'd marry you all over again" have an encouraging and stimulating power all their own. Tell your mate often how much you enjoy being with him or her.

 Of the five suggestions, place a check in the box by the one you plan to discuss with your spouse.

Suggestions for Men

 What would your wife say if she were asked how you could improve your sex life? My research shows that women often answer along the following lines. Husbands—as you read these, circle the number by the one(s) you will work on.

1. *Be romantic.* Women love to feel connection with their spouses, and nothing accomplishes this better than romance. By becoming a student of your wife, you can learn the best way to produce romantic feelings within her. For some it is flowers, cards, or a small gift. For others, it's sharing in work around the house and lightening her load. Still others look to a night out on the town, a concert, or dinner in a nice restaurant. Women love tenderness in a man. They always have, too—this is not just some "sensitive '90s man" fad. Women respond to romance, and most desire more of it.

 On a scale of 1 to 10 (the best) how would you rate the husband in your marriage in being romantic? _____

2. *Take time with foreplay.* You cannot lose by spending extra time touching, hugging, and cuddling your wife. These acts are like giving her an injection of pure energy. Ask your wife where and how she likes to be touched, and be responsive to her needs. Conversely, if something you desire makes her uncomfortable, respect her wishes. Remember also to freely touch your wife with caresses that won't necessarily lead to sex. Praise her, tell her how desirable she is, and give her spontaneous hugs.

 What can the husband in your marriage do to increase the joy of foreplay in your marriage?

_____

3. *Make yourself sexy.* Stan is a typical guy. He loves his wife, Andrea, and is always ready to make love at a moment's notice. Andrea is consistently amazed by this attribute. She was recently surprised when he came in the back door after gardening in the muddy dirt for four hours. Sweaty, dirty, smelly, and unkempt as he was, when he saw her bending over in the kitchen, he let out a low wolf whistle and offered her an invitation for some immediate fun.

Andrea, like most women, finds her husband attractive, but that isn't always enough. Did he really expect her to be interested in a sexual encounter after he had just finished four hours in the mud? No way!

At first Stan was hurt by her cool response. He prided himself on keeping in shape and looking good. So Andrea had to explain that she wasn't rejecting *him*. She just felt more inclined toward making love if there was "a total package," as she put it.

Husband, what would your wife say if she were asked how you could improve your sex life?

That included a clean and scrubbed, freshly shaven ("I hate stubble," she says), cologne-wearing Stan; clean sheets on the bed; soft light; and a classical CD playing softly in the background.

Andrea's reaction had nothing to do with Stan's fear that he was overweight or soft in areas that were once muscular. It was more about *atmosphere*. Stan needed to listen carefully to learn how to provide her idea of the perfect evening. It's only fair he learn from her, because, another time, he'll want her to try his idea of romance (in some room other than the bedroom when the kids are away at their grandparents' house).

 On a scale from 1 to 10 (the best) how is the husband in your family doing with sex appeal? _____

Suggestions for Women

 Many wives wish they could find the key to unlock the sexual aspect of their husband's life. So here are some ideas specifically for women. Wives— as you read these, circle the number by the one(s) you will work on.

1. *Understand his tremendous sexual needs.* As discussed earlier, the two of you probably view sex from different perspectives. More than likely, he desires sex more often than you. With that insight, there may be occasions when you're willing to have sex even if all four areas of intimacy are not in place for you. This should only be once in a while, however, not a regular pattern. He needs to be sensitive to your needs just as you're sensitive to his. For example, if your hormones make you wish your husband were in Siberia for several days, he needs to understand that and be patient.

If your husband ever struggles with impotence, which is commonly caused by performance anxiety, refer to the book *Intended for Pleasure,* by Ed and Gaye Wheat. Today there are a number of excellent books on the subject of "good sex."[1] It's not uncommon for older men to need stimulation from you to be aroused.

 What can the wife in your marriage do to be more understanding?

_____

2. *Find out what he really enjoys.* A man is thrilled when his wife asks him what he likes in regard to sex and then gives it a try. This does not mean you have to violate your inner convictions or participate in a sexual activity you find offensive. But there may be many things your husband thinks of in his fantasy life that you could fulfill for him and enjoy yourself.

The sexual relationship is a place where creativity should shine. God did not create sex to be dull, boring, or routine. Take the initiative to instigate some variety in your sex life. Few men will respond, "No, this isn't what I want. Let's go back to doing it exactly the same as we have for the last 20 years."

 Ask yourself *what does the husband in our marriage really enjoy?*

3. *Make yourself sexy.* Having read my account of Stan and Andrea, a woman could conclude that nothing is necessary on her part to keep the sexual fires alive. But in reality, a balance needs to be achieved. Just as a woman appreciates the "total package" from her husband, so a man is entitled to the same consideration from his wife.

Wife, what would your husband say if he were asked how you could improve your sex life?

You'll want to have those magical occasions when you take a leisurely bath, slide into something sexy, spray a little perfume around, dim the lights, and turn on the station that plays the late-night love songs. Your husband will enjoy that atmosphere just like you. It's another way to contribute to the variety that's so helpful to a healthy sexual relationship.

Offer a prayer thanking God for the physical attractiveness of your mate and sexual aspects He created for marriage.

---

[1]See Ed and Gaye Wheat, *Intended for Pleasure* (Grand Rapids: Fleming Revell, 1981); Bernie Zilberheld, *The New Male Sexuality* (New York: Bantam, 1992).

Day 5
Enjoying the Fruit of a Healthy Relationship

Many couples have a difficult time discussing sexual matters with each other.

Fortunately, Dennis and Lois were able to bring back some of the passion in their marriage. But it wasn't easy or quick.

Many couples have a difficult time discussing sexual matters with each other, so the thought of raising the issues with a third-party counselor is even more stressful. But many qualified counselors can provide confidential assistance in improving this area of your relationship. Add to that the vast number of good books, tapes, and study courses available, and it's exciting to see that so much help is accessible to you and your mate.

"I'll admit," Dennis told me much later in our counseling, "I was angry and embarrassed that our sex life had deteriorated to the point that we had to enlist the help of a counselor. That can be a bitter pill for any person to swallow—especially a man. But it really was one of the smartest moves I ever made. There was so much about Lois I didn't understand, along with a bunch of stuff I never even knew about her. These discoveries wouldn't have occurred without us reaching out for help."

As Lois summarized in one of our final sessions, "I now see the importance of putting sex in its complete context. Now Dennis and I think, feel, talk, and connect with each other. We're enjoying the *fruit* of a healthy relationship."

That was a good choice of words on her part, because a couple's sex life can be compared to an apple tree. If we nurture the tree and keep it healthy, we're going to have fruit on it. But if we neglect it and don't nurture it, it's not likely to bear much fruit. If we get impatient for fruit in the springtime, remembering the delicious taste of apples and complaining that we haven't had fruit lately, we might start picking the blossoms off. But they don't taste like fruit, and once you pick them off, you'll never get apples.

Don't settle for anything but the best. Don't let your sexual relationship deteriorate into just a physical act.

A healthy tree needs water, sunlight, air, and fertilized soil—it takes all four ingredients. Likewise, when we nurture a marriage verbally, emotionally, physically, and spiritually, we can watch the love and intimacy and knowledge grow. And as they develop, the marital tree will provide a steady supply of fruit. Then any time we want, basically, we can pick off the fruit and eat it, and it's delicious! Why? Because we've nurtured the sex tree—the relationship. Then we can have cinnamon-apple butter from time to time; French apple pie; apple dumplings with cinnamon and caramel sauce; and apple cobbler with ice cream. But we can't have any of those goodies unless we first have the apples.

Don't settle for anything but the best. Don't let your sexual relationship deteriorate into just the physical act. Enrich your life together in all four areas of intimacy, and watch your sexual-love relationship come forever-alive.

Every engaged couple I've ever talked with has an excited anticipation about married life. They look forward to being together, sharing every aspect of life together—talking, sleeping, hugging, and sexual intimacy. But every married couple knows how reality can change one's hopes and dreams.

 Fill in the lines to compose a prayer of thanksgiving for your marriage.

Lord, thank you for my spouse's physical appearance. I appreciate …

_____

Lord, thank you that in our emotional intercourse we …

_____

Lord, I thank you that spiritually we are intimate in …

_____

Lord, I praise you for verbal intimacy in …

_____

Lord, increase my sensitivity and intimacy with my spouse in the area of …

_____

Lord, increase my spouse's sensitivity in the area of …

_____

Thank you God for the gift of sexuality and the completeness that brings to my marriage relationship. Amen.

Making Love Last Forever

Couple Time

For you to complete

Now that you have completed this week's study, what are your expectations sexually in your marriage? Compare your response with your earlier response on page 190.

_____

_____

Rate your effectiveness in the four aspects of intercourse.

	Ineffective	Less Effective	So-so	Somewhat Effective	Effective
Verbal intercourse	1	2	3	4	5
Emotional intercourse	1	2	3	4	5
Physical intercourse	1	2	3	4	5
Spiritual intercourse	1	2	3	4	5

What idea presented this week stands out as the one you plan to work on in your marriage?

_____

For you to share with your spouse

1. Take turns sharing how you completed the above section.

2. Pray together the prayers you wrote on day 5, page 202.

3. Write a covenant that incorporates things both of you will start doing more of to increase your sexual intimacy. Both sign the covenant. Pray together for God to give you power and strength to keep your covenant.

WEEK 12

Divorce-Proof Your Marriage
with a Love That Lasts

I've learned a practical, simple principle that can work wonders in reviving love and keeping a couple happily together. In some ways it underscores most of the principles we've discussed at length. It's a good method to use—or mind-set to have—all the time. And it can produce immediate results when a marriage is in crisis.

A story from the early years of my own marriage will introduce the images I use to describe this great tool.

When Norma and I married, I was not very responsible financially. Growing up, I had never learned how to handle finances or even that it mattered. I didn't know anything about keeping a checkbook register or spending wisely. Norma, on the other hand, was a detail-oriented person who worked in a bank. So it was obvious that she should keep the books and pay the bills, which she was happy to do.

But problems arose right at the start and lasted five years. Each of us had a checkbook and wrote checks on one joint account. (Can you see the conflict brewing?)

I had my own system: I wrote checks as long as I had them in my book—until I ran out; I hoped—or assumed—there was enough in the bank to cover them.

But too often Norma would confront me: "We're overdrawn again."

"We can't be," I'd answer with a grin. "I still have checks in my book."

Sometimes she would be in tears. "I can't keep track of this. It's driving me crazy."

We also had a secondary conflict. We disagreed about when to pay bills. Norma preferred to pay them as soon as they came. But I wanted to hold on to our money as long as possible, paying our bills at the end of the month, just before pay day. I liked the idea of having money, because you never know when an emergency might come up. With my check-writing habits, however, there wasn't always enough left at the end of the month to pay all the bills.

"We have two late notices on this one bill," Norma would say, exasperated.

"Don't worry about it," I'd respond, which was not what she wanted to hear. My philosophy was that you don't have to do anything until you get the fourth or fifth notice. You just keep shuffling late notices to the bottom of the pile until they appear at the top again and can't be ignored any longer.

Then the day came when Norma had taken all she could. She tearfully approached me once more and laid all the bills, her checkbook, and the budget in my lap. "I've had it!" she declared. "I can't take it anymore. From now on, this area is all yours. It's up to you whether we sink or swim." Years later, she admitted her despair that day: She figured she was really giving away our home, our car, and the rest of our financial life, because there was no way I would be able to handle it properly.

Fortunately, with the pressure on, I decided to learn how to be responsible. I got some help, grew to respect a budget, and worked my way out of the mess I had created. For the next 15 years, I kept the books and paid the bills. I learned a crucial but simple principle: *You've got to have more money in the bank than you spend every month. Income has to exceed outgo.* That's about as basic as family finance gets.

Now let me make the application to how you can divorce-proof your marriage. The principle is simple, yet the impact is powerful. My hope is that this idea will become a part of your life, just like pearl counting and the other principles I've learned to live by and presented in this book. The principle is this: *To divorce-proof your marriage, make sure you are making more "deposits" to your spouse than "withdrawals."*

As you study this week, you will:

- develop skills toward balancing your joint marriage account;
- understand how deposits and withdrawals are made;
- develop a knowledge of what constitutes withdrawals and deposits;
- learn skills that decrease withdrawals while increasing deposits; and
- develop an attitude of commitment to your marriage.

As you complete this study, keep this verse in mind:

"The only thing that counts is faith expressing itself through love" (Galatians 5:6).

> *To divorce-proof your marriage, make sure you are making more "deposits" to your spouse than "withdrawals."*

Day 1 Basics of Marital Banking	Day 2 Personal Banking	Day 3 Banking with Your Spouse	Day 4 Deposits Have the Power to Save a Marriage	Day 5 The Love That Lasts Forever

Day 1
Basics of Marital Banking

When it comes to what I call *marital banking,* we can define a few terms.

A *deposit* is positive, security-producing—*anything that gives your mate energy!* It's a gentle touch, a listening ear, a verbalized "I love you," a fun, shared experience; the list could go on. Temperament, gender, and birth order influence one's personal definition of a *deposit.* Going for long walks in the woods with a spouse may energize an introvert the way a houseful of holiday company (entertaining) energizes an extrovert.

A *withdrawal* is anything sad or negative—*anything that drains energy from your mate.* It's a harsh word, an unkept promise; being ignored, being hurt, being controlled; the list could be long. Some withdrawals differ from temperament to temperament; something perceived as a withdrawal for one person might be a deposit for another person. But too much control or being absent too much, physically or emotionally, are always major withdrawals, and as I mentioned in week 8, these are the two biggest factors in unhealthy relationships.

The more you keep a positive balance in your relationship account, with "giving" deposits exceeding "draining" withdrawals, the more secure that relationship will be. There's something basic about the saying, "If you're happy, I'm happy. If you're energized, I'm energized." Enthusiasm—for life, for romance, for "us"—is contagious.

And if your marriage is in rough shape because you've been making a lot more withdrawals than deposits, beginning now with a concerted effort to make deposits can turn things around faster than anything else I've seen. By the way, once again, this will work in any relationship—with your friends, your children, your parents, and your coworkers, as well as with your mate.

Let me give you the biblical background for this principle. It's called "sowing and reaping." *Sowing* is depositing. *Reaping* is the reward–the harvest. Let's explore this biblical principle one step at a time.

 1. *Give and you will receive.* Read in your Bible Luke 6:31-38. In one sentence, write in your own words what Jesus is saying.

_____

Before we expect someone to make deposits into our lives, we need to begin depositing into their lives. God blesses us to be a blessing to others. In what way are you blessing your spouse? Write one thing you will give your spouse this week without expecting anything in return.

_____

 2. *Sow and you will reap.* Read in your Bible Galatians 6:7-10. Summarize in one sentence what this passage teaches.

_____

We receive a harvest based on the seed we sow. In the natural world, if we sow wheat, we do not expect a harvest of oats but of wheat. In relationships, if we sow love, mercy, and forgiveness, that's what we'll reap. If we sow anger, guilt, and hurt, that's what we'll reap. What kind of harvest do you want in your marriage? Dr. John Gottman, divorce prevention expert, says that the minimum ratio is five positives to one negative in a lasting and loving marriage.[1]

At the top of the next page are four sacks of seed. Label each one of them with the primary seed you wish to sow into your mate's life. It might be love, joy, faith, mercy, or healing. Ask the Lord to inspire you to sow what needs to be sown in his or her life.

A deposit is positive, security-producing—anything that gives your mate energy.

206

 3. *Be generous.* Read 2 Corinthians 9:6.

> Whoever sows sparingly will also reap sparingly, and whoever sows generously will also reap generously.

If you sow sparingly or grudgingly, then your harvest will be sparse. Ever ask yourself, why doesn't my spouse deposit more of (*you fill in your need*) in my life? Perhaps you are being a "scrooge" when *you* sow. Complete this sentence:

With my partner, I need to be more generous in …

_____

A withdrawal is anything sad or negative—anything that drains energy from your mate.

 4. *Treasure what's important in life.* Read in your Bible 1 Timothy 6:17-19. Summarize this passage in one sentence.

_____

Below are three treasure chests. Write in each chest one thing that you treasure in your spouse.

 5. *Be rich in good deeds.* What two or three good deeds do you need to sow (deposit) in your spouse's life?

_____

_____

Harvests always take time. You may sow something into your mate's life today that will not bear a harvest for years. You may deposit into your mate's life something for years and not make a withdrawal in that area for years. That's OK. We grow together for a lifetime. Continue to sow. God brings both the increase and the harvest.

Thank God for the privilege you have sowing into your mate's life.

---

[1]John Gottman, *Why Marriages Succeed and Fail* (New York: Simon and Schuster, 1994), 29.

Making Love Last Forever

Day 2
Personal Banking

You and your spouse both have a personal-relationship banking history. As in real banking, your current account balance is the direct influence of past deposits and withdrawals.

The first step in making personal-banking principles work for—not against—your marriage is for you to record and learn to understand your own personal-relationship banking history. Start by thinking through and writing down various withdrawals and deposits you remember from your younger years.

List one deposit each of the people from your past listed below made into your life

Mom: _____

Dad: _____

Siblings: _____

Friends: _____

Teachers: _____

Pastors /Youth Workers: _____

Coaches: _____

Bosses: _____

Others: _____

What Are Withdrawals to You?

In one of the TV commercials for my video series, you may have seen a couple, Kevin and Julie. They tell just a little of their story there. I'd like to tell you the rest of it here, because Kevin's experience illustrates the impact of childhood events.

Once married, Kevin made all kinds of withdrawals from Julie. For years he was controlling, harsh, critical, arrogant, angry, and abusive. That's when he was home. (He frequently wasn't.) Finally, Julie thought she couldn't take it anymore and got a court order to keep him away. She also had the locks changed on the house. When he arrived home that night and couldn't get in, he was, well, upset.

Kevin went home with a friend, who had some of my marriage-help videos. A sobered Kevin watched a few, including the one about marital banking. Acting on the advice to record the withdrawals made in childhood, he started writing phrases—actions, words, attitudes—that had caused him pain or drained him of energy as a young boy and teen.

When the withdrawals were on paper for him to contemplate, he saw that the withdrawals made to him looked amazingly like the actions, words, and attitudes that Julie complained about with him. The abuses done to him, he was passing on to others. He determined that he was going to do his best to stop the negative withdrawals and replace them with deposits. (More about that in a minute.)

Your current personal-relationship account balance is the direct influence of past deposits and withdrawals.

List one withdrawal in each category that others make from your life.

Actions that drain me: _____

Words that drain me: _____

Attitudes that drain me: _____

Circle any of the above that you do to others.

In my own life, a big withdrawal drained me any time someone—usually my father, later a boss—would exert excessive control over me. For example, I vividly recall going fishing with my father. If I started catching fish in one particular place, he would come over, literally shove me out of the way, and say, "Fish somewhere else."

Sadly but not surprisingly, that withdrawal done to me became a pattern for how I related to others. In time I became controlling with my wife, and I also got in the habit of making the exact same withdrawals from my kids. This was very evident one day when we were fishing in a Colorado stream and I was wheeling them in. When all three of my kids approached with their fishing poles, I said, "No, no, no!"

Greg knew what I was thinking. Finally he screamed, "Dad, we are not trying to fish here! Kari broke her leg!"

With that news, for a brief second I thought, *Ohhh, I'm going to have to leave this great fishing place!* I handed Greg my pole and said, "You fish here for a while so I don't miss anything." *Then* I took care of Kari. Even when we're aware of the reality—the record—of our childhood withdrawals, we can still not really understand how influential they are in terms of our current practice.

Below you will write down some of the withdrawals drained from your emotional-relational account as you were growing up. This can be useful to you in two ways:

1. It can help you, as it did Kevin, identify potential ways you are making withdrawals from your spouse's account. If a parent drained energy from you by doing x,y,z, are you similarly draining energy from your spouse?

2. It can help as you think through some things that are relational withdrawals for you today. What does your mate do that drains energy from you? Are some of these withdrawals connected to things that happened in your childhood?

 List ways your parents or siblings drained you and made emotional withdrawals from you as you were growing up.

_____

_____

As opportunities arise, share your childhood and current relational withdrawals with your mate (using "I feel" statements or word pictures, not accusations).

 In a couple of sentences, write a description for your mate of how one withdrawal that was made often in your life as a child still affects you now.

_____

_____

What Are Deposits for You?

What energized you as a child? As a young adult? While withdrawals frequently are caused by elements out of our control (an emotionally healthy person doesn't go seeking out draining withdrawals), deposits tend to be things we initiate or search out. And while withdrawals are often seen as being "done to" us, relational deposits are often things "done with" or "done for" us.

As for deposits in my own background, one of the biggest was singing with other people. Starting when I was in third grade, my sister taught me every popular song of the day, and I would harmonize with her. I got so much energy from that! Then I started singing with three or four friends. Rather than dating a lot as teens, we would go for long drives, singing on wheels. I enjoy close harmony so much, that sometimes I wonder if I should have been a singer instead of a speaker! (Then I listen to myself sing in the shower, and I know why I'm only speaking in public.)

 Think through your own childhood and up through the early years of your marriage. Look over the deposits that you listed earlier. Which kind of deposit do you need most from your spouse? List two or three.

_____

_____

Do you "make deposits" that are more suitable to your own needs than to your spouse's?

❑ Always   ❑ Sometimes   ❑ Rarely

It can also help you as you think through your current-day relational deposits. What does your mate do that energizes you? Are some of these deposits directly connected to things that happened in your childhood? Briefly write your response to those questions.

_____

If making deposits to your mate is difficult, pray for courage, sensitivity, and strength from God. Ask your spouse to pray for you to be sensitive to the kinds of deposits you need to make in his or her life.

Withdrawals tear your spouse down. Deposits build your mate up. Paul writes that the authority the Lord gave him was the authority "for building you up, not for tearing you down" (2 Corinthians 13:10).

Complete the following sentences as your closing prayer.
Lord, I thank you that I can build my mate up by …

_____

_____

> *While withdrawals frequently are caused by elements out of our control, deposits tend to be things we initiate or search out.*

Lord, I repent of tearing my spouse down by …

_____

_____

Day 3

Banking with Your Spouse

As you might guess from my descriptions of the first years of our marriage, when I eventually asked Norma to look back and reflect on those days, she was hard pressed to think of deposits I had made. Unfortunately she had no problem remembering plenty of withdrawals. She may have been charmed with me in our courting days, but living with me was no energizing venture.

For example, because I was so much into control, her stomach would turn every time I called a family meeting. She would say with her eyes and sometimes with her words, "I hate your meetings." For the longest time, I never understood why. Then I came to learn that too much control or too much distance in relationships drains people of their energy.

Evaluate your marriage. Check the items below that drain your marriage relationship.

❏ Too much control   ❏ Too much distance
❏ Unresolved anger   ❏ Unforgiveness
❏ Past guilt   ❏ Past hurt
❏ Irritating or bad habits ❏ Too many demands
❏ Other: _____

Another big withdrawal for her has to do with my driving habits. She's helped me understand the seed of this negative reaction to what I perceive as perfectly passable driving skills. When Norma was in high school, she was in a car that went over a cliff, and two of her friends were killed. Norma suffered a broken neck and was in a cast for a long time. It's perfectly reasonable that she has a healthy fear of a car going out of control. If I'm driving and get distracted and veer a bit too much toward the edge of the road, she'll say, "Ohhh, you're over too far." That's a withdrawal. And if I make light of her concern and tension, that's a serious withdrawal. On the other hand, if I make a point of driving carefully, that's a big deposit.

My snoring is another major withdrawal for Norma—keeping her from getting sleep and draining her of energy. This withdrawal doesn't fit the pattern I've previously presented—where something in childhood affects the present. Nor does it involve something I "do to" Norma. But it is something I do—or utter—that affects her negatively. And it is something I can make efforts to stop.

Of course she had to convince me of the reality of this annoying pattern. She once recorded the sounds and played the tape back to me so I couldn't deny the reality of my snoring. Can you imagine sleeping next to a rumbling diesel engine all those years? I've been kicked and told to roll over on my side many times. I've looked into new approaches to knocking out the noise. I was checked at a sleep disorder clinic in a hospital. I've just been fitted for a breathing devise that completely stops my snoring, and, by the way, I have twice the energy each day. It's been a miracle.

 Think about your experiences with your mate. Write actions, attitudes, or words (or noises!) you are sure she or he perceives to be withdrawals.

_____

_____

To increase the intimacy of your conversation and to confirm your assumptions, ask your spouse if your memories and perceptions are accurate.

When couples attending my seminars talk to each other about this, common withdrawals for women include "he treats me like I don't exist"; "he's never on time"; and "he travels too much in his job." Common withdrawals for husbands include "she's always on my case" and "she doesn't initiate sex."

 What can you do to reduce withdrawals you make to your spouse's account?

_____

_____

What Makes a Deposit to Your Mate?

Previously I noted that making a deposit in someone's account often involves doing something "with" or "for" someone. I've learned that for Norma, a huge deposit has to do with shopping—especially Christmas shopping. She likes to start shopping for presents in January. Now, I'm not big on shopping in the first place, and I hate to buy a present and then hide it somewhere; I want to give it to the person right away. So for the first several years of our marriage, I frustrated Norma and made big withdrawals by waiting until December 24 to do my shopping.

As we talked and I learned in this area, I came to understand that I could turn things around and make huge deposits just by changing my attitude toward shopping. So now, even though I still don't care to shop by myself, I make an effort to be enthusiastic when I'm doing it with her, whether she's buying presents or looking for a dress for herself. I try not to be like the guy who found out his wife's credit cards had been stolen, yet a year later he still hadn't reported it, because the thief spent less than his wife had!

Now, for me _fishing_ is my shopping. If she suggests taking a picnic on the boat, I know she's saying, "I love you." She doesn't actually go fishing with me. She would rather bring a book along and read. That's OK—I just like to be with her on or near the water.

During week 10 on conflicts, I suggested a couple have a love-language—actions you both know the secret meaning of: *I love you.* That love language is closely connected with this idea of marital banking. The energizing love language is based on an alphabet of deposits.

Today, Norma and I are best friends. We love finding out new things that make deposits into our accounts with each other. We go out of our way to make sure we're making more deposits than withdrawals.

When I ask seminar attendees for things they consider to be deposits, common responses include "him chatting with me when he gets home from work"; "daily verbal expressions of love"; "it's a big deposit when she initiates sex"; and "I love it when he plays with our kids." That last one is a prime example of something a man might never identify as a deposit unless he asks for feedback. My wife, too, has told me that it's a big deposit for her when I praise and encourage our kids—and especially the grandkids.

 List two or three deposits your spouse makes into your life.

_____

_____

 Close in prayer thanking God for your spouse and those deposits.

_____

_____

The best way to find out what your spouse "receives" as a withdrawal or deposit is to ask.

Don't Rely on Guess Work

What's the best way to find out what your spouse "receives" as a withdrawal or deposit? Ask! If you're both familiar with this concept, you might say as you do something with honoring intent: "I'm hoping this is a deposit with you. Does it work?" The response you get will tell you if you missed the mark or hit the bull's-eye.

I've touched on this before, but it bears repeating: In the best of marriages, one spouse may think he or she is making a deposit, but it turns into a big withdrawal. Considering this problem on the lighter side, perhaps you've heard of the couple who decided that a big deposit for them would be learning how to do something together—like duck hunting. They asked an expert what equipment of "outfit" they needed. He answered, "Well, if you're going to be successful, you've got to have a really good hunting dog."

So they bought a champion dog and then set out on their first hunting expedition. They started before sunrise and stayed with it all day, into the evening, but with no ducks to show for all their time and effort. Finally, exhausted, the man said to his wife, "I don't know. Maybe we're doing it wrong. I don't think we're throwing this dog high enough into the air."

Have you tried to make a deposit and it turned out somewhat like the "duck hunt"? You felt as if your "check" bounced?

What really matters to most spouses is that the mate *tried* to do the right thing. But if you find that your mate is reacting negatively to your well-intentioned deposit attempts, I suggest you allow some time to pass and feelings to cool. Then, by explaining the situation, you can redeposit the "check" in a different way.

Thank You! Thank You!

Ask your mate to *praise* you when you intentionally or unintentionally make a deposit into his or her relational account. This will reinforce your positive behavior. Who doesn't thrive on praise? That recognition will energize you, so your energy as a couple spirals upward. A deposit and then a thank you in return earns a couple mucho interest. Let's call it a *joint* high-interest savings account.

Of course this works two ways. Praise your spouse for deposits—and everybody wins double interest.

 One way I will ask my spouse to praise me is ...

_____

It's so important for you to speak the truth in love to your spouse. Too often, we think that "speaking the truth in love" (Ephesians 4:15) means to focus on the uncomfortable truth. However, it also means to express the wonderful truth. We get into the bad habit of always speaking what's wrong with our marriages and never sharing the truth of what's right.

 The truth about what's right in our marriage is ... (list several true, right things about your marriage–things that encourage) ...

_____

_____

_____

_____

_____

_____

 Close today's study in prayer thanking God for all the right things in your marriage.

*P*raise your spouse for deposits—and everybody wins double interest.

Day 4
Deposits Have the Power to Save a Marriage

Let me give you an update on Kevin and Julie's marriage: Kevin took this marital banking principle very seriously. With his new understanding, he worked hard to reduce his withdrawals from and increase his deposits to Julie's account. Gradually, this tremendous, sustained change in Kevin got through to Julie.

She later told me, "I could tell he wasn't really excited about saying 'I love you,' listening to me, and touching me gently. I could see he was forcing it. As he would listen to something I was saying, he would get preoccupied, but he was trying. When I saw his effort right in front of me, it was a major deposit, and he warmed my heart. That's why it was so easy to say, 'Let's keep going. I think we can make it together.'"

They did keep going, and Kevin did keep trying. If you saw them today, you'd be impressed with how sensitive he is and how responsive she is, and you'd never guess they had been to the brink of divorce just a few years ago.

This banking principle can save a marriage—even return it to days of joy.

What's your balance? How does your marital bank account look? If you were to ask your spouse today, "What's my balance?" what would the response be? Circle what you think your spouse would say if he or she answered based on the following graph.

$1	$10	$20	$30	$40	$50	$60	$70	$80	$90	$100

Whatever the answer, you can start improving your balance instantly by making deposits and refraining from making costly withdrawals. Do this regularly for a month—or two. Ask the question again. And watch your balance soar.

Another Scripture summarizes the principle of relational banking:

> Cast your bread upon the waters,
> for after many days you will find it again (Ecclesiastes 11:1).

Give love and you will receive love. This concept gives new meaning to the phrase "no deposit, no return." If you make no deposit, you'll get no return. Make deposits and you energize your spouse, your marriage, and your own life.

Let's look at a familiar parable Jesus told. Read in your Bible the parable of the talents in Matthew 25:14-30. Note what happened to those who deposited or invested their talents.

_____

What is one principle you learned from this parable that applies to your marriage?

_____

> "*Cast your bread upon the waters, for after many days you will find it again*"
> —*Ecclesiastes 11:1.*

Think of maintaining your balance as responsible relationship banking. Practice it and reap the bountiful rewards: the pleasure of seeing your love grow stronger with every passing year—as you and your spouse walk together into the forever.

 Write a prayer thanking God for your spouse and ask Him to deepen your relationship with each other as you both build your marriage accounts.

_____

_____

Enriching the life of another is often more satisfying than doing something for yourself.

Day 5
A Love That Lasts Forever

" 'Greater love has no one than this, that one lay down his life for his friends.' "
—John 15:13

For years I've been urging the thousands of people who read my books, watch my videos, and attend my seminars to see how much we need to help each other develop this "greatest" love. I call it *heroic love*—a love that sacrifices itself, that doesn't seek its own good but chooses to satisfy the desires of the beloved.

 Complete this sentence.
One way I'm laying down my life for my mate is …

_____

But don't get the impression that heroic love is all self-sacrifice. From looking at my own marriage and hundreds of others, I've come to understand that *enriching the life of another is often more satisfying than doing something for self.* As we reach out to another, our own needs for fulfillment and love are met.

I've seen that the most satisfied, joyous couples are those that have learned heroic love and practice it daily. When a husband and wife both want their partner to receive life's best before they do, you have a marriage that's going to exceed every wedding-day dream. Their love not only lasts; it continually grows.

Jesus calls us to be servants. That means we are to serve our mates and families as well as serve others. In fact, we really learn how to be servants in our families.

 Read the following passages on being servants and summarize what each one means to your marriage.

[Jesus], being in very nature God, …   _____
made himself nothing, taking the very   _____
nature of a servant, … humbled himself   _____
and became obedient to death—even   _____
death on a cross!" (Philippians 2:6-8).   _____

Submit to one another out of reverence for Christ. Wives, submit to your husbands as to the Lord. … Husbands, love your wives, just as Christ loved the church and gave himself up for her (Ephesians 5:22,25).

_____
_____
_____
_____
_____

"Whoever wants to become great among you must be your servant, and whoever wants to be first must be your slave" (Matthew 20:26-27).

_____
_____
_____
_____

A serving relationship is the kind of relationship Charlie and Lucy Wedemeyer enjoy. If our world could raise its vision of love to the level of this couple, I can hardly imagine what it would be like to live on this planet.

More than 15 years ago, doctors diagnosed 30-year-old Charlie Wedemeyer as having the progressively debilitating and paralyzing ALS—commonly called Lou Gehrig's disease. They gave the California high-school football coach one year to live. But Charlie proved them wrong. Despite the relentless, progressive nature of his illness, he continued coaching for seven more years.

When Charlie could no longer walk, Lucy drove him up and down the sidelines in a golf cart. When he could no longer talk, she read his lips and relayed his instructions to the players. And in his dramatic last season as a coach, after he had gone on 24-hour-a-day life support, his team won a state championship!

Lucy Wedemeyer is a heroic lover. She says that from the very beginning of Charlie's illness, they've focused on what they have together rather than on what they're missing. She admits it hasn't been easy, but she says in her book,

> I think we communicate and understand each other better today than we ever did. While I've learned to read Charlie's lips, I find I often don't have to. His eyes almost always tell me exactly how he feels, and his eyebrows punctuate those feelings as they bounce up and down or I watch his forehead furrow into a wrinkle. And if you don't think someone in difficult circumstances can find happiness and contentment, if you doubt the contagious quality of joy, well, you've never seen Charlie smile.[1]

When the ALS struck, the Wedemeyers had two young children and mountains of dreams they would never realize. One week after they were told of his impending death, while watching snow drift by the window of a borrowed mountain cabin, Lucy looked into Charlie's eyes and recognized the same raw emotions she felt churning inside herself. She had never felt more love for Charlie, or more loved by him, than she did that special evening. And yet, she says,

Jesus calls us to be servants to our mates and families as well as others.

I'd never in my life felt such pain. Such anguish. Tears filled our eyes. Neither of us dared speak for fear the floodgates would open. So we just sat silently, holding hands across the table, basking in the bittersweet warmth of that moment, wishing the romantic spell could somehow make time stand still. All the while wondering how much time we had left together.[2]

When I first met the Wedemeyers at one of my seminars, I couldn't help but see the radiant joy on Lucy's face and the contentment in Charlie's eyes. Each one represents the type of hero I would love to be like someday. No matter what I go through with Norma, we both hope to have people look into our eyes and see a similar enduring fire of love—for life and for each other.

Lucy prays daily for continued strength, because Charlie needs constant care. Some realities of her life are harsh and ever-present, and still she says, "I wouldn't trade my life for anyone else's. It's been so rewarding." How can she mean that? That's the beauty of heroic love. It can move mountains, cross rivers, and overcome any obstacle for the joy set before it. No one's life is laughing-happy every day, but people like Lucy have such a deep sense of satisfaction and love that, no matter what occurs, they rest on an underlying assurance that everything is still OK.

Every marriage will have its better and worse times, its springs and summers and falls and winters. Forever-love allows that full range of seasons. Enjoy the bright colors and warmth of good days. Accept the dark, rainy days, the cold of winter, and the hot summer winds of disagreement and of waiting for someone to say, "I'm sorry. I was wrong. I love you. Will you forgive me?"

 It is possible for husbands and wives to lay down their lives for one another and to become the best of friends in marriage. Which of the following biblical words or phrases describe the relationship you and your spouse have?

❑ Best friends   ❑ Mutual servants   ❑ Lovers *(agape)*
❑ Companions   ❑ Comforters   ❑ Believers
❑ Other: _____

With our society driven more and more by instant everything, many of us are losing the awareness that some of the best things in life take longer and aren't enjoyed until, like ripe fruit, they're ready to be picked. Charlotte, for example, came close to giving up many times with her husband, Mike. But if she had, it would have been too soon.

Mike, like me, didn't know how to love his wife in a way that made her *feel* loved. He and I struggled through many seasons—many ups and downs—together as we learned the things I teach in this book. And as he grew in his own happiness and in his sensitivity to her needs, she found herself in the kind of relationship she had dreamed about before they married.

Not long ago I got a letter from Charlotte. "I never thought the day would come," she said, "when my life with Mike would be so wonderful. As you know,

Some of the best things in life are like fruit—they take longer and aren't enjoyed until they are ready to be picked.

we've had our 'down times.' But this last year has been worth all we went through. Whatever we didn't have before has long since been forgotten because of what we have today."

Unfortunately, many couples don't wait for that exciting season that wipes out the memory of the difficult times. That good season is like picking delicious fruit after a hard winter, wet spring, and hot summer. The juicy apples need all three seasons to taste delightfully good.

But many other couples have come to realize that it's perfectly normal for a marriage to go through different seasons—of drought, worry, sadness, anger and also times of plenty, happiness, and overwhelming joy and laughter.

I close this study with my personal warranty: *No matter what struggle you may have right now that tempts you to leave your marriage, there's a workable solution for you!* Start by applying the principles in this study. Get professional counseling if you need it. Through the research and counseling expertise of many people, there's no shortage of excellent help for couples today.

Perhaps this study will give you all the help you need; at the very least, it will give you a big head start. If you'll work at applying the lessons of this study, and if you'll seek out whatever other assistance you may need, you, too, can one day bask in the delights of forever-love.

Don't give up until you find it.

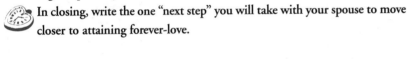 In closing, write the one "next step" you will take with your spouse to move closer to attaining forever-love.

No matter what struggle you may have, there's a workable solution for you!

_____

_____

 Pray a prayer of commitment to God. Seek God's power and guidance as you commit to taking this step together as husband and wife.

---

[1]Charlie and Lucy Wedemeyer, *Charlie's Victory* (Grand Rapids: Zondervan, 1993), 20.
[2]Ibid., 60.

Couple Time

For you to complete

What would God have you do as a result of this week's study?

_____

_____

For you to share with your spouse

1. Share with your spouse the best way he or she can make deposits into your life.

2. Share with each other which withdrawals are the most draining in your relationship.

3. Below is a stack of 20 $5 bills. Each of you put your initials on the stack indicating how much your spouse has on deposit in your life right now. Then offer suggestions to each other on how to increase the deposits.

4. Find 1 Corinthians 13 in your Bible. Read the passage to each other substituting your names for the word _love_. After you do this, say to each other:

> The truest part of that passage for me is …
> The part of that passage I will work on the most is …

5. Share with each other what God would have you do as a result of this week's study. Give each other a big hug and pray together thanking God for the forever-love He has given you in your marriage.

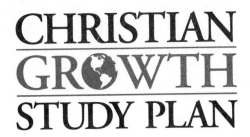

CHRISTIAN GROWTH STUDY PLAN

In the **Christian Growth Study Plan (formerly Church Study Course),** *Making Love Last Forever* is a resource for course credit in the subject area Home\Family of the Christian Growth category of diploma plans. To receive credit, read the book, complete the learning activities, show your work to your pastor, a staff member or church leader, then complete the following information. This page may be duplicated. Send the completed page to:

Christian Growth Study Plan
One LifeWay Plaza; Nashville, TN 37234-0117
FAX: (615)251-5067; E-mail: *cgspnet@lifeway.com*
For information about the Christian Growth Study Plan, refer to the Christian Growth Study Plan Catalog. It is located online at *www.lifeway.com/cgsp*. If you do not have access to the Internet, contact the Christian Growth Study Plan office (1.800.968.5519) for the specific plan you need for your ministry.

Making Love Last Forever
COURSE NUMBER: CG-0207

PARTICIPANT INFORMATION

Social Security Number (USA ONLY-optional)	Personal CGSP Number*	Date of Birth (MONTH, DAY, YEAR)
Name (First, Middle, Last)		Home Phone
Address (Street, Route, or P.O. Box)	City, State, or Province	Zip/Postal Code
Email Address for CGSP use		

Please check appropriate box: ❏ Resource purchased by church ❏ Resource purchased by self ❏ Other

CHURCH INFORMATION

Church Name		
Address (Street, Route, or P.O. Box)	City, State, or Province	Zip/Postal Code

CHANGE REQUEST ONLY

☐ Former Name		
☐ Former Address	City, State, or Province	Zip/Postal Code
☐ Former Church	City, State, or Province	Zip/Postal Code

Signature of Pastor, Conference Leader, or Other Church Leader	Date

*New participants are requested but not required to give SS# and date of birth. Existing participants, please give CGSP# when using SS# for the first time. Thereafter, only one ID# is required. **Mail to:** Christian Growth Study Plan, One LifeWay Plaza, Nashville, TN 37234-0117. Fax: (615)251-5067.

Revised 4-05